Electronic Portfolios 2.0

Electronic Portfolios 2.0

Emergent Research on Implementation and Impact

Edited by

Darren Cambridge
Barbara Cambridge
Kathleen Blake Yancey

Sty/us

STERLING, VIRGINIA

Published by Stylus Publishing, LLC
22883 Quicksilver Drive
Sterling, Virginia 20166-2102

Library of Congress Cataloging-in-Publication-Data
   Electronic portfolios 2.0 : emergent research on implementaton and impact /
edited by Darren Cambridge, Barbara L. Cambridge, and Kathleen Yancey.—1st ed.
      p.   cm.
      Includes bibliographical references and index.
      ISBN 978-1-57922-320-5 (cloth : alk. paper)—ISBN 978-1-57922-321-2 (alk. paper)
      1. Electronic portfolios in education.   I. Cambridge, Darren (Darren Robert), 1974–
II. Cambridge, Barbara L., 1943–   III. Yancey, Kathleen Blake, 1950–
LB1029.P67E43   2009
371.39—dc22
                                                                                      2008029938

13-digit ISBN: 978-1-57922-320-5 (cloth)
13-digit ISBN: 978-1-57922-321-2(paper)

Printed in the United States of America

All first editions printed on acid free paper that meets
the American National Standards Institute Z39-48 Standard.

Bulk Purchases

Quantity discounts are available for
use in workshops and for staff
development.
Call 1–800–232–0223

First Edition, 2009

10   9   8   7   6   5   4   3   2   1

CONTENTS

SECTION THREE

Establishing Identities: Roles, Competencies, Values, and Outcomes   81

SECTION FOUR

Organizational Learning   115

ACKNOWLEDGMENTS

We thank all who have contributed to the progress and findings of the Inter/National Coalition for Electronic Portfolio Research through participation and sponsorship. Research teams from colleges and universities in all five cohorts have provided collegial support for one another and for the Coalition. All the participating research teams listed here have institutions dedicated to student learning and knowledge building that have funded their work. In addition, important resources for the work have been provided by the American Association for Higher Education, the Pearce Center at Clemson University, George Mason University, NASPA (Student Affairs Administrators in Higher Education), the Centre for Recording Achievement, and the Higher Education Academy, the latter two in the UK. Chapters by research teams from within Cohorts I–III whose work is represented in this book were carefully compiled and formatted by Edith Kennedy.

As colleagues in both leading the Coalition and editing this book, we appreciate one another. As a leadership team, we work collaboratively on the basis of personal and professional commitment. Our incentive is intrinsic, linked to our belief that everyone can learn and can continue learning throughout a lifetime—both for the individual's good and for the common good. Because electronic portfolios support both these kinds of learning, we will continue to devote ourselves to fostering eportfolio practice and research.

Barbara Cambridge
Darren Cambridge
Kathleen Blake Yancey

Cohort I (2003–2006)

Alverno College
Bowling Green State University
Indiana University Purdue University Indianapolis
LaGuardia Community College
Northern Illinois University
Portland State University
Stanford University
University of Washington
Virginia Tech

Cohort II (2004–2007)

Clemson University
George Mason University
Kapi`olani Community College
The Ohio State University
Thomas College
University of Georgia
University of Illinois
University of Nebraska Omaha
Washington State University

Cohort III (2006–2009)

Arizona State University
California State Universities
Florida State University
Framingham State University
George Mason University
Minnesota State Colleges and Universities
Pennsylvania State University
Seton Hall University
Sheffield Hallam University
University of San Diego
University of Waterloo
University of Wolverhampton

Cohort IV (2007–2010)

London Metropolitan University
Queen Margaret University College
Sheffield Hallam University
University of Bradford

University of Cumbria
University of Groningen
University of Manchester Medical School
University of Michigan
University of Northumbria
University of Nottingham
University of Wolverhampton

Cohort V (2008–2011)

Kapi`olani Community College
Louisiana State University
University of Akron
University of Cincinnati
University of Denver
University of North Carolina Wilmington
University of Oregon
Virginia State University
Virginia Tech

INTRODUCTION

ON TRANSITIONS: PAST TO PRESENT

BARBARA CAMBRIDGE

*L*earning about portfolios in the past has become *portfolio learning* in the present through a shift in emphasis from implementation to inquiry. When *Electronic Portfolios: Emerging Practices in Student, Faculty, and Institutional Learning* (Cambridge) was published in 2001, many educators were exploring the possibilities for eportfolios, hoping that their initial forays into eportfolio use would improve documenting and assessing how students learn. Faculty and administrators were immersed in considering the conceptual and technical issues of beginning electronic portfolio practices and programs.

Two years later, in 2003, the Campus Computing Project Survey, an annual look at technology-related issues in colleges and universities across the United States, took the national pulse of electronic portfolios for the first time. K. C. Green, who conducted and analyzed the survey, concluded that "these first national data confirm that eportfolios are making the transition from an interesting innovation into routine implementations and operational imperatives at colleges and universities across the United States" (p. 7). Implementation and operation were key words, with colleges and universities surveying available technologies and investigating how to engage faculty and students in using

portfolios, mostly at the course and department levels.

Some educational leaders, however, thought beyond implementation and operation. In the 2004 book *The Quiet Crisis: How Higher Education Is Failing America,* Peter Smith, then president of California State University–Monterey Bay, called for "partnerships and passports" for lifelong learners. He advocated educational cooperatives that joined traditional colleges and universities with other community institutions such as museums, hospitals, and other nonprofits to provide and broker educational opportunities throughout people's lifetimes. He declared, "America's personal learners need an educational passport" that will enable "a cumulative, continuing appraisal of life experience and formal learning anytime and anyplace" (p. 153). At that time, however, Smith's visions were based more on aspiration and hope than on experience and evidence.

If electronic portfolios, which could be the potential passports that Smith described, were to gain the scale of use he espoused, evidence of their efficacy was essential. Thus the National Coalition for Electronic Portfolio Research was born in 2003. Coalition organizers, experienced with print and digital portfolios, recognized that research needed to catch up with practice. They realized that, as the power of electronic portfolios became more and more apparent, practitioners would want to work on a larger scale, a move requiring agreements about support for learning outcomes through portfolios and an infusion of resources justified by evidence. They realized also that, although many faculty members were asking excellent questions about their practices, designed inquiries into those practices were few and far between. The Coalition was established to bring together practitioners ready to ask penetrating questions about the practices of eportfolios and to apply findings to improve their practices and those of others.

FROM IMPLEMENTATION TO DESIGNED INQUIRY

A call for participation in a first cohort, limited to 10 institutions, evoked a flood of applications. Practitioners were hungry to do individual campus projects supported by critical friends in a cohort that included institutions of diverse kinds, sizes, and locations. As Pat Hutchings (2007), vice president of the Carnegie Foundation for the Advancement of Teaching, writes about a similar national project that brought together educators doing innovative work, "The single most important condition in allowing campuses to continue their work was the presence of one another working under a national project umbrella. Hard work needs good company" (p. 301). Research into the complex issues involved with electronic portfolios is hard work, so the good company of campus teams in each of the Coalition's cohorts, totaling five by 2008, portends well for generating the knowledge needed for widespread adoption of eportfolios.

The research in this book has been designed to gain answers to questions emerging from practice and to provide information to improve that practice. *Praxis*, the nexus of theory and practice, is the obvious location of many cohort members' projects. Because the Coalition was established to probe the ways in which eportfolios affect learning, research teams examined how they were used in order to generate questions about learning: How

does creating a portfolio affect student identity? How do students integrate learning from disparate sites in their lives as they choose portfolio artifacts? How does the reflection inherent in a learning portfolio change the way students make sense of their experiences? Whatever the scope of the research, the purpose was to highlight the interplay of practice and inquiry, symbiotic features of portfolio learning.

More and more faculty members in higher education recognize that this kind of inquiry into teaching and learning can and should be part of their professional lives. Researchers in the Coalition's cohorts have discovered, moreover, that achieving useful and important results can come without an abundance of new resources. Most teams in the cohorts have undertaken their research without outside funding or dedicated time or assistance. Many team members do not have "research" in their job descriptions, but they realize that answering questions about portfolio learning is crucial to creating educational environments in which students thrive and make progress toward and accomplish the learning goals of the 21st century.

In addition to teams doing projects about important educational issues, the Coalition also enables cohort-based inquiries. The first two cohorts, for example, homed in on reflection as an essential feature of eportfolios. The questions they asked and the method that the Coalition developed for addressing the questions are analyzed in Chapter 1, "Reflection and Electronic Portfolios: Inventing the Self and Re-Inventing the University." Because Cohort III comprised teams that represented student affairs and academic affairs in order to examine how eportfolios foster both in-class and out-of-class learning, integration became a central theme. Cohort IV, made up primarily of institutions in the United Kingdom, took up threshold concepts and effective practices as its two common themes. Such thematic inquiries are possible only because teams work hard to understand one another's contexts and projects and to build new knowledge about the theme by combining their answers to common questions.

Research in this book, then, means designed inquiry undertaken from practice in order to influence practice, and it is contextualized by involvement in a collaborative of individuals and institutions who are deliberate about understanding contexts and questions in order to support student learning.

FROM FORMAL SCHOOLING TO LIFELONG AND LIFEWIDE LEARNING

Initial interest in portfolios often emerged from a desire to assess student learning in a way that acknowledged its complexity, which is impossible to achieve through tests and grading of single performances. Faculty members and administrators knowledgeable about learning theories and educational research realized that current modes of testing were insufficient and did not promote students' ability to assess their own learning. These educators wanted to gain a more accurate picture of students' progress toward learning goals by helping students demonstrate their own development and self-awareness of where they came from and where they were going in their learning.

Portfolios containing only products and reflections about school-based learning, of course, could show only part of this developing knowledge and self-awareness. As Chapter 2, "Studying Student Reflection in an Electronic Portfolio Environment: An Inquiry in the Context of Practice," points out, nonformal education and informal learning contribute to what students can know and do and to who they are, so degrees and academic credentials are insufficient to paint an accurate picture. In the 21st century, students need evidence for themselves and others of their lifelong learning skills, including—as Chapter 3, "Using Eportfolios to Support Lifelong and Lifewide Learning," explains—"exploration and preparation for change" and "adaptability in both formal and informal learning environments." These skills are developed across the many roles that students play as family members, workers, and citizens, so portfolios need to represent lifewide learning. Cohort III moves in this direction by studying the ways in which eportfolios bring together co-curricular and curricular learning. Campuses in other cohorts

encourage inclusion of workplace products, reflections on multiple kinds of experiences, and feedback from multiple audiences. Eportfolios accommodate students' many roles and many sites of learning.

Recognizing the breadth of learning that contributes to what students know and do and to who they are, researchers have chosen to study the choices that students make in creating their eportfolios, including primary audience and design. For example, researchers in Chapter 6, "Making Connections: The LaGuardia ePortfolio," describe the surprise of finding that first-year students valued their families as a primary audience for their portfolios, families that often were not college-savvy and needed to understand what their family member was doing and learning. In Chapter 20, "Moving EFolio Minnesota to the Next Generation: From Individual Portfolios to an Integrated Institutional Model," the surprise came in finding that statewide eportfolio creators had personal planning as their primary objective, that is, themselves as audience.

The "Electronic Portfolio Technology and Design for Learning" chapters of this book, although they acknowledge the importance of technology choices, move beyond that consideration to show how students become agents in designing their eportfolios by employing skills acquired throughout their lives. Chapter 1, "Reflection and Electronic Portfolios: Inventing the Self and Reinventing the University," describes "a new kind of reflection that students are inventing in eportfolio environments" (p. 8). This section calls attention to *concept maps*—a design element that becomes the interface of the portfolio for the producer and the reader—as a feature that grows in complexity as students progress in their understanding and knowledge.

Moving to lifewide and lifelong learning does even more than provide a deeper and more accurate picture of students' progress in learning, however. The move enables students to be active in creating new life roles for themselves. For example, in Chapter 11, "A Values-Driven Eportfolio Journey: Nā Wa`a," students examine college learning in terms of established and ingrained cultural values, enabling themselves to move into and understand that they can operate in multiple cultures, expanding their identities rather than replacing one with another. In another example, graduate students in Chapter 21, "Assessing the Learning Potential of Eportfolios Through Thinking Sheets," learn that, in their role *as* graduate students, they can expect a predictable learning curve that may be different from the curve in other settings. They thereby know to be alert to the variability of learning curves in different situations and roles. Chapter 1, "Reflection and Electronic Portfolios: Inventing the Self and Reinventing the University," asserts, based on research by Cohorts I and II, that eportfolio practice furthers "the ability to see oneself," and "the ability to *see* oneself is the ability to see another way of being" (p. 14). The ability to see oneself leads to further learning across all the contexts of one's life.

FROM LOCAL SETTINGS TO LARGER CONTEXTS

Most campus examples in *Electronic Portfolios: Emerging Practices in Student, Faculty, and Institutional Learning* (Cambridge, 2001) described local settings. Single classrooms, single programs, and single institutions were implementing eportfolio practices through trial and error. Their experiences were and continue to be invaluable to others, a major reason for the continuing publication of that book.

Fortunately, research is now taking place for different purposes in higher education, often within larger contexts. For example, Chapter 19, "Revisioning Revision With Eportfolios in the University of Georgia First-Year Composition Program," and Chapter 8, "Influencing Learning Through Faculty and Student Generated Outcome Assessment," describe extensive and intensive research across writing programs at large state universities. Chapter 2, "Studying Student Reflection in an Electronic Portfolio Environment: An Inquiry in the Context of Practice," and Chapter 11, "A Values-Driven Eportfolio Journey: Nā Wa`a," report findings of long-term and shorter-term eportfolio practices, respectively, at the full institutional level

in two small colleges. In Chapter 12, "Eportfolios in an Undergraduate Psychology Research Experiences Program," inquiry into how eportfolios affect preparation for professional identity in the discipline of psychology brings disciplinary norms to bear across the profession. Chapter 20, "Moving eFolio Minnesota to the Next Generation: From Individual Portfolios to an Integrated Institutional Model," and Chapter 14, "Diffusing Eportfolios in Organizational Settings," describe analyses of an existing and a potential statewide program, respectively. "Moving Into the Future," the concluding section of this book, establishes that the work of this Coalition and of other initiatives signals the advent of more and more international research projects that cross national boundaries.

The work of the Coalition also signals other kinds of boundary crossings. The title of the earlier book itself, *Electronic Portfolios: Emerging Practices in Student, Faculty, and Institutional Learning,* signals three categories of focus that had potential for overlap and interaction but were often isolated. In the Coalition, however, many teams think strategically about their work, regardless of focus, in terms of institutional or statewide contexts. Even if the research shines light on a particular practice, the analysis of the research extends to effects of that practice beyond its initial site. This extension across boundaries of initial application is made possible partly by collaborations of individuals previously diffused in purpose or inquiry. Cohort III is a prime example: its teams are constituted of student affairs professionals, academic affairs faculty, and administrators. A shared commitment to student learning outcomes and the desire to investigate complementary modes of assisting students in reaching those outcomes characterize these teams and their various kinds of research.

In other cohorts, institutional researchers, classroom faculty, campus center personnel, teaching and learning center staff, and academic administrators constitute teams because of their interest in and commitment to finding out how to help student learners. Thus the cohorts bring together people who all too rarely cross the boundaries of their various roles. For example, the provost of Thomas College joined with faculty members and staff members in defining a research question and conducting the research to answer it. These new collaborations around research into electronic portfolios bode well for the larger collaborations necessary in the ever-changing circumstances of education in the 21st century.

Current discussions of higher education inevitably allude to one of those changing circumstances: the global nature of the world and the political, social, and economic interdependencies of countries. In the United States the mobility of students among various colleges and universities, the average of seven or more jobs people will hold in their lifetimes, and the diverse populations that continuously create new and different social arrangements signal the interactions among different sectors and circumstances that can be found in just one country. Education, work, and civic life in every country are connected within the country but also beyond its borders. For example, the Coalition went international after its first two cohorts in order to take advantage of learning from the similarities and differences in eportfolio practice in multiple, interconnected countries.

Taking a global view, The Knowledge Works Foundation has identified key trends and dilemmas facing education during the years 2006–2016. Technological advances are at the center of a number of them, advances that are common across national boundaries. For example, the Web makes "immersive learning environments" available to anyone at anytime. "An explosion of learning agents" includes seeing others as teachers and learners in venues far beyond schools. The result of this timelessness and expansiveness is "unbundled education," education that is available to anyone. The Coalition contends that part of that unbundled education includes electronic portfolios as learning agents themselves.

The Coalition has also been thinking ahead. In an exercise called "The View from 2030," participants have imagined the future by projecting themselves forward to 2030 and answering a set of questions as if they were living in that time. Three of the Coalition's 10 provocative questions illustrate our long-range thinking:

- At the turn of the century, the way information was encoded in electronic portfolios was either prescribed by standards created in isolation from practice or unique to an individual or institution. How were we successful in harnessing ethnoclassification to find ways of classifying and sharing information defined by actual portfolio authors?

- For a long time, we knew very little about how and why portfolio authors created links or associations between artifacts within and beyond their portfolios. We did little to help authors analyze and compare patterns of association. How did we succeed in mapping authors' associative thinking with the help of the numerical power of technology?

- Even as late as 2010, many readers of electronic portfolios did not know what to make of them, especially because they were increasingly asked to read portfolios of people very different from themselves, people from other contexts and countries. Now, in 2030, portfolio literacy is accepted as central to being an educated person and an effective organizational leader. All citizens are provided with and are able to use a rich array of portfolio tools and services. How did we succeed in helping lifelong learners and organizational leaders become portfolio literate?

The challenge for researchers and practitioners in higher education and beyond is to imagine how people can learn to benefit from the ubiquitous sources of education described by Knowledge Works. Imagining turns into practice and research as we enact our ideas about teaching and learning. As is evident in this book, researchers are beginning to show that eportfolio learning can prosper in larger and larger contexts with evidence of the impact of that learning on people and institutions. Readers are prompted to think both locally and globally, both about reports of findings and questions raised in their context of origin and in the wider context of unbundled education. This book features emergent findings *and* questions that we all need to ask about portfolio learning. In the transition from learning about portfolios to engaging with the scope and depth of portfolio learning, researchers and practitioners will continue to ask questions, posit answers based on designed inquiry, and use evidence to improve educational environments that are lifewide and lifelong.

REFERENCES

Cambridge, B. L. (2001). *Electronic portfolios: Emerging practices in student, faculty, and institutional learning.* Sterling, VA: Stylus (originally published by American Association for Higher Education).

Hutchings, P. (2007). From idea to prototype: The peer review of teaching. In R. Bacchetti & T. Ehrlich (Eds.), *Reconnecting education and foundations: Turning good intentions into educational capital* (pp. 301–302). San Francisco, CA: John Wiley.

Knowledge Works Foundation. (2006). *2006–2016 map of future forces affecting education.* Palo Alto, CA: Knowledge Works Foundation.

Smith, P. (2004) *The quiet crisis: How higher education is failing America.* Bolton, MA: Anker.

SECTION ONE

Introduction: Reflection in Electronic Portfolio Practice

In *How People Learn*, published by the National Research Council in 2000, editors John Bransford, A. L. Brown, and R. R. Cocking differentiate between expert and novice learners. Experts, who operate differently from less experienced learners, have a conceptual framework for information, notice features and patterns, organize content knowledge to reflect deep understanding, apply information in new situations, and monitor their understanding in a process of adaptive expertise, modifying concepts, identifying information gaps, and taking control of their learning. In *Electronic Portfolios: Emerging Practices in Student, Faculty, and Institutional Learning* (Cambridge, 2001), many students and faculty members were, if not novices, at least less experienced eportfolio practitioners. The chapters in this section reveal that the process of adaptive expertise in practice and research now enables more students and faculty members to warrant the label *advanced novice* or even *emerging expert* in portfolio learning.

FROM PRESCRIBED METHOD AND FORM TO LEARNER-GENERATED PROCESS AND PRESENTATION

When eportfolios were first being developed, teachers and students alike anguished over the "right"

format and the "right" process of collecting materials for the portfolio. Prescriptions of format and form, however, have been influenced by practice and, in some cases, eliminated, as practitioners have learned more about what leads to and constitutes portfolio learning.

According to researcher Helen Chen (Chapter 3), it is not degrees or academic credentials that mark lifelong learning but "transitions facilitated through the development of key work skills and personal competencies" (p. 31). Lifelong learning is based on the needs of learners as they progress in their professional and personal lives. The identification of those needs becomes more and more the responsibility of the learner over time. For example, although institutions may set desired competencies for students, with practice students begin to see how those competencies are important in their own lives and how their own experiences enact the competencies, including how the competencies can be represented. At Alverno College, for example, educators honor performances that students choose for demonstrating progress toward a long-standing set of college-wide competencies.

In fact, three continua of learning reported by Alverno researchers Bill Rickards and Lauralee Guilbault in Chapter 2 focus on developing expertise with setting frameworks and operating in those frameworks. The researchers' analysis reveals that students progress in their presented evidence from what Alverno calls "concrete and narrow" to "complex and interpretive." Students make evidence-based statements that move from "demonstrating an outcome" to "probing the meaning of the outcome," from describing a prescribed outcome to taking possession of the outcome in terms of the students' lives. On the third continuum, when students define a future self, they move from simple "personal narrative" about themselves in their school environment to seeing themselves "in a wider context."

Interestingly, faculty learners in the Inter/National Coalition's first two cohorts followed another kind of pattern of adaptive expertise. At first, they were uncertain about questions to ask, in this case feeling hampered by no prescription or even direction that might emerge from previous research, because the research was nonexistent. They turned to artifacts from student portfolios to build language and categories for analyzing reflective practices in eportfolios. They had to take the responsibility of creating an inquiry process that would be knowledge making. They reflected at multiple points upon the process, choosing to change it when it was less than fruitful and to document and extend what worked. They began to see the patterns that experts see and to modify their expectations as they generated and took control of their inquiry process.

Current practice and research in eportfolios reveals that the more the learner takes charge of the format and process, the deeper the learning.

FROM ARTIFACTS AS EVIDENCE OF IDENTITY TO IDENTITY THROUGH SELF-AWARENESS

Electronic Portfolios: Emerging Practices in Student, Faculty, and Institutional Learning (Cambridge, 2001) contains a number of screen shots, a helpful resource for people who want to know what a portfolio page looks like. In that book's section on student portfolios, information on collecting artifacts is plentiful: What should a student keep? Which

artifacts reveal what about the portfolio producer? What can readers make of the collection? The eye was often on the artifacts.

The shift from focus on the artifacts to the designer of the artifacts is revealed both in this section and in a later book section on design. Chen's Chapter 3 use of the term *curating* helps clarify the significance: Learners move from being consumers to producers as they take responsibility for their eportfolio presentations. Narrowing the point to reflection, Yancey (Chapter 1) uses the example of students' designing their own eportfolios through the use of concept maps. She poses both claims and questions about "materials, contexts, and practices" that make up "a new kind of reflection that students are inventing in eportfolio environments." This reflection operates during the making of the concept map and as an interface for their portfolios.

And in Chapter 2, Rickards and Guilbault describe one transformational learning cycle as a "progressive movement across successive domains," that is, "using metacognitive strategies—to restructure knowledge and enable thinking while performing—connects knowing and doing, reasoning and performance." The identity of the learner is both formed and made visible through reflection on and design of artifacts in an electronic portfolio.

FROM SINGLE INSTANCE AND CONTEXT TO MULTIPLE ITERATIONS AND CONTEXTS

Answering "What have we learned?" about the two Coalition cohorts who studied reflection in eportfolios, Yancey, in Chapter 1, tops her list with context: Audience makes a difference. Rhetorical situations demand different responses in formatting, amount and kind of evidence, and tone and register of language. Different occasions demand different portfolio presentations. Through creating rationales for different audiences and occasions, students realize that learning is a social engagement.

The cohorts' research revealed what has been verified elsewhere: Structures "are not innocent. Through arrangement, they signal what is valuable." Curricula are sometimes differentiated as delivered, experienced, and lived: In the Coalition research the lived curriculum is revealed through what students choose to include and reflect on in their eportfolios. Rickards and Guilbault state that "noting substantive differences in how students use evidence, in how conceptual understanding is advanced, and in how students recognize their own learning orientations and identity, teachers can make sense of student differences important in diagnosing class and individual needs." In other words, not only do portfolio producers learn from creating portfolios for multiple audiences, but their work influences the larger world through curricular and pedagogical consequences.

Authors in this section all consider the influence of time on learning. Chen's emphasis on lifelong learning implies multiple opportunities through an eportfolio to represent stages of development throughout a lifetime. In analyzing the research finding about students' developing a future self, Rickards and Guilbault note that moving from personal narrative to relationships in context is marked in part by the extent of observing changes in oneself. In addition, Yancey states that cohort researchers advocate building in time for reflection so that students become aware of influences on their identities, especially the influence of their own acts as they create and re-create their eportfolios.

These influences and changes occur iteratively and cumulatively in a way that recognizes the importance of time.

The evolution of eportfolio research reveals a move from prescribed method and form to learner-generated process and presentation, from artifacts as evidence of identity to identity through self-awareness, and from single context and instance to multiple contexts and iterations. As you read these chapters that allude to research at a single institution, across two cohorts of institutions, and across a range of colleges and universities, watch for emergent findings and common questions. As you read, you may well generate additional questions for research of your own.

REFERENCES

Bransford, J., Brown, A. L., & Cocking, R. R. (Eds.). (2000). *How people learn: Brain, mind, experience, and school* (Expanded ed.). Washington, DC: National Research Council.

Cambridge, B. (2001). *Electronic portfolios: Emerging practices in student, faculty, and institutional learning*. Sterling, VA: Stylus (originally published by American Association for Higher Education).

1

REFLECTION AND ELECTRONIC PORTFOLIOS
Inventing the Self and Reinventing the University

KATHLEEN BLAKE YANCEY
Florida State University

Print and electronic portfolios historically have featured *reflection* as their centerpieces. By *reflection*, educators have typically meant both the processes in which students have engaged and one or more reflective texts. In print portfolios, these texts are often a reflective essay or a reflective letter, both of which introduce and interpret the portfolio contents to one or more readers, sometimes a teacher but also the student. As portfolios have gone electronic, reflective texts have taken myriad forms—from concept maps to written texts to streaming video. In this shift from print to electronic, the claims for reflection have widened and increased as well. Three of these claims are that (1) through reflection, students make knowledge by articulating connections among portfolio exhibits, learning, and self; (2) reflective activities introduce students to new kinds of self-assessment, often an outcomes-based self-assessment, that they carry into life outside of and beyond educational settings; and (3) through engaging in reflective activities, students develop the stance and practices of a reflective practitioner who can synthesize multiple sources of evidence and make contingent and ethical sense of them.

Collectively, institutional members of the Inter/National Coalition for Electronic Portfolio Research, like many portfolio advocates, have found considerable promise in reflection. As a research entity, however, the Coalition wanted to know if the claims for reflection could be substantiated. We had many related questions: What counts as reflection, and what evidence of learning do we see in reflection? Does the medium matter, and, if so, how? Are students who practice reflection more engaged than other students? Do students who practice reflection stay in school longer? Do these engaged students graduate at a higher rate than non-portfolio practitioners? To inquire into the efficacy of reflection, then, we began a multiyear study of reflection. Our processes were, like portfolio processes themselves, *reiterative*: that is, we began with one question, considered a related question, and returned to the first, seeing the first question anew through a new context. More specifically, Coalition participants engaged in five iterations. We

1. began with reflection itself, including definitions of and research about reflection;
2. analyzed a reflective artifact;
3. reviewed a reflective artifact in the immediate context of the entire eportfolio;
4. considered reflection and electronic portfolios in larger institutional contexts; and

5. created a "catalog entry" for a reflective artifact.

In taking up these questions, we engaged in several kinds of learning. We understood reflection anew, as we saw reflection-as-text differently—through multiple contexts. We traced the development of students as they reflected. We were able to link students' reflective practices with their school performance, thereby documenting the claim that reflection enhances learning. Most significantly, through reflective activities, we saw students inventing themselves as they coinvented our universities.

FIRST ITERATION

Our initial focus on reflection enabled us to define it, especially in the context of an electronic portfolio. In a first exercise, we took up seven questions, which together functioned as a heuristic for understanding the place of reflection in electronic portfolios.

1. Our first question inquired into the materials of reflection and the evidence of reflection. What are the materials of reflection, and what counts as evidence of reflection? Given the context of the Coalition's diverse set of institutions, what are the ways that reflection is defined, solicited, and valued at different institutions? Is reflection a distinctive feature of electronic portfolios? What role do linking, coherence, and accessibility play in reflection? Is there sufficient commonality among definitions that we can talk about reflection in some useful way?

2. Our second question focused on guiding principles and practices. What are those principles and practices at individual schools? How do electronic portfolios appear to inside stakeholders and to outside stakeholders?

3. Our most challenging question was the third: Do electronic portfolios enhance student learning, and, if so, in what ways? Key to this

question, of course, was the idea of learning: how would we define it? One approach involved a taxonomy like Bloom's; a second involved national outcome statements like the Writing Program Administrator's Outcomes for First-Year Writing; a third approach was to use locally developed statements of outcomes or competencies.

4. Because electronic portfolios are by definition digital and can be networked, we asked, Which literacies are fostered by eportfolio use?

5. Because electronic portfolios were being sponsored by different units on campuses, from first-year composition programs to career centers, we asked the following questions: What are the uses of eportfolios? Can these uses or purposes be categorized?

6. Student engagement, as a proxy for learning or as evidence of learning, could be connected to reflection. How might we correlate these two dimensions?

7. Because in electronic portfolios success is not defined in conventional ways—either grades on one end of the spectrum or nationally normed tests on the other end—what *does* count as success in eportfolios? What are the criteria for success for specific disciplines or outcomes? What counts as evidence of student learning? Is reflection part of that evidence, and by reflection, do we mean metacognition and/or something more?

SECOND ITERATION

Our second iteration focused on a detailed description of a single artifact as a mechanism for defining reflection more specifically, and the artifacts taken together for reading across institutional examples of reflection (Figure 1.1).

Question 1: Describe the context of your chosen artifact. (What assignment generated this artifact? Was it required? Graded? Given feedback? What was the desired outcome?)

Question 2: Provide a thick description of your chosen artifact from a student electronic portfolio.

Question 3: What is the impact of the artifact on student learning and the educational environment?

Question 4: Please use this space to pose questions to your Inter/National Coalition colleagues regarding student electronic portfolios.

THIRD ITERATION

Our third iteration was influenced by our sense that a detailed description was not enough: context was essential. To explain and analyze the reflective properties of the artifact, we needed a fuller picture of the *artifact-in-context*. We hoped that this iteration would enable us to look at artifacts relative to each other as we continued to ask: How does reflection supported by electronic portfolios influence learning? To focus on the artifact-in-context, we designed a set of six questions that formed an hourglass: beginning at the scope of a portfolio, narrowing to one artifact, and moving out again to all the identified artifacts in the portfolio.

1. Choose *one student portfolio* that you can share. List all the *possible artifacts* from that portfolio that you would categorize as examples of reflection. List only artifacts that are reflective.
2. Of these, *which three* are most useful for analysis about reflection. Why?
3. *Which artifact* will you choose to analyze first? Why?
4. What information would a reader (such as a member of the Inter/National Coalition) need in order to *understand* how this artifact shows reflection?
5. Is there *evidence* that the act of composing this reflection, in itself, contributed to the student's learning?
6. How is this artifact *congruent* or not congruent with what you learn about the student's ability?

FOURTH ITERATION

Our fourth iteration took a different turn, toward prior work on reflection and the intellectual development of college students. We considered research on transfer of knowledge, especially that presented in the National Research Council volume *How People Learn* (Bransford, Brown, & Cocking, 1999), paying special attention to the mental maps characterizing expertise. We considered Donald Schön's (1983) scholarship on reflective practice, with its attention to reiterative practice and to the results of unsuccessful reflection, in over-learning and counter-learning. We reviewed Marcia Baxter Magolda's (2001) work on epistemological reflection, with its three-part framework: validating the student as knower; situating learning in the student's own experience; and defining learning as jointly constructed meaning. Finally, we considered how interviews themselves, particularly because of the dialogue characterizing them, construct a reflective space and how the reflective interview, even when not captured, constitutes a legitimate form of reflection.

FIFTH ITERATION

Our fifth iteration focused on developing a catalog of Coalition-reflective artifacts. For each artifact, we looked for the following:

School and Contact Person
Artifact
Medium/Media/Genre
Context
Focus/Intent
Practices Surrounding/Supporting Reflection
Special Features

CATEGORIES OF FINDINGS

Our findings from these processes fall into three categories: a set of findings linked to the relationship between eportfolios, structure, and reflection; evidence of the efficacy of eportfolio-reflective practice

Figure 1.1

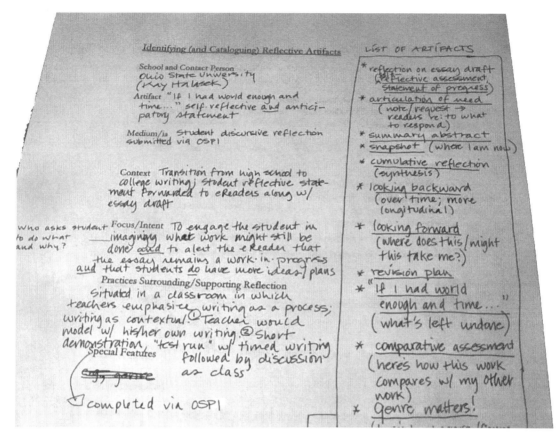

on students; and a set of claims—and new questions emanating from them—about the materials, contexts, and practices of a new kind of reflection that students are inventing in eportfolio environments.

Eportfolios, Structures, and Reflection

One of the more surprising findings across institutions was that of eportfolio structures and of the ways that established or student-created eportfolio structures invite, foster, and support reflection. The University of Washington's composition program, for example, worked with IT personnel to create a structure specific to desired writing outcomes for students, outcomes linked to a national outcomes statement. In addition, this structure, represented in an eportfolio shell, includes curricular support—for example, reminders to students about their task and a rationale guiding student selection of texts (see Figure 1.2). The shell, therefore, is not a shell but a resource, in this case about the genre of the eportfolio. The shell provides guidance with prompts

such as, "Does one of your papers demonstrate especially compelling support for a claim? Talk about how you found and developed this evidence to make your argument." Students then can work in the context of both structure and guiding questions.

A structure that works toward different aims is designed into the general education electronic portfolio at Indiana University Purdue University Indianapolis (IUPUI). Keyed to the general education competencies—the PULs, or principles of undergraduate learning—the IUPUI framework offers students a number of possibilities (see Figure 1.3). Perhaps most obvious is the developmental structure; students can include exhibits at one of three achievement levels: introductory, intermediate, and advanced. In addition to exhibits from schoolwork, there is a column for exhibits completed outside of school. Through the inclusion of both academic and nonacademic learning samples in the matrix, IUPUI invites the student to create a whole composition of learning in and through

Figure 1.2

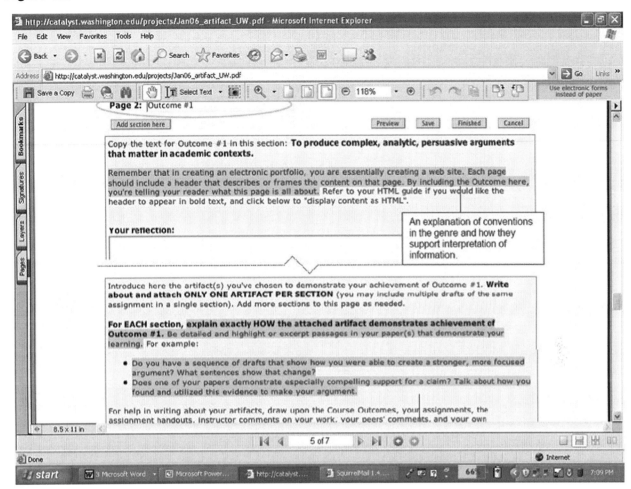

the portfolio. In addition, the electronic portfolio is itself an interactive *environment* where students can receive response to their exhibits. As important for consideration of reflection, the designers of the electronic portfolio see in it both structure and invitation for advanced reflective thinking:

> Our findings included the predictable discovery of more evidence of advanced reflective thinking in our seniors than in our first-year students, which also provided a level of confirmation for the construct of our developmental framework for reflection. Much more noteworthy, however, was our discovery of a phenomenon that we call "matrix thinking," the kind of reflective thinking that results when students combine the elements of a matrix and use the resulting conceptual construct as a lens through which to revisit work initially created in a different context for a different reason.

In other words, and as Hamilton and Kahn explain in Chapter 10, the matrix itself shows students how to *see doubly*. This ability to see in multiple contexts is one characteristic of reflection.

Drawing from a review of student work and from research on learning, the Alverno model of reflective development is a structure used as a context for student development by several other campuses—among them IUPUI and Portland State University in the United States, and Sheffield Hallam University in the United Kingdom—as a context for student development. In this single structure, three dimensions associated with reflection—self-assessment, understanding of how knowledge is created, and identity as a lifelong learner—are crafted into a single developmental schema. Such a schema is valuable for at least three reasons. First, each dimension is developmentally articulated, and each level is fully operationalized.

Figure 1.3

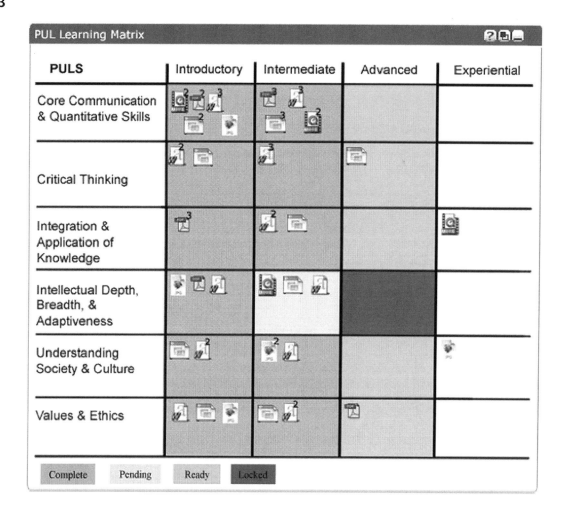

Thus, the advanced learner understands not only how knowledge is constructed but also how to construct it himself or herself. Specifically, the advanced learner incorporates feedback and past performance in constructing further performance and learning plans; uses his or her growing command of knowledge structure (e.g., expertise, discipline, theory, abilities) as a foundation for further learning; and understands his or her own performance as a learner and transfers learning strategies to multiple contexts (see Chapter 2).

Second, because the dimensions are all included but crafted *onto* a schema rather than woven together, a student's differentiated development can be acknowledged, with progress rewarded and support provided as appropriate. Third, because of its comprehensiveness, the easily adoptable and adaptable schema offers potential for a context for reflection operating across multiple institutions, thus supporting students and providing a foundation for additional interinstitutional research.

The last set of structures, created by students themselves, takes the form of concept maps where students plot their understandings as a function of visual and verbal relationships. As explained by an accounting student at the University of Waterloo, "The biggest challenge I faced when creating my concept map was trying to identify relationships. It was very easy to name accounting concepts, but developing relationships between the concepts was a challenge." A key shift is that students create the concept maps that used to be *given* to them in textbooks and syllabi and by faculty.

Through creating, students construct their own map of learning, one congruent with the digital medium of an electronic portfolio (see Figure 1.4). For example, at Clemson University, psychology students created eportfolios that produced another

Figure 1.4

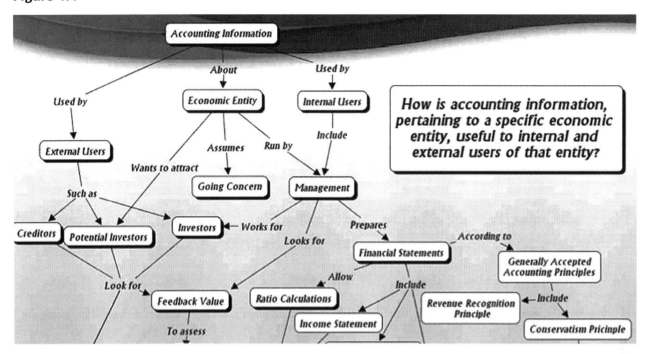

Figure 1.5

kind of map directly related to learning. In this project, the links that students created to connect different exhibits in initial eportfolios were compared with those they created for later eportfolios. In this analysis, a developmental pattern emerged; the sunburst heliocentric structures of early eport-

folios expanded and elaborated into the more complex structures of the final eportfolio (Figure 1.5). In this eportfolio model, students literally link their way to connectedness and meaning. An important motivator in this linking is the audience, which for these students, as Clemson faculty member

Clemson Eport Structures

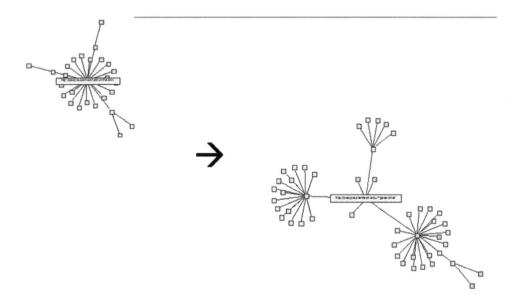

Ben Stephens notes in Chapter 12, was plural and yet differentiated:

> These structures may reflect the interns' concept mapping of the content of the portfolio designed to appeal to various social audiences for the eportfolio. Some nodes in the hierarchy seem useful for the mentor and graduate schools (e.g. the research project) while others are designed for the instructor (e.g. class activities node). Likewise, many interns constructed nodes that seem directed towards peers; these often contained links to their home institution and/or to photos of summer program peers and social activities. In addition, these concept maps may serve a dual purpose: they may aid both communicator and audience (Wang & Dwyer, 2006). In sum, the development of these maps in our intern eportfolios seems to suggest an awareness of how artifacts connect to self as well as to the needs of valued social audiences.

EFFICACY OF EPORTFOLIO-REFLECTIVE PRACTICE ON STUDENTS

Findings about the efficacy of eportfolio reflection were equally, or perhaps more, important. Four different electronic portfolio projects, at four very different institutions, provided co-relational and institutional evidence of student learning. Put differently, data support the claim that eportfolio reflection, as defined here, is directly related to student success.

Kapi`olani Community College (KCC) introduced into a Hawaiian values class an eportfolio that helps students succeed in the explicit context of native cultural values. KCC has used several measures to assess this eportfolio-based approach to learning, including the nationally normed Community College Survey of Student Engagement (CCSSE) and a set of local questions. As the leaders of the KCC effort point out in Chapter 11, six local questions received responses worthy of note:

> The six questions that were significantly more positive than national and local benchmarks addressed the use of values, critical thinking, writing, teamwork, and a level of engagement. [In addition] students' spontaneous, open-ended comments in the survey support our hypothesis that working on the ePortfolio with the values approach is leading students to engage more deeply in their learning, to mention the values in their reflections, and to relate the values to their understanding of their learning.

One student, in commenting on the value of the eportfolio, especially in the context of native values, noted the role of reflection in learning, the role of time as a factor in learning and the new space for learning provided by the eportfolio: "I like reflecting on what I've learned or hope to in the future. Makes it so much easier to focus on what it is I'm trying to learn when I know there is a place for me to reflect upon my work at a later time."

At La Guardia Community College, the eportfolio seeks to serve many purposes—increasing academic achievement by strengthening learning and assessment; aiding career development by assisting students to become prepared for employment; and encouraging student expression by providing a site where personal representations are welcome. This eportfolio model also invites students to include two cultures, their home culture and the academic culture, a particularly appropriate structure, given the largely immigrant population of the school. In reviewing the efficacy of their effort, the leaders at La-Guardia drew from a varied set of data, including CCSSE data and local data on course completion rates and retention rates. As at KCC, the student engagement data, here specifically CCSSE data, indicate higher than expected positive responses for eportfolio students:

> On virtually every question, students in these ePortfolio-intensive courses tended to score higher in engagement than the collegewide reported by the LaGuardia Office of Institutional Research. For example, on one critical thinking-related question—Question 5a from the 2005–6 survey: "How much has your coursework emphasized synthesizing and organizing ideas, information, and or experiences in new ways?"—the collegewide mean is 2.85 (a substantial .18 points above the national

mean of 2.67). The mean for students in ePortfolio courses was 3.12, an additional .27 points higher than the already positive college mean. The pattern was similar for questions about writing, effort, technology, and classroom collaboration.

At two very different schools literally halfway around the world from each other, and in two very different models—one a single-class model; the other an institutional, multiyear model—students report higher levels of engagement on questions inquiring into practices critical for academic development and success: writing, critical thinking, and teamwork. And interestingly, at LaGuardia, that engagement is translating into higher course completion and retention rates:

> Retention data is similarly positive. For example, analysis of the transcripts of a sample of nearly 2,000 students in ePortfolio-intensive courses in 2005–6 showed an average one-semester return rate that is 5.6 percentage points higher than the college average.

A student's explanation of the value of this work, of course, is not located in the world of data. As she puts it, it is in the world of seeing anew:

> Not only did I gain technical skills, but I learned how to express myself as a student. The different sections of my ePortfolio made me realize important things about how I see myself starting at LaGuardia, how I see myself now and in my future. My experience with ePortfolio at LaGuardia has made me see more of who I want to be.

At another university, the University of Nebraska–Omaha (UNO), eportfolio researchers took another focus. UNO, a major urban institution, has as one of its goals the use of electronic portfolios for disciplinary development and achievement, in this case for teacher education candidates. The eportfolio is a database-driven repository for exhibits from coursework activities throughout a teacher candidate's undergraduate program, which is itself keyed to a set of standards. UNO's research focused on the role that the eportfolio and its accompanying reflec-

tion play in helping students learn required content. The results were bimodal: students who used it infrequently found little value, whereas those students whose teachers integrated it into the program and who worked on it consistently found it a valuable means of learning:

> The respondents that reported consistent use of ePortfolios indicated more often that the ePortfolio had a positive impact on their learning of content. The open-ended comments also confirmed this idea, with several respondents who were generally positive about ePortfolio mentioning the consistent use and generally those who were negative toward ePortfolios indicating there was not a consistent use. Also, elementary education majors were much more positive about ePortfolio than secondary education majors, and we know that the elementary program is much more consistent in the use of ePortfolios than the secondary program.

As is the case in earlier examples, student comments provide a window into the findings. In this case, the student makes a point echoing that of the LaGuardia student about the ways that portfolio and reflection provide a means of *seeing* oneself in action: "I feel it was helpful in making me more genuinely reflective as I was able to actually see myself in practice." The ability to *see* oneself is the ability to see another way of being.

The Clemson model is also oriented toward disciplinary development, in this case in psychology and specifically through a summer internship program. One measure of success for the summer program was the ability of the interns to conceptualize their learning in an appropriate hierarchy. To assess this feature, the leaders at Clemson focused on the "interrelationship among artifacts" within the electronic portfolio:

> To determine the interrelationship among artifacts, we calculated a "Hierarchy" score, computed as the weighted average of all website pages where the entry page was equal to 1.0, pages linked to the entry page were equal to 2.0, and so on. The average hierarchy score for the group was

2.74, indicating that many eportfolios were richly structured within organizing themes.

Moreover, as previously indicated, the Clemson researchers believe that audience may be a compelling rationale for this arrangement. Learning is thus conceptualized with both intellectual and social dimensions. In this model, students formally reflect at mid-experience and at the end of the experience, and that reiteration reveals how students value time and a *planned* reiterative process. At midterm, this student looks backward as she casts a glance into the future:

> For the remaining six weeks of the program, I imagine we'll encounter these questions [about pure and applied research] again. Next time, I'll also provide a larger reflection on my particular project, discoveries I have made, how it contributes to this knowledge base, and how, somewhere along the "continuum," it can be directly applied.

In the reflective conclusion, she notes not only what has been learned but also what might be learned as a function of the initial experience. Interestingly, the identification of weakness—a point made in the Alverno developmental schema—is understood *not* as a problem but rather as a *prerequisite for learning* that the student herself wants to acquire:

> Even though I have faced many of the challenges of psychological research this summer and now understand where my weaknesses lie, I am all the more interested in conducting further and *better* research my upcoming senior year and throughout graduate school. After recognizing what limitations, complications, and problems my study had this summer, I feel a strong need to improve upon my research and the research of others.

Put more observationally, what is it that we think we have learned? We understand the following:

- Reflection always happens in context. Contexts, like purposes, vary. Where contexts connect with students, where they include cultural and personal values, where they encourage a process view of learning, they are more likely to engage students.
- Portfolio structures are not innocent. Through arrangement, they signal what is valuable.
- Structures that we provide shape reflection. Where the structure provides scaffolding, and where it stimulates connections, it invites the meaning-making characteristic of deep learning.
- Asking students to create their own structures may be a critical move, allowing students to articulate both curricular understandings and personal connections, in the process demonstrating the mapping development associated with expertise.
- Reflection comes in many forms and in reiterative processes: building in reiteration explicitly builds in time, which in turn fosters the identity of a learner.
- "Materials" of reflection warrant further study. Those materials include the use of visuals like images and maps, developmental frameworks, and even the thinking sheets created at George Mason University; these sheets, which are a low-tech way of recording reflective processes that go into eportfolio making, constitute one form of raw material for reflection (see Figure 1.6 and Chapter 21).
- Responses of students to reflection, as defined here, are remarkably similar both in terms of student engagement data and in terms of student articulation of their experience. Although there is evidence of many kinds, there are patterns in the evidence.
- The audience for reflection is not a trivial matter: it motivates students, it often includes peers and other personal audience members, and it may motivate the acquisition of content.
- Reflection as a knowledge-making activity—like the making of knowledge in science and the design of art and performance—relies on reviewing, recontextualizing, and reiterating, processes functioning as means of discovery and development.
- The role of the personal is important in securing learning, perhaps especially in reflection.

Figure 1.6

George Mason Thinking Sheets

Name:_____

Date_____Length of time for this

session_____

(spaced out for fill in space)

Feel Free to use the back of this sheet as necessary
1.) What do you intend to accomplish this session?

2) As you work on the portfolio this session, please note what artifacts (text, links, documents, pictures, audio/video, etc.), or design elements you create or change and briefly explain your reasons for doing so.

3) What issues came up this session?

4) How did you seek out help or work with others during this session?

5) What do you think you achieved/ learned this session?

- The power of collective expertise enables insight into student learning. The Coalition's set of reiterative activities has contributed to the success of the Coalition in addressing questions about student learning. We shared a common question and allowed it to play itself out across different sites. We established a set of questions and used the rhythm of the questioning as a way to pace learning and as a means of learning. We learned, especially in the two artifact exercises, how important it is to document practice and how useful it is to have an external audience who needs that documentation and who is interested in reviewing it and assisting in making sense of it. We learned about the role of inquiry and the need to engage in it. As we moved outward, we found that larger sets of data—such as course completion rates and CCSSE data—allowed us to contextualize our own findings and to discern larger patterns.

QUESTIONS: MATERIALS, PRACTICES, AND CONTEXTS

We do have further questions. Several institutions are now using a version of the Alverno reflective framework, and we are eager to see how it supports reflection and how it might be locally adapted. Other institutions are interested in using a coding schema to inquire into the quality of reflection. Still others are inviting employers to review reflection. And research teams are eager to know more about reflection itself: What is the best medium for it? Does that definition vary by student population, by level of development, and/or by discipline? How else might we encourage quality in reflection, and how else might we scaffold it? What is the role of reflection in disciplinary contexts, in professional contexts, and beyond school gates?

REINVENTING THE UNIVERSITY

In 1985, rhetoric and composition scholar David Bartholomae (1985) coined the expression *inventing the university* to explain the basic task of the postsecondary student aspiring to success: "He must learn to speak our language." In connecting *our* language and students' invention of the university, Bartholomae highlighted a need for students to accommodate to and assimilate into *us*, into *our* institutions. Such accommodation does not always succeed, however, as we see in stagnant student retention and graduation rates and in disengaged students who are dropouts in waiting.

There are other ways to think about the university, of course. One way is through the lens of three curricula. In addition to the "delivered" curriculum of our catalog copy and syllabus, there are two others—the *experienced* curriculum, which is what students make out of our delivered curriculum; and the *lived* curriculum, which occurs prior to *and* alongside *and* after our institutional curricula conclude (Yancey, 2004). In the best of all instances, electronic portfolios can provide a common site for these three curricula, and reflection can provide a specific opportunity to see each, to talk across them, to connect them, to trace the contradictions among them, and to create a contingent sense of them. In this sense, reflection is itself a site of invention, a place to make new knowledge, to shape new selves, and, in so doing, to reinvent the university.

That is the promise of reflection, a promise we continue to explore and support.

REFERENCES

Bartholomae, D. (1985). Inventing the university. In M. Rose (Ed.), *When a writer can't write: Studies in writer's block and other composing-process problems* (pp. 134–165). New York: Guilford.

Baxter Magdola, M. B. (2001). *Making their own way: Narratives for transforming higher education to promote self-development.* Sterling, VA: Stylus.

Bransford, J. D., Brown, A. L., & Cocking, R. R. (1999). *How people learn: Brain, mind, experience, and school.* Washington, DC: National Research Council.

Schön, D. (1983). *The reflective practitioner: How professionals think in action.* New York, NY: Basic Books.

Yancey, K. B. (2004). *Teaching literature as reflective practice.* Urbana, IL: National Council of Teachers of English.

2

STUDYING STUDENT REFLECTION IN AN ELECTRONIC PORTFOLIO ENVIRONMENT

An Inquiry in the Context of Practice

W. H. RICKARDS and LAURALEE GUILBAULT
Alverno College

> I believe that you are sincere and good at heart. If you do not attain happiness, always remember that you are on the right road, and try not to leave it. . . . What seems to you bad within you will grow purer from the very fact of your observing it in yourself.
>
> Dostoyevsky, *Brothers Karamazov*, 1880/1990

> Reflective practices that are intellectually credible can promote resiliency and resourcefulness in the face of life's dynamic challenges and encourage habits of individual and collective attention and analysis that can sustain higher education as it works to address the problems of society.
>
> Rogers, 2001, p. 37

As Dostoyevsky suggested, systematic attention to ourselves creates a context for learning, growth, and change. Reflection has long been an important dimension of adult and advanced learning. Digital technology has enabled new ways of using tools like portfolios to scaffold reflective activities—by storing and making accessible multiple artifacts of student performance and records and by structuring a context for analysis and interpretation. But these opportunities have also created challenges for research and pedagogy. We need to understand the use and potential of the portfolio as a tool in the context of educational practices.

In 1999, Alverno College, an undergraduate women's college of liberal arts and professional studies, introduced a Diagnostic Digital Portfolio as a tool to support all students in the critical work of understanding and building on their own learning (www.ddp.alverno.edu; patent number 6,651,071). Since that time, the college has monitored this process, sampling student and faculty experiences and conducting targeted studies (Ehley, 2006). In reflective writing in which students examine multiple assessed performances and analyze patterns of learning, the college's faculty and researchers have worked to understand and describe this process of student construction, including what different characteristics of the reflections imply for teaching practices (Rickards et al., 2006, 2008). During collaborative and deliberative inquiry, faculty members and the Office of Educational Research and Evaluation staff produced a matrix of descriptors that has contributed to continuing discussions about reflection, learning, and teaching. Rather than an examination of particular practices at Alverno, the current work summarizes the process of studying reflection within the portfolio with further attention to (a) ways digital portfolio practices are located in the larger educational program of Alverno College, (b) themes within the reflection descriptors, and (c) implications for educational practice, specifically relating to portfolio-based environments.

THE IMPORTANCE OF REFLECTION AND ITS ROLE IN PEDAGOGY: PORTFOLIO-BASED PRACTICES IN THE EDUCATIONAL PROGRAM AT ALVERNO COLLEGE

It is useful to understand the larger system of practices in which Alverno's portfolio and the studies described here emerged.

Alverno College Learning Principles and Practices

For over three decades, Alverno College faculty members have deliberated extensively on student learning and targeted learning outcomes across multiple disciplines (Alverno, 1979/1994). From early in the process, shared assumptions about characteristics of learning included *integrative/experiential, characterized by self-awareness, active and interactive, developmental*, and *transferable*. The college's longitudinal research and continuing deliberations of the faculty elaborated the principles, and the notion that "learning that lasts is self-aware and reflective, self-assessed and self-regarding" (Mentkowski & Associates, 2000, pp. 232–235) was examined from developmental and curricular perspectives. Focusing on conceptual relationships and performative aspects of learning, these statements emphasized that as students are more actively engaged in learning and consciously attend to learning processes and

outcomes, they can consolidate their learning and increase the potential for transfer.

In similar constructions, Boud, Keogh, and Walker (1985); Kitchener and King (1981); Kolb (1984); Schön (1983); and others have emphasized how—in *reflection*—past experiences, prior learning, personal frameworks, and performance can be engaged and analyzed, resulting in some combination of new learning, frameworks, and constructs; deeper understanding of personal capacity; and readiness for new and diverse contexts. Specifically, reflection on experiential aspects of learning, performance, and interactions becomes a richer source of learning.

In the Alverno curriculum, in a context of explicit learning outcomes, performances, feedback, and self-assessment, reflection was included to expand the capacity to integrate learning and to transfer it to new contexts of performance. Through learning activities that involved analysis, mental rehearsal, goal setting, and other personal means, students could prepare for and better understand performance. In this form, reflection was pursued as a part of learning activities.

In performance assessments of varying types and with sustained study, self-assessment developed as a critical aspect of learning (Alverno, 2000). Although self-assessment and reflection frequently overlap in practice, in general, self-assessment is more directed at specific performances and evaluative judgments in relation to criteria, whereas reflection is an approach to learning, often from the analysis of multiple performance experiences. But self-assessment and reflection each involve processes of analysis, interpretation, and construction for the future. Because portfolios are sustained performances that engage students in their own learning as they gather and analyze multiple performance and artifacts, students also examine their own processes for developing and interpreting the portfolio as a conscious, metacognitive take on their learning. (For further discussion of reflection and self-assessment, see Yancey, 1998.)

Integrating Learning and Development

Based on a longitudinal study of two complete classes from college entry through graduation and up to 5 years beyond, Mentkowski and her colleagues (2000) proposed an *educational theory of learning that lasts* that consists of

1. domains of growth in the person (*reasoning, performance, self-reflection, and development*) integrated through transformative learning cycles, and
2. learning and action principles expressed through a narrative language of learning with essential elements of curriculum and college culture for learning that lasts.

Using the longitudinal data from cognitive developmental measures; curriculum performance; open-ended, in-depth interviews with students and alumnae; and performance interviews with alumnae 5 years after graduation, researchers described three transformational learning cycles that supported progressive movement across successive domains:

- *Using metacognitive strategies*—to restructure knowledge and enable thinking while performing—connects knowing and doing, reasoning and performance.
- *Self-assessing role performance*—using criteria and standards from diverse sources—fosters identity as a learner and professional.
- *Engaging diverse approaches, views, and activities with breadth and depth*—appreciating multiple perspectives and mutuality, engaging others, and independent learning—leads to personal transformation.

These findings are striking in the context of learning portfolios: Reflecting on multiple artifacts from diverse contexts becomes an engine for individual change. This approach also emphasizes the fundamental purpose of the portfolio as a learning tool rather than a product for external review (O'Brien, 2006).

The Diagnostic Digital Portfolio

Alverno educators developed the Diagnostic Digital Portfolio (the DDP) over a period of years (Ehley, 2006; O'Brien, 2006). Responding to students' needs to see their academic progress in a more specific format, educators designed the DDP

as a theory-based electronic tool consonant with the college's researched practices and learning principles to support student learning and development through a range of cognitive and reflective actions. Residing on the Web, the DDP allows students, faculty members, and academic staff to upload assignments and assessments, feedback, and self-assessments for review on a regular basis. Each entering cohort of students has access to the DDP, selected assessments in general education are fully integrated into the eportfolio, and additional assessments are added each year. Some, such as the Mid-Program Portfolio Assessment examined in this study, are designed specifically to include reflection on work across courses as part of the performance. The college's expansive research studies about the portfolio have helped in understanding the complexity of portfolio practices and the challenges of large-scale implementation (Ehley, 2006).

A MIXED-METHOD RESEARCH PROGRAM: REFLECTION IN A PORTFOLIO ENVIRONMENT

As Alverno's DDP was implemented at scale from the beginning, faculty members and the college's Educational Research and Evaluation office collaborated to monitor the process and record the experiences of faculty and students. Targeted efforts were also pursued in selected programs and classes.

Watching the portfolio's implementation over an extended period and understanding the patterns of faculty and student use have been critical. Although it may seem axiomatic, it was important to recognize that the educational value of a learning portfolio derives from the learners' uses. How these are supported by faculty, curriculum, physical access, prior preparation, and institutional policy all become variables critical to learning. The degree of variance in these factors complicates study of learner impact outside of a controlled laboratory situation (Rickards et al., 2008). Although this complexity complicates making claims about the tool as an intervention, that complexity is also the basis for increasing the accuracy of electronic portfolio descriptions that relate learning outcomes, practices, and technology tools.

Alverno's research involved a multi- and mixed-method approach: using individual interviews, classroom observations of students using the DDP during initial implementation, and then survey techniques to estimate patterns of use. Simultaneously, faculty and researchers addressed questions about student reflection to increase understanding of this aspect of portfolio use. Collaboration with peer institutions was an important part of the research process; as a part of the Inter/National Coalition for Electronic Portfolio Research, members of the college participated in discussions and deliberations that helped advance our thinking about reflection. Most recently, faculty in science, mathematics, and technology have been addressing how the portfolio can enhance problem solving and analytic reasoning with additional opportunities to study self-assessment and reflection as integrated elements.

Modeling Portfolio Use:
Steps Toward an Assessment Practice

Following the initial period of implementation, the observational data were used to identify kinds of student use of the DDP and how numerous and various factors were involved in the interaction of those uses (including, for example, access to the Internet, faculty orientation, prior student experience, course-based uses of self-assessment, and so forth). A simplified version of five terms is presented in Figure 2.1.

Faculty educational practices shape the teaching-learning program that is targeted to student learning outcomes; the portfolio is a part of the teaching, learning, and assessment activities and consists of key performances already assessed, with assessor feedback and student self-assessment; the hypothesized contribution of the portfolio to learning comes through the student's use of the portfolio primarily as a tool for reflection. At the same time, the portfolio and the learning behaviors of the

Figure 2.1

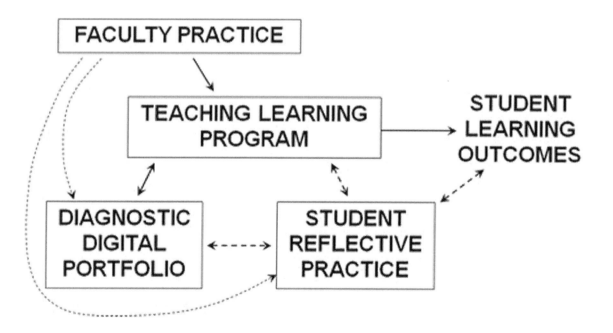

student—particularly in regard to reflection—are to some extent shaped by the faculty's use of the portfolio in connection to teaching, learning, and assessment. This modeling of portfolio use emphasizes the potential importance of student self-reflections on academic performance and learning as a means to understanding the impact of portfolio use in the context of related educational practices.

A MATRIX OF REFLECTION AND LEARNING: A PERFORMANCE-BASED DESCRIPTION

To more fully understand reflection, faculty members and researchers conducted a deliberative inquiry into samples of written essays from a digitally based Mid-Program Portfolio Assessment in which students examine their academic work in three or more semesters. Students complete the Mid-Program Portfolio Assessment after their third semester; using the DDP and other sources, they examine work from the previous semesters and analyze patterns in their learning, describing their findings in a brief, reflective essay.

Working with written essays from this performance, a team of 5 faculty members and 2 researchers examined essay characteristics and themes in the students' essays to develop a shared understanding of the variability across them. A sample of 20 students was drawn from those taking the assessment over a 1-year period; 10 were students who had gone on to graduate with honors, and 10 were randomly selected from non-honors students. With the students' identities masked, the team used three frameworks through which to examine the samples, selecting salient aspects for applications with the student performances: the *Self-Assessment* framework, developed from the college's own practices (Alverno, 2000); a cognitive approach to knowledge acquisition and concept development based on Bransford, Brown, and Cocking's (2000) *How People Learn*; and the transformative learning cycles that students use to integrate reasoning, performance, self-reflection and development from *Learning That Lasts* (Mentkowski & Associates, 2000).

The team's process of recursive and thematic analysis resulted in a matrix of descriptors organized by these frameworks and by potential ordinal levels (Table 2-1). Note that the descriptive statements are observations, not criteria for assessment.

APPLICATIONS AND STUDENT PERFORMANCES

Table 2-1 provides an organized statement of the observations that the team made from analyzing the student writing. But it is also useful to see these in relation to specific performance samples, particularly in relation to the differences among students that can be interpreted at different levels and from different perspectives.

For example, some students tended to use vague claims about their learning and achievements, in some cases giving evidence only in the form of affirmations from instructors or assessors, even to the extent of quoting the simplest phrases from feedback ("he said I did well"). However, with more experience, a student may use an affirmative quote but also deepen her understanding with other observation. But individual cases can also be quite complex. For example, in the following passage, the student discusses her analytic abilities using some simple affirmative quotes without trying to explore or unpack any real meaning of the ability. However, these simple statements are also offered in a larger analysis with attention to her own process of reflection:

I consider analysis to be one of my strengths because I feel that in my assessments and homework I have consistently done a good job in examining the details of problems/questions in order to draw well thought out conclusions . . . In reviewing past self-assessments and instructor feedback I found that analysis was repeatedly mentioned as one of my strong points. For example, [the faculty member] said in some feedback from [a religious studies class] that I "have again done exceptional work, evidencing keen analytic abilities." In addition, for [an assessment in beginning science, another] stated that the best part of my whole assessment

Table 2-1. Developmental Perspectives on Reflection and Learning[1]

Frameworks and Themes[2]	Observations From Student Examples of Reflection on Prior Work		
	Beginning	Intermediate	Advanced
Self-Assessment Framework[3] Observing performance Using evidence, feedback Finding and analyzing patterns Making judgments	Vague, global judgments, asserted without evidence Simply repeats description, judgment of assessors Sees performance as same as assignment (e.g., did what was told to do) Sees feedback as affirmation and evidence Offers procedural stories, describing action without perspective on ability Uses observations without inference	Relates judgments/conclusions to multiple sources of evidence (inference) Deepens understanding of ability Uses feedback to expand understanding of ability Realizes connections and links in plans Recognizes cause and effect relationships Uses designated discipline frameworks	Makes connections and applications and uses them to move forward Observes intentional changes as a basis for complex learning Uses multiple frameworks from disciplines and beyond Probes own work and meaning of ability Uses abilities as a framework for learning and assisting others
How People Learn[4] Understanding how concepts, alternative concepts, and misconceptions develop Understanding knowledge construction Understanding and using metacognition	Sees feedback as external and not subject to control and analysis Sees knowledge construction as only what is received through assignment/assessment Sees meaning of ability as limited to the terms given in the assignment or assessment Employs personal theories, more or less consciously, but without exploration or analysis	Sees feedback as a means for understanding links between her performance and target abilities Uses diverse tools and notes own changes in own patterns of performance Begins to have an understanding of the tools being employed and the metacognitive nature of one's decisions and planning Uses explicit theory applications	Incorporates feedback and past performance in constructing further performance and learning plans Uses growing command of knowledge structure (e.g., expertise, discipline, theory, abilities) as a foundation for further learning Understands own performance as a learner and transfers learning strategies to multiple contexts
Learning That Lasts[5] Using metacognitive strategies Self-assessing role performance Engaging diverse approaches, views, and activities	Observes own behavior with concrete relationships to broad criteria Utilizes criteria and generalized notions of effectiveness/success as the basis for reflection Uses global self-evaluations that minimize the opportunity to find connections between performance and reflecting on performance	Self-identifies as a learner, constructing meaning in experience Employs a concern for a future self and performance Includes personal values and identity in own narrative Recognizes and analyzes personal change Recognizes multiplicity Questions personal assumptions Uses abilities as a framework for criteria through which to interpret situations Clear conception of challenges, with positive attitude or confidence in ability Develops self-assessment as a basis for personal improvement	Elaborates own identity as person, learner, and professional Employs an internalized construction of effectiveness Uses multiplicity as a basis for developing identity Moves between questioning personal assumptions and construction/articulation of commitments Situates personal narrative in relation to a wider narrative history (e.g., becoming a professional) Develops personal identity in relation to mature commitments Uses self-assessment and reflection to transfer ability and capacity to new situations Integrates personal effectiveness as part of a developing future self

1. Rickards et al. (2008).
2. In each framework, the working groups selected relevant themes for application with the student performances, recognizing that these represent incomplete interpretations of the frameworks.
3. Alverno College Faculty (2000).
4. Bransford, Brown, & Cocking (2000).
5. Mentkowski & Associates (2000).

was the analysis of the facts of respiration and photosynthesis. Even in [a sociology class], [the professor] said that I had shown thorough analysis in one of the assessments.

Two attributes distinguish what could have otherwise been a shallow reflection: The student evokes a sense of the processes used to study her performances (reading across performance records), and she uses comments from multiple faculty members across very different courses. She then self-identifies a tendency to overevaluate, use too much time, overcomplicate, and reduce her efficiency. In this deeper analysis of what she views as a strength, she also shows her capacity to learn from her reflections and self-assessments. Seen through the self-assessment framework, she is developing more complex, multiplistic ways of providing evidence and deepening her understanding of the ability. In dealing with her problems of social interaction and group work—and integrating her own development as a learner—she finds a corresponding form in which her tendency to overanalyze works against her:

In a panel discussion in biochemistry I was told I didn't speak up enough or challenge other group members. If I can remember correctly, I said about a total of 2 full sentences during the whole discussion and it wasn't due to a lack of preparation. In fact, I had spent hours preparing and I even had notes present . . . My quietness might also be related to my tendency to analyze everything. All the stuff that I probably should be saying out loud to my group I am saying to myself in my head instead. I tend to think about what I am going to say before I say it.

From this point, she goes on to construct a dimension of her future performances and the work that she has ahead.

The perspective developed in the matrix from *How People Learn* (Bransford, et al., 2000) emphasizes concept development and metacognitive strategies. As one student stated,

Throughout my academic career at Alverno, analysis has been the ability that I particularly excelled

at and where I have been most consistent. It's ironic because it was this ability that I was most apprehensive about when I started out. I just thought things out the way that I always have and hoped for the best, but through time and experience I have grown more aware of my thought process and the implications of them and I now use them as a tool. My experience in the United Nations class that I took this past fall says it best. As a part of the class we had to research the country we were going to represent in the UN simulation in Chicago.

Describing the research approach that she used and its effects on her performance and process, she identifies how the concepts and analytic processes become tools for her achievements. She includes commentary from the assessor's feedback but deals specifically with how the feedback led to an expanded sense of the ability. She quotes her assessor as saying:

You used strong research skills to gather appropriate information about [your country] and its position on foreign policy. You wrote a clear position paper and drafted an ambitiously complex resolution in advance of the conference. I was impressed by your focus and dedication, as well as by your grasp of the issues in your committee.

With an elaborated description of the ability rather than a simple endorsement or affirmation, the student uses this description to support her forward movement:

I have some strengths and some weaknesses, but because I am conscious of them both . . . I will be able to continue to develop as a learner and accomplish more.

The collaborative task group frequently returned to questions of how growth was represented and understood in the student statements. Different perspectives varied in emphasis but together provided an integrated version of individual development. In the following example, the student compares an assessment involving analysis of policies and actions in a dam construction project in Africa and an English class:

> After researching the real life situation, we had to make a recommendation (there was no sitting on the fence). This was an interesting and challenging task, since fact obviously had more relevance than fiction. This project called for careful analysis of many separate, and equally valuable, factors. [By comparison, my English] class has focused on ambiguity as a part of advanced level abilities, which changed my concept of analysis. We have explored the concept of multiple perspectives on one issue, yet holding that our own opinion or analysis of the situation is the one that makes the most "sense" to us. This is certainly challenging at times; it would be easier to have concrete answers. However, I think thoroughly about my analyses, I question my judgments, I always try to see another opinion on the same issue. This move towards ambiguity is occasionally confusing, but I think it is realistic and meaningful to allow for curiosity and uncertainty. (Sometimes knowing what you do not know can be your greatest asset!)

Her focus on self-assessment of abilities is integrated with her understanding of the cognitive and conceptual tools involved, as well as a sense of herself as a developing learner with future responsibilities. This approach allows her to look at group work in very full terms:

> It is only recently that I began to appreciate group work as a truly vital learning tool. Since I am a reflective learner, it is tempting, and sometimes more convenient, to complete tasks on my own, so I can internalize the results. And of course, group work involves conflicts, scheduling, etc. There are times when I wish that I could have work time by myself. Group work, though, is growing more and more valuable to me . . . In preparation for an oral assessment, I spent over two hours working with my group . . . We have to defend Keynesian economic theory in a debate . . . As we sat down to our group session, we told each other how difficult the theory was for each of us, and quickly realized that we needed to help

each other gain a better understanding. I was one of the first to admit that this theoretical perspective was confusing and difficult for me, but two-and-a-half hours later, we were all thanking the others for being so wonderful and helpful.

The points that emerged from the collaborative task group's deliberations also indicated some pedagogical considerations. For example, during a semester, multiple versions of a performance or a learning strand offer students an opportunity to practice and learn through performance, but they also mean that students can observe their own development related to different factors, such as context, task, abilities, and assessors. The feedback from these performances as well as feedback on the self-assessments and reflective processes can also strengthen student learning.

MAJOR PERSPECTIVES AND DEVELOPMENTAL STRANDS

The collaborative team developed their observations into a matrix organized by perspectives and levels. Although there was a strong sense that the notion of levels was problematic and needed to be further refined, it was accepted for the current analysis. All students in the samples were at similar points in their studies, having successfully completed the assessment being studied by the team, so the use of the terms *beginning*, *intermediate*, and *advanced* signaled only distinctions in the nature of the reflective writing. The matrix, therefore, was not a rubric in the typical sense but a set of observations from selected samples from students designed to explore areas of difference and to make framework-based observations.

With acceptance of these cautions, it is useful to note salient characteristics that emerged through analysis using each of the three research frameworks. Using the *Self-Assessment* framework, two themes recurred across the observations: analysis of student performances in terms of evidence, a dimension that moved from *concrete and narrow* to *complex and interpretive*, and evidence-based statements related to ability development, from *demon-*

strating an outcome ("I demonstrated the ability when I . . .") to *probing the meaning of ability* and seeing an ability as a *framework for continued learning*. The group using *How People Learn* highlighted aspects that included knowledge acquisition and conceptual development, with use of diverse analytic tools and a sense of personal changes in performance, cognitive dimensions, and dealing with the student's own understanding and misunderstanding of concepts. Lastly, those using the *Learning That Lasts* framework tended to emphasize the elaboration of identity, including (a) moving between challenging personal assumptions and construction of commitments within a field of study and (b) developing a future self and personal narrative in relation to a wider context, such as becoming a professional or developing civic responsibility.

But equally important, persistent features extended across different framework perspectives, including observing changes in self, transfer of abilities and learning across contexts and situations, and encountering multiplicity and complexity.

- *The extent of observing changes in self*: In beginning-level performances, students tended to focus on a single performance and give narrow attention to assessor comments as the source of evidence, making no observation of personal growth. More thoughtful and reflective performances showed a fuller awareness of self across multiple experiences. Some reflections showed a sense of personal change and development as a basis for further learning.
- *Transfer of abilities and learning to other contexts and situations*: For beginning-level examples, transfer was limited to similar tasks or potentially repeating the same task. At higher levels, students interpreted observations across very different contexts and recognized that their learning could support performance in new and different situations.
- *Encountering multiplicity and complexity*: Beginning examples tended to refer to contexts or frameworks in fairly concrete terms—for example, those explicit in a class

or assessment—whereas the more advanced examples involved students working across multiple disciplinary frameworks. For example, they might see and address the potential conflicts between disciplinary, civic, or professional frameworks at the same time that they analyzed how these frameworks illuminate one another.

There are also some potential patterns in the distinctions between levels in the matrix. The general flow is toward increasing complexity and an increasing personal engagement with ideas and constructs. In terms of using evidence, from the *Self-Assessment* framework, beginning or preliminary performances involve verifying that criteria were met, often relying on an assessor's judgment ("my feedback was that I was successful . . ."). In more complex examples, students deal with what they understand about an ability as a result of their experience and growth. From a more cognitive perspective, students initially deal with concepts as claims of what they are learning, staying close to the examples and terms discussed in class; more complex examples involve students discussing the larger structure of knowledge in which particular concepts occur and how this serves in transferring an ability. From a framework of integrated learning and development, examples at the beginning level involve limited, self-evident, and concrete attributions between criteria and performance while more complex examples build on the role of the self—in terms of identity, commitments, abilities, responsibilities—as the source of past performances and in projecting a developing future self.

CURRICULUM ELEMENTS AND PERSISTENT QUESTIONS

By developing pictures of meaningful differences in reflective performances, educators can better understand distinctions among students. Noting substantive differences in how students use evidence, in how conceptual understanding is advanced, and in how students recognize their own learning orientations and identities, teachers can make sense of student differences important in diagnosing class and individual needs.

In another teacher role, developmental perspectives on learning and reflection can be used in giving feedback to students that helps them move to higher or targeted levels of performance. Observed characteristics may illuminate ways to give individual feedback or guide students through learning activities. Students who approach feedback and criteria achievement in concrete terms need to be comfortable with those terms at the same time that they are challenged to look at their performances and learning in more complex terms. They can then move to the edge of a comfort zone as they respond to more complex and ambiguous situations. They can also be asked to take more authority for constructing their own performances and dealing with more complex material and frameworks.

For both teachers and students, the complexity of the developmental matrix suggests the need to become effective portfolio users. An analysis of student portfolio use, particularly one targeted to student learning outcomes, often leads to observations about the importance of preparing students and faculty for the responsibilities and capacities involved in making effective use of portfolios. In *Educating the Reflective Practitioner* (1987), Schön makes a case about how reflective practices help a person continue development in professional contexts through becoming more adaptable and effective, learning from the complexities rather than waiting to be trained.

The combination of elements that enable reflection also points toward specific pedagogical concerns. Giving instructions, giving guidance for analytic processes, using flexible criteria that enable student engagement in making qualitative judgments, giving feedback, and providing opportunities to practice reflective processes in context all contribute significantly to student development and use of reflection. Through course-based activities, faculty need to support, model, and guide reflective activities. Students need to engage in reflective activities in the electronic portfolio through assignments, demonstrations, assessments, and other teaching and learning activities.

CONTINUED STUDIES AND USE

Major observations from this study have informed continued work at Alverno. Most recently, researchers have completed an NSF-funded project using the DDP in the study of problem solving and analysis in science, technology, and math (STM) that extends our understanding of the interactions between technology, self-assessment and reflection, and curriculum. This work also provides a way to further analyze the observations about student reflection in a digital portfolio environment.

The analysis of reflective writing and the production of the preliminary matrix of developmental perspectives on learning and reflection point to major considerations:

- Differences in student reflective writing and self-assessments can be observed in relation to ways students deal with evidence and developing abilities; their growth in conceptual knowledge and knowledge frameworks; their identifications as individuals, learners, and performers in disciplines and professions; and the ways they recognize and make use of changes in their own learning
- Digital portfolios provide specific contexts for reflection and self-assessment that need to be addressed and adapted through pedagogy.
- Students need knowledgeable faculty, course-based activities, and plentiful resources to take advantage of reflection and self-assessment opportunities in multiple ways. They need iterative activities that create multiple opportunities to review learning and practice reflection and self-assessment processes.

The recent work with the DDP/STM project provides another way of seeing these same dimensions and practices in operation. For example, in organic chemistry, one of the participating classes, follow-up interviews with seniors on their uses of reflection in the DDP give further insight. At the time of the study, the organic chemistry faculty member had recently revised the course that students usually take in their third or fourth semester. The integrated theme of the course, green chemistry, engages students in conceptual, practical, and ethical issues of the professional chemist in an ecologically conscious world. Students complete five self-assessments, stored in their DDPs, that cover different types of performance, such as group problem solving and analysis, and a final reflection on the semester. As students complete these self-assessments, they receive feedback about their observations and about continued development. This faculty member's approach uses DDP technology for supporting self-assessment and reflection or, in Sadler's (1998) term, personal evaluative expertise in learning. In addition, however, the college seeks to understand learning from the student perspective, so, in follow-up interviews, students were asked to review the course and their portfolio-based reflections.[1] Sandra, a chemistry major preparing to enter pharmacy school, presented a perspective that combined performance evidence and her growing sense of herself as a learner:

In my introductory classes, I seemed to always be with students who had fewer interests and less preparation in science than I did, and I would push myself in leadership positions and get overdramatic. Organic Chemistry was my first experience with students who all had similar preparation and interests. We were sharing our ideas with each other. I learned that I could take from others . . . share the learning. But I also found that I could take that into other classes like [electives in humanities] . . . and share and give.

Jean, a biology major looking to a career in science, noted in her final reflection and interview that her learning could adapt in different situations and was also connected with her future performances:

When it comes to analysis tasks, I always think of myself as working alone, and I think that is often how we think of scientists. In Organic, we had to work in groups a lot and I learned a lot about how to communicate and also to be patient. I

know I will still tend to approach analytic problems on my own, but I know that I can work in a group and communicate, and that will also be part of my work life.

Some students also described how individual approaches to self-assessment and reflection could be direct and plainspoken but not less complex or personally significant. Kendra, who will be entering medical school, reflected that

[self-assessment] is an inherent part of science in regard to how to look at what you've done and how to improve it . . . Because you get into this culture of science once you start doing research or whatever you go into and it's kind of just the way you do things. You just follow a culture basically. I realized that when I started my internships that it's just a way that you do research, it's a way that you keep records and you know that it's right and you go back and look and say how could I improve this technique later or how could I improve this protocol to meet this end.

Nura, who has been accepted to dental school, also offered a perspective that combined awareness of class procedures, her understanding of ability, and the relation to professional frameworks:

In fact my lab experiment kept failing. I used all the resources I could find—reading, interviews, on the Net, with the [faculty]—and I would have kept at it until I succeeded, but part of the class was also about learning from failures. [The faculty's] feedback helped me understand what this could mean to me. And that persistence is something I will take with me.

Analysis of the use of the matrix across the college and the analysis of applications within specific contexts of practice such as chemistry help address, if not yet answer, questions about pedagogical roles for reflection and reflection's critical place in digital portfolio learning. Alverno will continue to study the reflective practices of its students and to apply its research findings to continued improvement of its Diagnostic Digital Portfolio.

_____

1. Student quotes have been edited for clarity and confidentiality and are used with the students' permission.

ACKNOWLEDGMENTS

The authors base much of their material on the work of a task group on the Student as Learner from Alverno College's Research and Evaluation Council; the group is composed of Rickards, Guilbault, Mary Diez, Linda Ehley, Georgine Loacker, Judith Reisetter Hart, and Paul Smith. In addition, a portion of the work described here was supported by National Science Foundation Award Number 0404986 for research on teaching analysis and problem solving using Alverno's Diagnostic Digital Portfolio.

REFERENCES

Alverno College Faculty. (1994). *Student assessment-as-learning at Alverno College*. Milwaukee, WI: Alverno College Institute. (Original work published 1979, revised 1985 and 1994.)

Alverno College Faculty. (2000). *Self assessment at Alverno College* (G. Loacker, Ed.). Milwaukee, WI: Alverno College Institute.

Boud, D., Keogh, R., & Walker, D. (Eds.). (1985). *Reflection: Turning experience into learning*. London: Kogan Page.

Bransford, J. D., Brown, A. L., & Cocking, R. R. (Eds.). (2000). *How people learn: Brain, mind, experience, and school* (Expanded ed.). Washington, DC: National Academy Press.

Dostoyevsky, F. (1880/1990). *Brothers Karamazov*. (R. Pevear & L. Volkhansky, Trans.). New York: Farrar, Straus, and Giroux, 58.

Ehley, L. (2006). *Digital portfolios: A study of undergraduate and faculty use and perception of Alverno College's Diagnostic Digital Portfolio*. Unpublished doctoral dissertation, Cardinal Stritch University, Milwaukee, WI.

Kitchener, K. S., & King, P. M. (1981). Reflective judgment: Concepts of justification and their relationship to age and education. *Journal of Applied Developmental Psychology, 2*, 89–116.

Kolb, D. A. (1984). *Experiential learning: Experience as the source of learning and development*. Upper Saddle River, NJ: Prentice Hall.

Mentkowski, M., & Associates. (2000). *Learning that lasts: Integrating learning, development, and performance in college and beyond*. San Francisco: Jossey-Bass.

O'Brien, K. (2006). E-portfolios as learning construction zones: Provost's perspective. In A. Jafari & C. Kaufman (Eds.), *Handbook of research on e-portfolios*. Hershey, PA: Idea Group.

Rickards, W. H., Diez, M. E., Ehley, L., Guilbault, L. F., Loacker, G., Reisetter Hart, J., & Smith, P. C. (2006). *Learning, reflection, and electronic portfolios: Stepping toward an assessment practice*. Paper presented at the annual meeting of the American Educational Research Association, San Francisco.

Rickards, W. H., Diez, M. E., Ehley, L., Guilbault, L. F., Loacker, G., Reisetter Hart, J. & Smith, P. C. (2008). Learning, reflection, and electronic portfolios: Stepping toward an assessment practice. *Journal of General Education, 57*(1), 31–50.

Rickards, W. H., & Ehley, L. (2005). Portfolio reflections in a digital environment: Evaluating an unfinished tool. In D. Shamatov (Chair), *Emerging dimensions in higher education applications: E portfolios, technology, and learning*. Paper presented at the annual meeting of the American Evaluation Association, Toronto, Ontario, Canada.

Rogers, Russell R. (2001). Reflection in higher education: A concept analysis. *Innovative Higher Education, 26*(1), 37-57.

Sadler, D. R. (1998) Formative assessment: Revisiting the territory. *Assessment in Education: Principles, Policy and Practice, 5*(1), 77–84.

Schön, D. A. (1983). *The reflective practitioner: How professionals think in action*. New York: Basic Books.

Schön, D. A. (1987). *Educating the reflective practitioner: Toward a new design for teaching and learning in the professions*. San Francisco: Jossey-Bass.

Yancey, K. B. (1998). *Reflection in the writing classroom*. Logan: Utah State University Press.

3

USING EPORTFOLIOS TO SUPPORT LIFELONG AND LIFEWIDE LEARNING

HELEN L. CHEN
Stanford University

The expressions *lifelong learning* and *lifewide learning* are not very common yet in U.S. educational policy circles. But in Europe, increasingly they are, in part as an effect of a fall 2000 report issued by the Commission of the European Communities. This report, which included guidelines for implementing lifelong learning in the European Union, specifically identified lifelong learning as a guiding principle for directing the successful transition of the European Union into a knowledge-based economy. Not surprisingly, this report is producing significant changes in the direction of policy and action in both governmental and private sectors as well in individual citizens (Commission, 2000). As important for eportfolio practitioners, theorists, and researchers, the plans for achieving such a vision of lifelong and lifewide learning represent an opportunity to which eportfolio pedagogy and technology are uniquely suited to contribute and support.

DEFINING LIFELONG AND LIFEWIDE LEARNING

Skolverket, the Swedish National Agency for Education, describes lifelong learning as a holistic approach to education, recognizing learning on two dimensions, lifelong and lifewide. The *lifelong* dimension emphasizes the "spread of learning" across the various stages of life, whereas the *lifewide* dimension comprises the range of environments in which learning occurs—formal, nonformal, and informal (Skolverket, 2000). *Formal learning* is defined as the education that occurs in the classroom, from elementary to postsecondary education. *Nonformal education* is organized education outside the formal education system including tutoring, continuing studies, in-service training, and professional and organizational education in the workplace. Lastly, *informal learning* takes place outside of any formal environments such as the learning taking place within society, family, community, and daily work. A possible third dimension is intentionality of learning, which can differentiate formal and nonformal learning from informal learning, a recognition that although learning may be an unintentional consequence or side effect of some other factor, it can still exert significant influence on an individual's thinking and understanding.

In Figure 3.1 a conceptual model of the two axes of lifelong and lifewide learning is plotted. Formal or organized education, presented in the upper left-hand quadrant, is what many think of when considering the role of education in lifelong learning, but as indicated in the model, it provides only one location for learning. And the model itself, with its multiple locations for learning, provides a useful starting point for discussing the ways different kinds of learning experiences and environments can be characterized as well as the sites where eportfolios can be used to support activities and tasks associated with both dimensions.

THE CHANGING ROLE OF FORMAL EDUCATION RELATIVE TO LIFELONG LEARNING

Over the last century, life expectancy in developed countries has increased by an average of 30 years (Stanford). Whereas only 4 percent of the population in the United States was aged 65 or over in the year 1900, by the year 2030 one in four people will be over 65 (Friedland & Summer, 1999; Rice, Läken-hoff, & Carstensen, 2002). This segment of the population will also be healthier and better educated than previous generations (Friedland & Summer, 1999; Rice et al., 2002). This extended life course has many implications for how an individual might choose to optimize his or her education, work, family, and personal pursuits (Carstensen & Charles, 1998). Most notably, the 12 to 16 years one might spend in primary, secondary, and postsecondary education becomes somewhat less significant relative to the nonformal and informal educational experiences encountered during one's *entire* life course.

Increased longevity also presents an opportunity to imagine how one might restructure one's learning trajectory in order to take advantage of these additional years. We know, for example, that individuals will hold several jobs and change careers several times in their working lifetime. Currently, according to the U.S. Bureau of Labor Statistics, the average person born in the later years of the baby

Figure 3.1

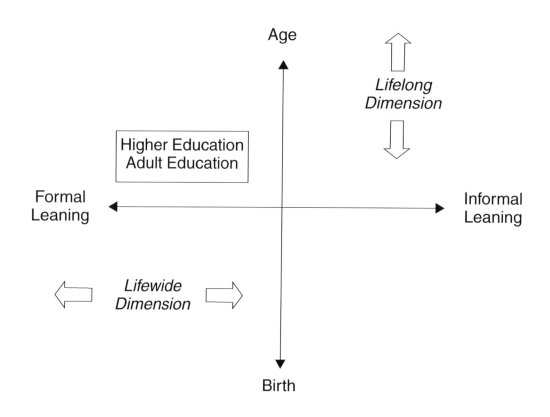

boom has held 10.5 jobs from the ages of 18 to 40 (Bureau, 2006). Given the projected increase in life span, there is an immediate and critical need to help individuals think less in terms of terminal degrees and academic credentials and more in terms of transitions facilitated through the development of key work skills and personal competencies.

Our current model of education age largely dictates what should be taught and learned, whereas lifelong learning, in contrast, places the *needs* of the individual at the forefront where "at every state of an individual's life-span, there should be education and learning opportunities based on the needs of the individuals, their background and competence" (Skolverket, 2000). The implications of such an extended life course for the kind of higher education we will need to provide include two issues: the importance of exploration and preparation for change and adaptability in both formal and informal learning environments.

At Stanford, we have begun interesting work in this area in the context of a new emphasis on the individual and on the benefits of providing learners with tools such as an eportfolio system. The hope is that students can use these tools to track the integration of various learning experiences and to define a collection of artifacts representing their learning career. In this work, we define a *learning career* as the individual trajectory of one's learning as it develops over the course of an undergraduate education, within the university environment and beyond. Our longitudinal study tracks a cohort of thirty Stanford undergraduates from 1998 to 2003. Sponsored by The William and Flora Hewlett Foundation, the Learning Careers project was established on the principle that a community of people engaged in an ongoing conversation about learning can produce a comprehensive picture of what learning actually is and the ways it occurs within the higher education environment and beyond.

Experimentation with an "eFolio" prototype and training in the skills of reflective thinking helped the study cohort articulate the connections among their courses, activities, and plans for the future. One significant outcome of the Learning Careers project was the design of learning activities and best practices for *folio thinking*, a learner-centered pedagogy

focused on providing structured opportunities for students to create learning portfolios for the purpose of fostering coherence and making meaning. Drawing upon the literature and research in experiential learning, reflective thinking, mastery orientation toward learning, and metacognition, folio thinking capitalizes on the specific context of students creating learning portfolios keyed to reflection on the pursuit of defined learning outcomes. These portfolios also served as the basis for explicit conversations with peers and coaches about the development of a *lifelong* learning career.

The Learning Careers project is one example of how specific features of an eportfolio tool in conjunction with folio thinking practices and culture can support self-assessment when a student considers next steps in a career, in that consideration identifying which knowledge or skills are needed as well as what other sources should be sought out. In addition, meaningful and comprehensive documentation of students' learning experiences, including all competencies acquired throughout life, will prove useful to students as well as prospective employers (Flynn, 2004). Serving both as a repository for past experiences and a means for evaluating and reflecting upon those experiences, the eportfolio can be a valuable resource for guiding this process over time.

AN EMPHASIS ON INDIVIDUAL RESPONSIBILITY FOR LEARNING

Reconceptualizing formal education according to individual needs rather than age relies upon a corresponding shift to individual responsibility for one's learning. The emphasis on learner-centered education, which can be conceptually linked to notions of individual responsibility, is an underlying principle in the pedagogical practices of many eportfolio programs, where the individual is the common denominator among the wide range of experiences in and outside the classroom that together comprise one's learning trajectory.

Microsoft's MyLifeBits project has taken up issues around such a project, and its findings to date are instructive. Project leaders are designing a platform to record, store, and access a personal lifetime archive, so the storage issue, even for thousands of texts per digital eportfolio composer, is being addressed (Gemmell, Bell, & Lueder, 2006). More important, perhaps, is the effect of storage—or what the researchers call a "surrogate memory"; the researchers observed that "having a surrogate memory creates a freeing, uplifting, and secure feeling" (Gemmell et al.). We could also imagine the value of such a digital memory of one's learning experiences, built over a lifetime, to enhance personal reflection. The MyLifeBits project has implications as well for the role of the successful organization and categorization of data, such that an eportfolio creator can classify items according to time as well as to various "lives" (personal and professional; active lives, including current projects and position; and past lives, including data from college years or regarding relationships with a former company or organization). With such a large collection, the "killer app" is the screen saver that randomly selects artifacts and pleasantly refreshes memories while also encouraging comments and ratings for future exploration. The Microsoft team is also exploring more advanced search capabilities that support linking of metadata with digital memories across media formats.

For both eportfolios and the MyLifeBits project, the capture of artifacts is easy relative to the time-consuming steps of annotation and self-organization. Both tools share the same goal of achieving an understanding of what knowledge has been acquired and, perhaps more importantly, how to access and reuse that knowledge when needed. However, what distinguishes an eportfolio from a digital archive is the process of selection, not the act of collection. This point is emphasized by Lee Shulman (1998): "What is declared worth documenting, worth reflecting on, what is deemed to be portfolio worthy is a theoretical act." As we consider the possible implications of advances in technology for capturing, archiving, and managing digital information, Neal Beagrie (2005) makes one last important point, that the most significant parts of the process are also the most expensive: "digitally it is becoming cheaper to collect and more expensive to select, and cheaper to

search than to organize." In sum, individual ownership and responsibility for the "cradle-to-grave, lifetime personal web space that will enable connections among personal, educational, social and business systems" proposed by Cohn and Hibbits (2004) is a necessary prerequisite for any personal collection, electronic or otherwise, that is consistently updated, effectively maintained, and truly meaningful.

For lifelong and lifewide learning, several portfolio theorists—Barrett (2007), Chen (2003), and Paulson and Paulson (1991)—highlight the use of the story or narrative stream as the "universal information structure" and primary means for managing, organizing, and essentially *curating* one's eportfolio. This approach is particularly appropriate given the emergence of *Generation C* (for *content*), a consumer trend shifting interest away from passive consumption in order to take advantage of technologies offering creative avenues to create and produce digital content (Generation C, 2004).

DISSOLVING THE BOUNDARIES BETWEEN POLICY SECTORS

Lifelong and lifewide learning also shifts responsibility for education and learning from the public to the private spheres (Commission, 2000). Formal institutions such as schools and universities no longer have a monopoly on education, and recognition of other kinds of educational and learning environments demonstrates that the formal education system is just one of many environments in which learning occurs. As individuals move from formal education to the workforce, cooperation among those making and implementing educational policy, labor policy, industrial policy, regional policy, and social policy will be required in order for lifelong and lifewide learning to succeed (Skolverket, 2000). As the individual begins to take a more proactive role in his or her own learning, he or she will need to have supported both motivation and the ability to take advantage of opportunities for continuing education.

Although Skolverket (2000) asserts that lifelong learning is "dependent on the individual's desires, motivation and attitudes to education and learning," this is not to say that the state has no responsibility whatsoever. In fact, the state must expand upon, invest in, and create conditions and the opportunities for individuals to take advantage of education and learning. The eportfolio has enough flexibility in its design to be able to incorporate all forms of learning experiences, regardless of the environment in which they were generated or conducted, and current research is investigating how this incorporation works in different situations. The third cohort of the Inter/National Coalition on Electronic Research, for example, has as one of its goals documenting such multisite, curricular, and co-curricular learning, be it in leadership portfolios at George Mason University or in competency-based portfolios at the University of Waterloo and Florida State University. The concept of integrative student learning is thus an institution-based mechanism focused on including new learning outcomes, stakeholders, and partnerships inside and outside campus boundaries.

Another example of how these various silos can be overcome using eportfolios is seen in the eFolio Minnesota initiative providing an eportfolio for all residents of the state. eFolio Minnesota represents a partnership among the Minnesota State Colleges and Universities with state workforce and education organizations. The primary users are students, educators, and workers or individuals seeking employment. Survey results found that these users do not differ significantly from Minnesota residents in terms of age, race, and ethnicity (eFolio, n.d.). With over 80,000 users, this project has demonstrated success in how various organizations and policy sectors can collaborate to provide a resource for individuals with varying educational experiences and backgrounds, and their own education and career objectives. Interview data showed eFolio Minnesota supporting role shifting as users transitioned among student, educator, and worker. Individuals would often transition among multiple roles at once, change between roles over time, or carry different roles simultaneously, depending on their specific purpose and need to present themselves via the eFolio (Cambridge, 2008).

Collectively, these research findings from the eFolio Minnesota demonstrate the significant contributions of an eportfolio to support lifelong and lifewide learning for a large number of diverse individuals by providing a venue for professional and personal self-representation and a means and process for integrating multiple roles. The eFolio Minnesota initiative also emphasizes the importance of using partnerships among educational institutions, workforce development organizations, nonprofit organizations, and the Department of Labor to expand access by secondary school students and less-educated users.

Access to continuing education has typically been the privilege of the wealthy and well educated. However, the successful introduction of eportfolios at LaGuardia Community College provides another case study documenting the universality of eportfolios and the opportunity they present to immigrants and to low-income and first-generation college-goers (Clark, Eynon, Graciano, & Gross, 2006). Corresponding efforts in Europe are seen in the Keypal project (coordinated by the European Institute for E-Learning [EIfEL]) and the "More self esteem with my ePortfolio" (MOSEP) project (managed by Salzburg Research Forschungs-gesellschaft). Both of these projects are aimed at engaging disenfranchised young adults by exploring the use of eportfolios to support, assess, and validate the acquisition of key skills such as interpersonal and civic competencies and entrepreneurship as they occur in a variety of formal and informal settings.

A common theme among all of these projects is the emphasis on transitions—whether from school to training/employment, college to university, or employment to study, occasions where reflection about one's personal goals and plans for the future most naturally occur. Hartnell-Young, Smallwood, Kingston, and Harley (2006) describe how eportfolio tools, practices, and content can support these transitions, as illustrated by the efforts of the Regional Interoperability Project on Progression for Lifelong Learning in the United Kingdom, a model for cross-sector collaboration in the domain of personal development planning and employability.

The vision of a lifelong and lifewide learning career cannot be achieved without overcoming the significant obstacles relating to cultural and socioeconomic inequalities and providing underserved populations with a way to acquire education. Ensuring that there is equality in access among all groups including the unemployed, immigrants, and individuals who have had no or limited formal education will be one of the greatest challenges to authentic and widespread lifelong and lifewide learning. This can occur only if we raise both the demand and the supply for learning, particularly among those who have benefited the least from education and training (Commission, 2000).

REFERENCES

Barrett, H. (2007). *Online personal learning environments: Structuring electronic portfolios to support lifelong and lifewide learning.* Retrieved August 22, 2007, from http://docs.google.com/Doc?id=dd76m5s2_42cscw4g

Beagrie, N. (2005, June). *Plenty of room at the bottom? Personal digital libraries and collections.* Retrieved August 1, 2007, from http://www.dlib.org/dlib/june05/beagrie/06beagrie.html

Boström, A. K., Boudard, E., & Siminou, P. (2001). *Lifelong learning in Sweden: The extent to which vocational education and training policy is nurturing lifelong learning in Sweden.* Retrieved February 15, 2007, from http://www2.trainingvillage.gr/download/publication/panorama/5112en.pdf

Bureau of Labor Statistics. (2006, August 25). Number of jobs held, labor market activity, and earnings growth among the youngest baby boomers: Results from a longitudinal survey. *United States Department of Labor Press Release.* Retrieved August 4, 2007, from http://www.bls.gov/news.release/pdf/nlsoy.pdf

Cambridge, D. (2008). Audience integrity and the living document: eFolio Minesota and lifelong and lifewide learning with ePortfolios. *Computers and Education, 51*(3), 1227–1246.

Carstensen, L. L., & Charles, S. T. (1998). Emotion in the second half of life. *Current Directions in Psychological Science, 7*(5), 144–149.

Chen, H. L. (2003, Winter). Symposium: Learning reconsidered: Education in the digital age. *Journalism and Mass Communication Educator, 57*(4), 292–317.

Clark, J. E., Eynon, B., Graciano, H., & Gross, N. (2006). ePortfolio@LaGuardia: A learning project. *In Transit: The LaGuardia Journal on Teaching and Learning, 1*(2), 19–24.

Cohn, E. R., & Hibbits, B. J. (2004). Beyond the electronic portfolio: A lifetime personal web space. *Educause Quarterly, 27*(4). Retrieved August 1, 2007, from http://www.educause.edu/apps/eq/eqm04/eqm0441.asp?bhcp=1

Commission of the European Communities. (2000, October 30). *A memorandum on lifelong learning.* Retrieved February 15, 2007, from http://ec.europa.eu/education/policies/lll/life/memoen.pdf

eFolio Minnesota. (n.d.). Retrieved February 15, 2007, from http://www.efoliominnesota.com/

Flynn, W. J. (October 2004). *Electronic portfolios—Digital documentation for competitive advantage* (National Council for Continuing Education and Training Abstract). Retrieved February 15, 2007, from http://www.nccet.org/associations/2158/NCCETEPortfolio.pdf

Friedland, R. B., & Summer, L. S. (1999). *Demography is not destiny.* Washington, DC: National Academy on an Aging Society.

Gemmell, J., Bell, G., & Lueder, R. (2006, February 20). *MyLifeBits: A personal database for everything* (Microsoft Research Technical Report, MSR-TR-2006-23). Retrieved February 15, 2007, from ftp://ftp.research.microsoft.com/pub/tr/TR-2006-23.pdf

Generation C. (2004, June). Retrieved August 22, 2007, from http://www.trendwatching.com/trends/GENERATION_C.htm

Hartnell-Young, E., Smallwood, A., Kingston, S., & Harley, P. (2006). Joining up the episodes of lifelong learning: A regional transition project. *British Journal of Educational Technology, 37*(6), 853–866.

Keypal. (n.d.). Retrieved August 22, 2007, from http://www.eife-l.org/activities/projects/keypal.

MOSEP: More self-esteem with my ePortfolio. (n.d.). Retrieved August 22, 2007, from http://www.mosep.org/

Paulson, P. R., & Paulson F. L. (1991, March). *Portfolios: Stories of knowing.* Paper presented at the 54th annual meeting of the Claremont Reading Conference (ERIC Document Reproduction Service No. ED377209).

Rice, C. J., Löckenhoff, C. E., & Carstensen, L. L. (2002). Chasing independence and productivity: How Western cultures influence individual and scientific accounts of aging. *Revista Latinoamericana de Psicología (Latin American Journal of Psychology)*, 34, 133–154.

Shulman, L. (1998). Teacher portfolios: A theoretical activity. In N. Lyons (Ed.), *With portfolio in hand: Validating the new teacher professionalism* (pp. 23–27). New York: Teachers College Press.

Skolverket. (2000, January). *Lifelong and lifewide learning.* Retrieved February 15, 2007, from http://www.skolverket.se/publikationer?id=638

SECTION TWO

Integrative Learning

*E**lectronic Portfolios: Emerging Practices in Student, Faculty, and Institutional Learning* (Cambridge, 2001), recalled the difficulties of Kalamazoo College, an innovator in eportfolios for integrative learning. Aware that students made few connections between learning during study abroad and in on-campus classes, the college developed eportfolio practices to help students make sense of their college learning on all sites, including at work and in co-curricular settings. Barriers to success toward this goal, however, included too little scaffolding to help students learn how to make connections, too few pedagogical supports for integrative practices, and the lack of mutual understanding between faculty members and advisors as to the value of the eportfolio learning.

Fortunately, we in higher education now know more about the power of integration through eportfolios and the strategies that support it. Thanks to the public sharing of early pioneers like Kalamazoo and of current practitioners and researchers like the University of Wolverhampton in the United Kingdom, the University of Waterloo in Canada, and LaGuardia Community College in the United States, more thorough understanding of integration can guide our practice and research.

INTEGRATION IN THE SHORT TERM AND IN THE LONG TERM

Darren Cambridge, who begins this section in Chapter 4 with a piece that analyzes what he calls network and symphonic selves, distinguishes between integration that demonstrates agility and flexibility in day-to-day practices as learners reflect on their experiences and integration that is more about continuity, enduring value, and "in-depth intellectual engagement and sustained creativity." These two kinds of integration, both valuable, are optimal at different times in the learning process.

The University of Waterloo and the University of Wolverhampton, for example, both comment on the importance of day-to-day attention to learning through eportfolios. As described in Chapter 7, at Waterloo a history course endeavors to teach students "to think historically" through historical artifacts, historical memory, a historical lens, and historical interpretation. The eportfolio that accommodates practice in and evidence of these elements increases student learning in the course. As detailed in Chapter 5, at Wolverhampton in teacher preparation courses students reveal and reflect on day-to-day situations in classrooms, including through using blogs and other social networking technology.

But both institutions also insist that students do more integration and make more sense of their learning across courses and learning environments. Waterloo states that "students often do not understand 'why' they are developing their eportfolios until they have an opportunity in another learning context to make a connection" (p. 74). Wolverhampton values the integration of former and evolving identities that happens over time: "The ongoing construction and questioning of professional knowledge and identities are key" (p. 57). Cambridge suggests that more attention has been given to the networked self, present in the shorter-term integrative work, than to the symphonic self, which becomes apparent over time as "personal engagement" makes "the practice of inquiry a guiding principle of living lives of integrity in which new opportunities are connected to enduring commitments over time" (p. 43).

Cambridge suggests, outside of the demands of daily practice, where a "different pace and disposition" lead to a more unified understanding of learning. Through research on interdisciplinary learning communities, LaGuardia Community College found that "quantitative data collected over 3 years reveal that students value each element of the ePortfolio" but also "the combinative of diverse elements into a single integrated whole" (p. 61). Cambridge calls this the "provisional assertion of capability and consistency."

Cambridge asserts that different kinds of technology help foster these two kinds of thinking. Blogs, wikis, YouTube, Flikr, and Facebook, for example, promote the kind of engagement characteristic of folio thinking. On the other hand, the Open Source Portfolio, the Angel system, and the University of Georgia's EMMA (see Chapter 19) provide more support for matrix thinking. Pebble Pad combines the two, providing contexts for both the network and the symphonic self.

PORTFOLIO THINKING AND MATRIX THINKING

Another way to get at the distinction that Cambridge is making is to consider what Helen Chen calls "folio thinking" (see Chapter 3) and what Sharon Hamilton calls "matrix thinking" (see Chapter 10). Portfolio thinking is a habit of mind that develops as students use portfolios to explore and document their learning across experiences and sites. As students begin to reflect naturally and continuously about how day-to-day events overlap in their learning, they do what both Wolverhampton and LaGuardia call border crossing. Wolverhampton states that the "leaky seams" between making sense of different experiences are "the most interesting 'border' work." In Chapter 6, LaGuardia describes its students as "constantly navigating intersecting boundaries of nationality, race, gender roles and expectations, language, religion, economic class, and educational background" (p. 59) An integrative habit of mind, folio thinking, improves abilities at border crossing on a daily basis.

Matrix thinking, on the other hand, operates as

A NEW DIGITAL RHETORIC: INTEGRATION OF THE WRITTEN AND THE VISUAL

Elizabeth Clark at LaGuardia Community College contends that the electronic portfolio constitutes a new digital rhetoric. The integration of the written and the visual is an essential literacy in the 21st century in which technological advances enlarge the capabilities that we have to generate and exhibit knowledge. Exhibits on the LaGuardia Web site (http://www.eportfolio.lagcc.cuny.edu/advanced_gallery.html) demonstrate ways in which text and image are symbiotically effective in revealing integrative learning. LaGuardia's research findings are significant in revealing how this new digital rhetoric affects individual and institutional objectives.

LaGuardia examined student engagement, pass rates, and retention. Using data from the Community College Survey of Student Engagement (CCSSE) regarding Academic Challenge and Active Learning, especially in relation to critical thinking, writing, technology, and collaborative learning, researchers found that students in courses that required eportfolios were more engaged than students in courses that did not require eportfolios. Institutional concerns were also affected by eportfolio use: Both pass rates and retention were higher in courses employing eportfolios.

LaGuardia researchers attribute these positive effects of using eportfolios chiefly to interdisciplinarity and to the integration of the written and the visual. "In our experience, visual creativity is key, as are interdisciplinary linkages." LaGuardia concludes, based on CCSSE, self-designed surveys, qualitative feedback, and key student outcomes like pass rates and retention, that "our successes demonstrate, in a preliminary way, ePortfolio's viability as an integrative tool" (p. 59).

The phrase "in a preliminary way" characterizes the research findings about integrative learning through eportfolios at many institutions, mainly because institutions have been doing this kind of research for short periods of time and have been experimenting with methodologies to answer their context-specific questions. Questions about integrative learning as fostered by eportfolios are many, but, as Julie Hughes from Wolverhampton in the United Kingdom says, "Being in the swim—transatlantic at this moment—is a thrillingly unstable and exciting place to be." As you dive into this section, look for ideas, assertions, and findings that tantalize you and that provoke you to ask your own questions about the eportfolio's influence on integrative learning.

4

TWO FACES OF INTEGRATIVE LEARNING ONLINE

DARREN CAMBRIDGE

George Mason University

Integrative learning is emerging as an important way to see how higher education can be improved to better prepare students for a changing world. It has been a focus of publications and programs of the American Association of Colleges and Universities and the Carnegie Foundation for the Advancement of Teaching (American Association of Colleges and Universities, 2002, 2007). Major funding agencies in the United States, such as the Fund for the Improvement of Postsecondary Education and the National Science Foundation, have supported projects focused on integrative learning, and, in the United Kingdom, the Higher Education Academy has established a multimillion-pound Center for Excellence in Teaching and Learning focused on integrative learning. Mary Huber and Pat Hutchings's survey of the literature on integrative learning suggests that it is a broad category that includes many recent educational theories and innovations, including those related to reflection, metacognition, and intentional learning (Huber & Hutchings, 2004). It has also long been a key theme in literature on interdisciplinarity (Klein, 1996).

The connection to electronic portfolios is immediate. Portfolios are fundamentally integrative, being composed of heterogeneous artifacts, the connections between which are explored through reflection. Portfolios are used to integrate across contexts, often looking beyond individual assignments, courses, or disciplines. In the Inter/National Coalition for Electronic Portfolio Research (hereafter "Coalition"), many campus research teams address issues of integrative learning, both explicitly and implicitly. Many of the ideas about integrative learning explored in this chapter are emergent in their work. The ideas were also shaped by work done by a cross-campus group of Coalition participants who worked together over several months exploring the relationship between learning supported by electronic portfolios and students' high level of engagement with social networking tools such as Facebook and MySpace (Cambridge et al., 2006).

In both portfolios and social software, students create virtual identities. Which tools and processes we advocate they use in this online self-representation shapes the form of these identities. Taking up a question first posed by Coalition co-director Kathleen Yancey, I'm asking, "What kinds of selves do our digital portfolio models invite from students?" (Yancey, 2004).

I'd like to suggest two types of selves that parallel dimensions of integrative learning, the networked and symphonic selves. The *networked self* focuses on creating intentional connections. Crossing boundaries such as those between courses, disciplines, institutions, and groups, the networked self creates new relationships. Through reflection, the networked self makes independent choices about which connections to make and why they are important. In contrast, the *symphonic self* focuses on achieving integrity of the whole. Through examining and articulating how the sum of its experiences and ideas has an overall coherence, the symphonic self articulates enduring commitments and systemic understanding.

The two types of selves relate differently to the literature on integrative learning and portfolio pedagogy. With its emphasis on agility and flexibility, the networked self is more consonant with recent integrative learning discourse. However, the symphonic self, through producing an overall account that explains and predicts, is better synchronized with the tradition of portfolio pedagogy.

These two faces of integrative learning are not, and cannot be, mutually exclusive. Both are urgently needed, and figuring out how they work together is a key challenge for educational leaders. Although such a synthesis is beyond the scope of this chapter, I will here be able to examine some distinctions between the two that may point toward a solution. When enacted through self-representational practices using information technology, the networked and symphonic selves differ in the values they embody, the activities in which they engage, the genres their representations tend to take, and the technologies used to create and communicate them. (These contrasts are summarized in Table 4-1.) Each of these differences has implications for how we frame the integrative learning of electronic portfolio composition for students.

VALUES

The networked self values flexibility and agility. Its focus is on intentionally cultivating connections to create new opportunities for growth and collaboration across boundaries. To the extent that there are overall patterns in the work of the networked self, they are emergent from this local connection making. The value of each new connection, whether it expands a personal network, finds common ground between disciplinary techniques, or suggests new ways of working across institutional structures, is determined through a rapid process of analysis and experimentation. Play is encouraged, rules of thumb are helpful, and speed and frequency are of the utmost importance.

Students who master the networked self exemplify student engagement. They get involved in numerous organizations and activities, on and off campus, and apply what they have learned in one setting to another. They build relationships with faculty and staff who share their interests and put them to work in the service of their learning. They are regularly on the lookout for new ways to interweave their numerous activities and ideas, making decisions about where to invest their time through reflective conversations with their friends and mentors and online self-representations through blogs and social networking systems.

They embody one of liberalism's central principles, what former labor secretary Robert Reich calls the "terrific deal" (Reich, 2000). In college and university environments rich with opportunities to make and dissolve connections in search of a better deal, situated within a society in which such opportunities are becoming more and more common, students composing their networked selves have many rewards at their fingertips. Less important than long-term engagement is the entrepreneurial spirit of creating something new that can yield rapid returns.

The symphonic self, in contrast, stresses integrity and continuity. Connections are valued not just for their immediate impact but for their coherence with a long-term narrative of how a person's actions in multiple spheres add up to a whole that embodies enduring values (Sennett, 1998). The symphonic self focuses on achieving balance among its many relationships and commitments. The symphonic self is intentional not just about where and why to make new connections but about the value and meaning of those connections within the whole, viewed over months or years, rather than hours or days. Such meaning making requires in-depth intellectual engagement and a more sus-

Table 4-1. Distinctions Between the Network Self and the Symphonic Self

	Network Self	Symphonic Self
Values	• Play, emergence, entrepreneurialism, flexibility, agility • Analysis • Liberalism • Student engagement • Folio thinking	• Integrity, commitment, intellectual engagement, balance • Creativity • Humanism • Personal engagement • Matrix thinking
Activities	• Ease, speed, low-cost integration • Embeddedness in day-to-day life • Connection • Aggregation, association • Collection • Reflection-in-action, constructive reflection • Revision • Continual learning	• Time, effort, high-cost integration (author, context, and audience) • Stepping out of daily work • Articulation, reframing • Synthesis, symphony • Selections, projection • Matrix thinking, reflection-in-presentation • Iteration • Moments of mastery, accomplishment, celebration
Genre Characteristics	• Space • Openings • Relationships as end, heuristic, invention • Relationships between things • Atomized, aggregated • Collection, list, link, datum, snapshot	• Text, composition • Boundaries • Relationships as organization • Relationships between relationships • Holistic, integral, systemic • Theory, story, interpretation, map
Technologies	• Web 2.0 tools, social software, identity 2.0 providers, PLEs and other aggregators, MyLifeBits • Atom, RSS, FOAF, Flikr API, Open ID, etc.	• Eportfolio systems • Concept mapping systems • IMS ePortfolio, Topics Maps, RDF
Impacts	• Low yield—incremental and by accretion • Greater connectedness and intentionality • Learning in the network	• High yield—occasional and intensive • Synthesis, coherence, integrity • Learning in the individual

tained creativity (Sill, 2001). Moving beyond student engagement, students who master the symphonic self exemplify what I have called "personal engagement," making the practice of inquiry a guiding principle for living lives of integrity in which new opportunities are connected to enduring commitments over time (Cambridge, 2006b). Such students engage in the "educationally purposeful activities" that characterize student engagement not just for their own sake, but as part of a larger, longer-term project of building a coherent identity (Kuh, 2003).

The symphonic self embodies the values of humanism in its focus on whole person. It is a traditionally valued outcome of a general, liberal education. Well-supported by the post-WWII bureaucratic society in which patterns of long-term commitment and cumulative growth were the norm in both the home and the workplace, the symphonic self is both more difficult to craft and more urgently needed in an era where the boundaries between these two spheres are increasingly permeable and in which disruptive change is an increasingly common reality in both (Bateson, 1989; Hardt & Negri, 2001; Sennett, 2006).

The way in which portfolios have been used traditionally suggests values that correspond with the symphonic self. In rhetoric and composition, portfolios have traditionally helped students and faculty see a student's writing as a whole over an extended period of time—a semester, 4 years in a undergraduate major—creating a reflective narrative of how that writing has changed over time, how diverse pieces add up to something more than the sum of the parts, and what that means for future writing. In professional fields such as teacher education, portfolios help students map their diverse activities and achievements within a framework of enduring commitments of the professional community of practice that they are joining.

My own research on how people use portfolios to learn throughout life supports the importance of the symphonic self. Over 80,000 residents of the state of Minnesota have used eFolio Minnesota to create and share electronic portfolios. Representative of the population of the state overall in terms of age and race, many are not currently, or never have been, enrolled in a college or university. More than 20 percent of these portfolio authors surveyed reported that their experiences with eFolio had a very strong impact on their learning and relationships with others. Integrity was one of two primary characteristics these experiences had in common (Cambridge, 2008). Most eFolio users who reported a very high impact shared in interviews that they valued their portfolio because it gave them a place to represent and articulate the relationships between the different spheres of their lives—personal, professional, and academic—showing how they achieved a balance that embodied the values that infused all three. In the words of one informant, eFolio allowed her to represent her "whole human being" (Cambridge, 2008).

The campuses involved in the Coalition are representative of an international trend toward extending these disciplinary models and insights from lifelong learning to the larger educational project of colleges and universities. Programs such as University Studies at Portland State and New Century College at George Mason University, and institutions like IUPUI, Kapi`olani Community College, and Arizona State Polytechnic have begun encouraging students to create integrative explanations of their work through electronic portfolios that tell stories of achievement in conversation with outcomes and values embraced by the academic community. Sharon Hamilton has called this process of rearticulating one's work in relationship to a shared conceptual framework "matrix thinking" (Hamilton, 2006). In most cases, students are encouraged to combine evidence of learning from within and

beyond the classroom, considering both what they gained from formal educational programs and how that learning has shaped their larger identity. Although these projects value intentional connection making, the connections are situated within a larger whole that, if successful, presents an integrated and balanced picture of a symphonic self.

Other Coalition campuses, however, are also applying electronic portfolios to the challenges of the networked self. At Stanford, engineering students are writing reflectively in portfolio blogs and wikis to make connections, day to day, between ideas and with each other, making considered choices about how to invest their time and energy in learning informed by the emergent relationships they discover through writing and responding. Although not producing a portfolio, this work engages students in much of the same thinking processes as researchers have observed when students composed portfolios. Helen Chen and her colleagues call these ways of learning "folio thinking" (Chen, 2003 and Chapter 3). At the University of Wolverhampton, through writing regularly within a shared eportfolio environment, education students working in real classrooms for the first time make sense of their experiences, applying ideas from course texts and discussions, exploring connections between the cognitive and affective aspects of teaching, and receiving support and new ideas from peers and advisors (see Chapter 5). Rather than emphasizing an overarching synthesis of the teaching experience, this "everyday theorizing" focuses on helping students improve their performance and maximize their learning in the midst of the relentless demands of a new professional environment (Hughes, 2006).

ACTIVITIES

These differences in emphasis between the networked and symphonic selves lead to different varieties of activity. The networked self tends toward activity that can be completed quickly and with the least effort necessary. The focus is on adding value at the edges of existing activities, in brief, discrete acts of making connections and reflecting upon them that can provide quick wins. The work of the networked self is embedded day-to-day practice. It is most effective and sustainable when frequent and unobtrusive, adding value without drawing away attention from the tasks at hand.

In this sense the work of the networked self includes the type of reflection Kathleen Yancey terms "reflection-in-action," the process of "reviewing, projecting, and revising" that is undertaken in the midst of completing a learning project (Yancey, 1998). The longer-term value of the networked self is aggregate. Through collection of diverse artifacts of learning and performance and many acts of reflective dialogue with them over time, meaningful connections accumulate and compound. This process of "developing a cumulative, multi-selved and multi-voiced identity" is "constructive reflection" (Yancey).

Such identity is in a constant process of revision. Each new activity and new connection is an opportunity to add, adjust, and remix. Asked to constantly adapt to new tasks, tools, and structures of collaboration, the networked self is in a constant state of change that requires improvising and calculating what is sufficient at each moment. Unlike the traditional model of apprenticeship, which sometimes serves as a metaphor for learning in the midst of practice, the networked self's learning is continual throughout life without the promise of graduating into mastery (Rikowski, 1999).

The activity of the symphonic self, in contrast, has a markedly different pace. Finding the relationships between relationships in one's learning and performance requires a significant investment of time and effort. Integrating the process of synthesizing insights and evidence into a unifying theory or story of one's learning takes sustained creativity and careful thought, and these in turn require time to think and compose outside of the immediate demands of daily practice (Levy, 2001; Sill, 2001). In addition to requiring more from its author, the symphonic self also produces more complex representations that call for more work on the part of their audiences, and the work of producing them requires more formal and extensive support from the institutions and communities supporting their production. All this cannot be achieved in the interstices of business as usual. Composition of the symphonic self requires a periodic stepping out of day-to-day practice. Finding the space for this stepping out, for the effective communication of its results, and for action on the basis of them may often require significant change to the normal practice itself.

During these periods of stepping out, portfolio authors create representations of the symphonic self that arrange their many voices and relationships accumulated over time into a cohesive account that can be shared with others. Thus, they move from constructive reflection to "reflection-in-presentation" (Yancey, 1998). While this reflective process continues to generate and evaluate connections, it moves beyond aggregation toward integration and synthesis.

Although temporary, these representations of the symphonic self say to their audiences, this is who I am, what I have done, what I stand for, and the basis on which I choose to act going forward. They make commitments, which will need to be revisited at some point in the future, but not immediately or continuously. The work of the symphonic self is thus more of iteration than of revision. In this respect, the symphonic self can also celebrate mastery. Although not the permanent facility claimed by the traditional matriculating apprentice, it is a provisional assertion of capability and consistency for some period against the background of the "permanent white water" some proponents of the networked self suggest characterizes our lives (Vaill, 1996).

Many of the Coalition campuses most successful in engaging students in learning through electronic portfolios have found ways to change their practice to accommodate the time and support needed to represent the symphonic self. Most campuses—even those that haven't been able to achieve it—recognize the value of integrating the portfolio process within the curriculum, through course assignments contributing to portfolios, capstone courses organized around them, and general education credits awarded over multiple semesters in recognition of portfolio work. LaGuardia and Clemson have extended this curricular space into physical space, offering students support for their portfolio writing through special studios that offer both technical and conceptual assistance.

Also at LaGuardia, students have benefited from creating multiple iterations of their portfolios over time, each involving an overarching reconsideration of both content and architecture (see Chapter 6). This process of iteration can be supported by occasions for public celebration, such as the contests hosted by the University of Washington (see Chapter 15) and Florida State University's and La-Guardia's showcasing of exemplary portfolios.

Other campuses have thus far focused on supporting the processes of collection and connection that form the networked self. Several campuses, such as Bowling Green, have concentrated their efforts toward providing a space for all students to collect and share documents related to their learning over the course of their undergraduate careers (see Chapter 16).

GENRE CHARACTERISTICS

Space is one of the defining features of the genres of representation associated with the networked self. Although called by many names—portfolios, profiles, blogs, aggregators—networked self-representations tend to emphasize openings and possibilities for new connections. Relationships in representations of the networked self serve a dual role both as the goals of self-representation in themselves and as heuristics, helping to create, discover, or construct more connections.

These relationships most often are between small, discrete items of content: a video clip, a URL, a blog post, the name of one's favorite book, one's job title, a picture, a comment, or the name of a trusted associate. Capturing or translating complex evidence of learning and performance into this format means atomizing it, breaking it down into easily digestible chunks, and aggregating it, bringing together many items in one place. The end product is a list or collection, an inventory rather than a story or an explanatory framework. Its organization is typically chronological or essentially arbitrary, reflecting how the material was collected or named more than what it means. The boundaries of the collection in many cases are not fixed. They depend on what the reader decides counts within the network. Connections within the networks are also most often discrete links between individual items such as a person or site listed on a blog roll or buddy list. Alternately, connections may serve to classify, assigning a tag, rating, or keyword.

In networked self-representations, connections aggregate and relate the parts, but they rarely articulate boundaries. Representing the symphonic self, in contrast, requires a focus on the whole. Through visual design and verbal explanation, a sense of how the items included add up to something more than the sum of their parts is communicated. It is clear what is part of the whole, what is outside of it, and why. Relationships here serve as organization, as both structure and content. They are created not just to classify and associate but also to arrange in service of a global argument or narrative. More than a space, these relationships define a composition, a text in which each element is purposefully placed.

The items and their relationships combine to form a theory, story, or map that explains and predicts what the author has done, values, and can do. As I've argued elsewhere, the tradition of portfolio pedagogy in the United States suggests that this integrative character is what distinguishes a portfolio from other kinds of self-representations (Cambridge, 2005, 2006b). Helen Barrett's recent work also highlights the importance of narrative as a central feature of electronic portfolios, stressing the need for significant student control over the design, contents, and organization of the portfolio in order to convey an integrated picture of the student as a learner who has ownership of the portfolio (Barrett & Wilkerson, 2004).

Several Coalition campuses committed to the symphonic self are investigating the effectiveness of two-dimensional grids as structures for helping students recontextualize their experiences to show how the experiences make a whole in relationship to shared interpretive frameworks, literally using matrices to capture matrix thinking. At IUPUI, this framework is supplied by a set of principles of undergraduate learning articulated across several stages of an academic career (see Chapter 10). At

Kapi`olani Community College, it is a set of six Hawaiian values and the metaphorical stages of the journey of an outrigger canoe (see Chapter 11). At other campuses, matrix thinking happens through alternatively integrative structures, such as the concept maps being used at George Mason to help students present a coherent picture of their learning in relationship to course goals and college-wide competencies. This work parallels applications of concept mapping to portfolio pedagogy in Norway (Lavik & Nordeng, 2004).

Still others invite students to employ a wider range of hypertextual and visual organizations through creating portfolios, often in the form of standard Web pages. A key resource for articulating the symphonic self in these portfolios is internal linking. Work at Clemson is beginning to identify patterns in the way students make links within their portfolios that may inform us about how their integrative thinking develops. Another key resource is visual design. At the University of Washington and at George Mason, researchers are examining how students' visual design choices connect to the narrative and persuasive power of their portfolios (see Chapters 18 and 21).

At campuses where the focus is on the networked self, students are generally invited to create briefer, more discrete blog posts or wiki pages, connecting their work with those of peers and faculty through comments and collaborative revision rather than contextualization within a larger, explicitly defined explanation. Reflections and connections accumulate into a powerful collection of evidence of networked learning, but space is not always carved out for students to synthesize this material into a unified and bounded self-representation.

TECHNOLOGY

Genre and technology go hand in hand. Tools have affordances and constraints that make certain kinds of self-representations easier to achieve than do other tools (Norman, 1990). In recent years, an explosion of development of software supports representation of the networked self. With their focus on making it easy to post, comment on, tag,

and aggregate discrete pieces of content, most tools that are beginning to be called Web 2.0 fall into this category (O'Reily, 2005). In addition to blogs and wikis, they include media posting sites like YouTube and Flikr, social networking tools like Facebook and LinkedIn, social bookmarking and categorization sites such as del.icio.us and 43 Things, and tools for aggregating content from multiple sources, such as Bloglines and PageFlakes. A growing number of applications more explicitly focused on learning incorporate multiple features and ideas from these tools. Elgg, software initially presented by its developers as an eportfolio system, is one example that has garnered much attention, combining blogging and social networking in an explicitly academic space.

Many similar projects focus on building Personal Learning Environments, individually controlled spaces for creating, collecting, and distributing information in support of learning (Wilson & Milligan, 2006). Such integration is made possible through a rapidly growing set of technical standards and specifications, such as the ubiquitous RSS and Atom, the use of which has expanded beyond blogs to atomizing and aggregating a wide variety of content. Friend of a Friend (FOAF) provides an open way to represent the profiles and buddy lists common in social networking systems. The adoption of systems that allow individuals to manage their identity across multiple systems is growing, and consensus is beginning to form around OpenID.

What otherwise impressive systems like Elgg lack is functionality targeted at helping their users represent the symphonic self. Through tools such as the matrix included in the Open Source Portfolio and Angel systems, true electronic portfolio systems are beginning to better support representation of online identity as a coherent whole. The University of Georgia's EMMA system allows students to add semantic markup to the texts they include within their portfolios, providing new ways to show how different artifacts are related.

However, not much significant innovation has taken place over the last 3 years in improving eportfolio systems to support the creating of narratives, theories, or maps. Much of the integrative work within these systems is still achieved through writing and hyperlinking, as it has been with online portfolios since the dawn of the Web. More promising is the growing power of concept mapping systems such as Tuft's Visual Understanding Environment, the Institute for Machine and Human Communication's CMap Tools, and BrainBank Learning, each of which has been used for creating portfolios.

Corresponding with these tools that support the symphonic self is a set of specifications and standards, although here too there has been less work in recent years. IMS ePortfolio Specification, which allows for portfolios to be moved between systems, has been implemented in several systems, such as Guinti's LearnXPress ePortfolio and PebblePad, along with the British Standards Institution 8788 LEAP draft standard, which it largely parallels (Cambridge, 2006a; Cambridge, Smythe, & Heath, 2005). Other standards associated with the Semantic Web, such as Resource Description Framework and Topic Maps, could be used to represent the overall structure of meaning within a portfolio. BrainBank Learning represents its concept map portfolios internally as Topic Maps (Lavik & Nordeng, 2004).

PebblePad, developed at the University of Wolverhampton and used by several other members of the Coalition's third cohort, is a leading example of the attempt to support the representation of both the networked self and the symphonic self. PebblePad supports the reflective conversations often associated with blogging tools focused on the network and the hypertextual design associated with Web design in service of the symphonic. Although the network capabilities seem to be receiving the bulk of attention in how the system is currently being used by students, the software might also be used to support the integration of the two styles of integrative learning.

IMPACT

Differences in values, activities, genres, and technologies all combine to produce contrasting impacts from work representing the networked and symphonic selves. The yield of the daily work of the networked self is modest, but over time it grows by accretion, constructing a cumulative identity out of which richer gains might emerge. It results in greater connectedness and increased intentionality. The work of the symphonic self is both less continuous and more intensive. The complex products of these periods of sustained integration achieve a synthesis that provides a sense of coherence and integrity.

Both outcomes are essential for each individual who seeks to live a fulfilling life and make the world a better place. The future challenge for electronic portfolio practice, and integrative learning more generally, will be to perfect the interface between the networked and symphonic.

REFERENCES

American Association of Colleges and Universities. (2002). *Greater expectations.* Washington, DC: American Association of Colleges and Universities.

American Association of Colleges and Universities. (2007). *College learning for the new global century.* Washington, DC: American Association of Colleges and Universities.

Barrett, H., & Wilkerson, J. (2004). *Conflicting paradigms in electronic portfolio approaches: Choosing an electronic portfolio strategy that matches your conceptual framework.* Retrieved from http://www.electronicportfolios.com/systems/paradigms.html

Bateson, M. C. (1989). *Composing a life.* New York: Grove Press.

Cambridge, D. (2005). *The integrity of electronic portfolios in the United States.* Paper presented at Constructing, Using, and Evaluating E-Portfolios, London, England.

Cambridge, D. (2006a). Integral ePortfolio interoperability with the IMS ePortfolio specification. In A. Jafari & C. Kaufman (Eds.), *The handbook of electronic portfolio research.* Hershey, PA: IDEA Group.

Cambridge, D. (2006b). Personally engaged information literacy in general education through information ecology and fieldwork. In C. Gibson

(Ed.), *Student engagement and information literacy* (pp. 143–168). Chicago: Association of College and Research Libraries.

Cambridge, D. (2008). Audience, integrity, and the living document: eFolio Minnesota and lifelong and lifewide learning with ePortfolios. *Computers and Education, 51*(3), 1227–1246.

Cambridge, D., Cummings, R., Day, M., Lane, C., Vanek, T., & Yancey, K. (2006). *Electronic portfolios and social networks*. Paper presented at the Assessment Institute, Indianapolis, IN.

Cambridge, D., Smythe, C., & Heath, A. (2005). *IMS ePortfolio Specification v1.0* (Final Specification Version 1.0 ed.). Burlington, MA: IMS Global Learning Consortium.

Chen, H. (2003). Symposium: Learning reconsidered: Education in the digital age. *Journalism & Mass Communication Education, 57*(4), 292–317.

Hamilton, S. (2006). A principle-based ePort goes public (and almost loses its principles!). In A. Jafari & C. Kaufman (Eds.), *Handbook of ePortfolio research* (pp. 434–446). Hershey, PA: IDEA Group.

Hardt, M., & Negri, A. (2001). *Empire*. Cambridge, MA: Harvard University Press.

Huber, M. T., & Hutchings, P. (2004). *Integrative learning: Mapping the terrain*. Washington, DC: AAC&U.

Hughes, J. (2006). *Eportfolio storytelling as "everyday theorizing": Exploring professional learning narratives, digital "becoming" and blogging as transformative socio-cultural spaces*. Paper presented at the International Conference on Researching and Evaluating PDP and e-Portfolios, Oxfordshire, England.

Klein, J. T. (1996). *Crossing boundaries: Knowledge, disciplinarities, and interdisciplinarities*. Charlottesville: University Press of Virginia.

Kuh, G. D. (2003). *The National Survey of Student Engagement: Conceptual framework and overview of psychometric properties*. Retrieved January 6, 2006, from http://nsse.iub.edu/pdf/conceptual_framework_2003.pdf

Lavik, S., & Nordeng, T. W. (2004). *BrainBank learning—Building topic-map based e-portfolios*. Paper presented at Concept Maps: Theory, Methodology, Technology, Pamplona, Spain.

Levy, D. M. (2001). *Scrolling forward: Making sense of documents in the digital age*. New York: Arcade Publishing.

Norman, D. (1990). *Design of everyday things*. New York: Doubleday.

O'Reily, T. (2005). *What is Web 2.0: Design patterns and business models for the next generation of software*. Retrieved March 6, 2007, from http://www.oreillynet.com/pub/a/oreilly/tim/news/2005/09/30/what-is-web-20.html

Reich, R. B. (2000). *The future of success: Working and living in the new economy*. New York: Vintage.

Rikowski, G. (1999). Nietzsche, Marx, and mastery. In P. Ainley & H. Rainbird (Eds.), *Apprenticeship: Toward a new paradigm for learning*. London: Kogan Page.

Sennett, R. (1998). *The corrosion of character: The personal consequences of work in the new capitalism*. New York: W.W. Norton & Company.

Sennett, R. (2006). *The culture of the new capitalism*. New Haven, CT: Yale University Press.

Sill, D. J. (2001). Integrative thinking, synthesis, and creativity in interdisciplinary studies. *Journal of General Education, 50*(4), 288–311.

Vaill, P. B. (1996). *Learning as a way of being: Strategies for survival in a world of permanent white water*. San Francisco, CA: Jossey-Bass.

Wilson, S., & Milligan, C. (2006). *A reference model for personal learning environments*. Paper presented at the CETIS Personal Learning Environment Meeting, Manchester, England.

Yancey, K. B. (1998). *Reflection in the writing classroom*. Logan, UT: Utah State University Press.

Yancey, K. B. (2004). Postmodernism, palimpsest, and portfolios: Theoretical issues in the representation of student work. *CCC, 55*(4), 738–761.

5

BECOMING EPORTFOLIO LEARNERS AND TEACHERS

JULIE HUGHES

University of Wolverhampton

> Many of the group were apprehensive about adding an IT element to an already difficult task of reflecting, and fears were certainly expressed! We could never have imagined that the . . . e-portfolio was to be one of the few constants in the following months of rollercoaster change that we experienced, becoming a picture frame of our thoughts and experiences.
>
> Karim-Akhtar (2006)

In our thinking about eportfolios, the missing views are often those of students. Through articulating eportfolio experience, students, collectively, can help us examine eportfolios and the ways that they may foster integrative learning and enact identity construction(s). In their accounts, however, students also raise questions requiring response; for example, they question the role of the eportfolio teacher and the impact of the eportfolio itself. Taking up these questions, this chapter presents a case study of how an eportfolio community shared blog might support the dialogic reflective writing and teaching practices associated with the transition from student to professional, specifically from student teacher to qualified teacher status. In presenting this case study, I reflect upon the identity work made visible by iterative writing, noting how a framing discourse on networked and symphonic selves, such as that presented by Darren Cambridge (Chapter 4), paints a richer picture of student learn-

ing and engagement. And not least, this study also considers how a commitment to supporting integrative learning as pedagogical strategy may create both openings and tensions for learners, teachers, and researchers operating within traditional text-based curricula dominated by professional standards such as those for teacher education.

A word about the framing device of selves used here: As Cambridge suggests, the two selves—networked and symphonic—are not either/or, and each of them merits consideration. In exploring the networked/symphonic relationships, we must take care to both avoid binaristic readings of eportfolio learning that privilege the symphonic self unproblematically and move beyond humanist ideals/discourses. A mastery metaphor, albeit momentarily glimpsed within the symphonic self, is a powerful and enduring educational ideal, but it is one that sits somewhat uncomfortably within other theoretical frameworks. For example, one danger in the pursuit of coherence and synthesis is that evidence of process in learning may be lost/censored/cleansed by an eportfolio learner, an issue defining a key tension in being an eportfolio learner and teacher. Here, I offer the possibility of exploring further selves as our eportfolio research grows. In this way the symphony includes, in addition to coherence, a provision for the performance of discordant selves, both individual and communal, the orchestration of which changes over time (Figure 5.1).

INSTITUTIONAL CONTEXT

In September 2005, the University of Wolverhampton (http://www.wlv.ac.uk) became the first U.K. university to provide an eportfolio system, PebblePad (http://www.pebblepad.co.uk), to all staff and students (see Figure 5.2.) The eportfolio is being used for learning, teaching, and assessment; for support of PDP (Personal Development Planning); for appraisal and professional accreditation; and for support of individual and group research clusters. Eportfolio pedagogical use and research is an emerging area in the United Kingdom, generating much interest across the HE sector. And given the U.K. context, government policy drivers for the compulsory education sector will inevitably impact upon postcompulsory provision in its demand for an online (eportfolio) presence for all learners by 2008.

Wolverhampton's response to policy drivers was to design and develop a custom-made eportfolio system that would fulfill the external requirements but also, importantly, provide learners with a personal learning system (Dalziel, Challen, & Sutherland, 2006; Sutherland, 2005). Individual and institutional research interests (Duncan-Pitt & Sutherland, 2006; Hulme & Hughes, 2006; Maiden et al., 2007) that have grown out of this innovation focus on the individual "user" experience.

Figure 5.1. One of my teaching webfolios

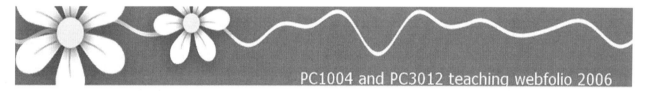

PC1004 and PC3012 teaching webfolio 2006

Welcome PGCE cohort 2006

Welcome!

This is Julie Hughes' teaching webfolio for PC1004 and PC3012, your reflective practice modules. This webfolio will grow over time and will provide you with links to resources.

Where to start? Well, what about the PGCE blog? This is a shared space to ask questions, upload resources or just chat.

During induction you probably felt bombarded by all the information you were given. I introduced you to some subject resources and to some of the child protection and vulnerable adult issues that we have to be aware of as teachers. Emma and I also introduced you to the fabulous world of pebblePAD and blogging ! We asked you to begin your Learning Autobiographies - remember that this first piece for your teaching portfolios can be creative and imaginative using any media. Why not share yours with me and I'll post them on here.

Remember that staff are happy to answer your questions, click here for contact details. We do hope that you enjoy this year. You may adapt your view of this webfolio through the options menu on the top left of your screen.

Click here for PC1004 webfolio and good luck on your pgce!

Figure 5.2. PebblePad.

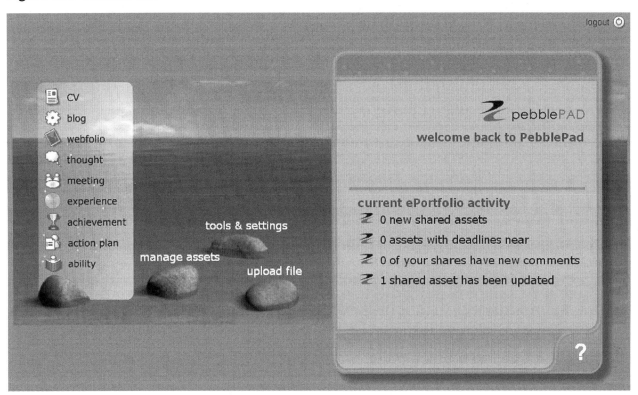

METHODOLOGIES

The research context for this project is located in concepts of felt sense and of research as occurring in reiterative waves. As articulated by Kathleen Yancey and Irwin Weiser (1997), this research can be seen as

> developing in waves, with one wave of practice preparing the next wave of theorizing about that practice, with an intermediate wave extending new practice. By such reflective "wave action" is knowledge created. A knowledge that is responsive to and incorporates "felt sense," a knowledge that is grounded in reflective analysis, a knowledge that always turns to practice as a source for knowing.

The presence of earlier reflective wave action and the "felt sense" of research are both a comfort and a challenge to the eportfolio practitioner/researcher. Admittedly, reflective research occurring in waves is a wonderfully slippery concept aptly supported by fluid cyclical metaphors. But be-

cause of three dimensions—ability to capture process; ability to accept discordant views and voices; and ability to provide a space for sharing findings—eportfolios provide new opportunities to embody this felt sense and to document learning as it occurs. The integrative learning framework applied to eportfolio research, for example, allows us to make explicit the messy complexities and tensions inherent in ongoing narratives of learning. Likewise, adopting an eportfolio hypertext format for presentation of research supports the sharing of ongoing narrative(s) with audiences, demonstrating both networked reflections and the interface between networked, symphonic, and other selves (see Figure 5.3).

Key to my research is the Interview Plus research model, a method identified by Helen Beetham utilizing

> individual interviews supported by appropriate learning artefacts. These artefacts would normally be created by the learner during a learning episode and may include items such as learning diaries,

Figure 5.3. Creating the conditions for dialogue—encouraging talkback.

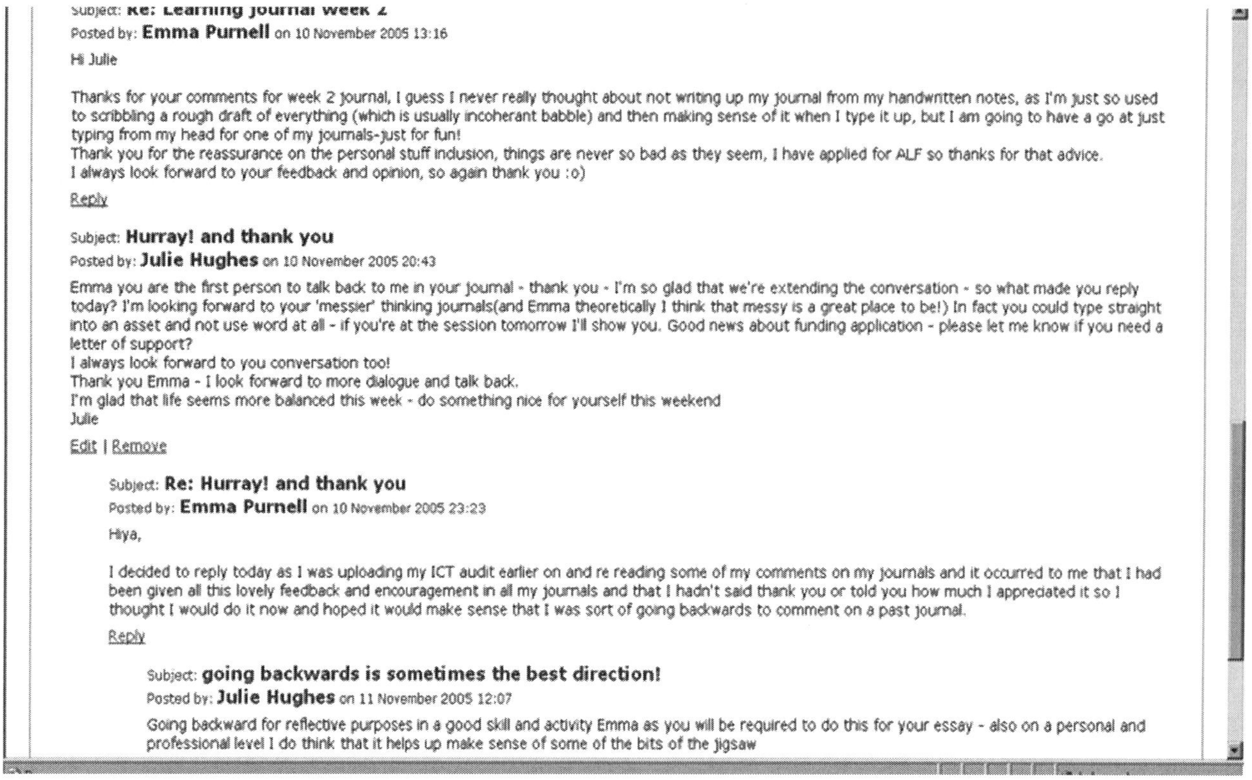

> Subject: Re: Learning Journal week 2
> Posted by: **Emma Purnell** on 10 November 2005 13:16
>
> Hi Julie
>
> Thanks for your comments for week 2 journal, I guess I never really thought about not writing up my journal from my handwritten notes, as I'm just so used to scribbling a rough draft of everything (which is usually incoherent babble) and then making sense of it when I type it up, but I am going to have a go at just typing from my head for one of my journals-just for fun!
> Thank you for the reassurance on the personal stuff inclusion, things are never so bad as they seem, I have applied for ALF so thanks for that advice.
> I always look forward to your feedback and opinion, so again thank you :o)
>
> Reply
>
> Subject: **Hurray! and thank you**
> Posted by: **Julie Hughes** on 10 November 2005 20:43
>
> Emma you are the first person to talk back to me in your journal - thank you - I'm so glad that we're extending the conversation - so what made you reply today? I'm looking forward to your 'messier' thinking journals(and Emma theoretically I think that messy is a great place to be!) In fact you could type straight into an asset and not use word at all - if you're at the session tomorrow I'll show you. Good news about funding application - please let me know if you need a letter of support?
> I always look forward to you conversation too!
> Thank you Emma - I look forward to more dialogue and talk back.
> I'm glad that life seems more balanced this week - do something nice for yourself this weekend
> Julie
>
> Edit | Remove
>
> > Subject: **Re: Hurray! and thank you**
> > Posted by: **Emma Purnell** on 10 November 2005 23:23
> >
> > Hiya,
> >
> > I decided to reply today as I was uploading my ICT audit earlier on and re reading some of my comments on my journals and it occurred to me that I had been given all this lovely feedback and encouragement in all my journals and that I hadn't said thank you or told you how much I appreciated it so I thought I would do it now and hoped it would make sense that I was sort of going backwards to comment on a past journal.
> >
> > Reply
> >
> > > Subject: **going backwards is sometimes the best direction!**
> > > Posted by: **Julie Hughes** on 11 November 2005 12:07
> > >
> > > Going backward for reflective purposes in a good skill and activity Emma as you will be required to do this for your essay - also on a personal and professional level I do think that it helps up make sense of some of the bits of the jigsaw

blogs, transcripts of asynchronous discussions and e-portfolios which are used as prompts to instigate discussion and encourage deeper reflection. (Creanor, Trinder, Gowan, & Howells, 2006)

The idea of exploring the active construction of eportfolio learning with the learner may create the conditions for exploring the construction of eportfolio selves within an integrative learning framework. The concepts of becoming, growth, and change are intrinsic to this approach for the development of reflective and reflexive practices among becoming teachers. The construction metaphor may also apply to the researcher himself or herself as a bricoleur who—engaged in the storying, theorizing, and mapping of the eportfolio learning experience (Kincheloe & Berry, 2004)—actively constructs research methods from the tools at hand. In sum, the adoption of an Interview Plus approach invites an *eportfolio learner* (as student and teacher) to create and present stories of learning located in the reflection of networked self, and including in that reflection the performance of discordant stories that may move the learner into the symphonic realm.

MAJOR FINDINGS

Students were enrolled in the "PGCE," a 9-month program that requires attendance at the university for 2 days per week and attendance at a placement college for 2 days per week. This pattern changes during January and May when students are in placement full-time. During the academic year 2005–6, all new teachers created individual journal blogs and eportfolios for assessment, drawing upon image, video, music, metaphor, and text to represent their journey to becoming teachers, engaging in reflection both in real time and online. Following earlier practices, a shared group weblog was introduced in November 2005, 6 weeks into the professional program; students were to post and to receive feedback from their peers.

The posts from the blog reveal the experiences of these new teachers as they shared their weekly journals for community feedback, beginning in February 2006. The first journal, shared by Mark, could have potentially disrupted the group, as he recounted a failed lesson observation. However, the sharing of this crisis encouraged the growing support for reciprocal dialogue. As Mark reflected in his eportfolio at the conclusion of the PGCE,

the term was made easier by writing down journals and sharing, often I found the journals getting longer and enjoyed awaiting the comments as much as the writing down of the experiences. Commenting on responses and pondering further was taking reflection into other directions. It was becoming exhilarating and I often thought a journal without a response was like "skiing without snow." Journeying was a combination of emotions . . . sharing with others was making it work.

Tess, a dyslexic student, also viewed the eportfolio and blogging as a vital support for the PGCE which she likened to the film *Speed* in that the group had to maintain 50 mph simply to survive.

Interestingly, she also perceived the eportfolio as a supportive writing frame where she had "learned new ways" to present herself and her work. She comments that

after struggling for years as a dyslexic student I feel that pebblePAD has aloud [*sic*] me to be at the same level as everyone else and in some cases ahead . . . I'm sure that you can imagine what this does to my confidence and self esteem (being at the top of the class instead of the bottom).

Although space considerations prevent a full exploration of how writing and sharing within an eportfolio space can contribute to confidence and self-esteem, Tess's observations echo those of several other students during my 3 years of eportfolio practice.

The *pattern* of eportfolio communication tells another story. As Figure 5.4 demonstrates, during the block placements of November 2005–January 2007 there was considerably less blog activity than during the frantic last semester of February to early

Figure 5.4. Eportfolio community blog activity November 2005–January 2007.

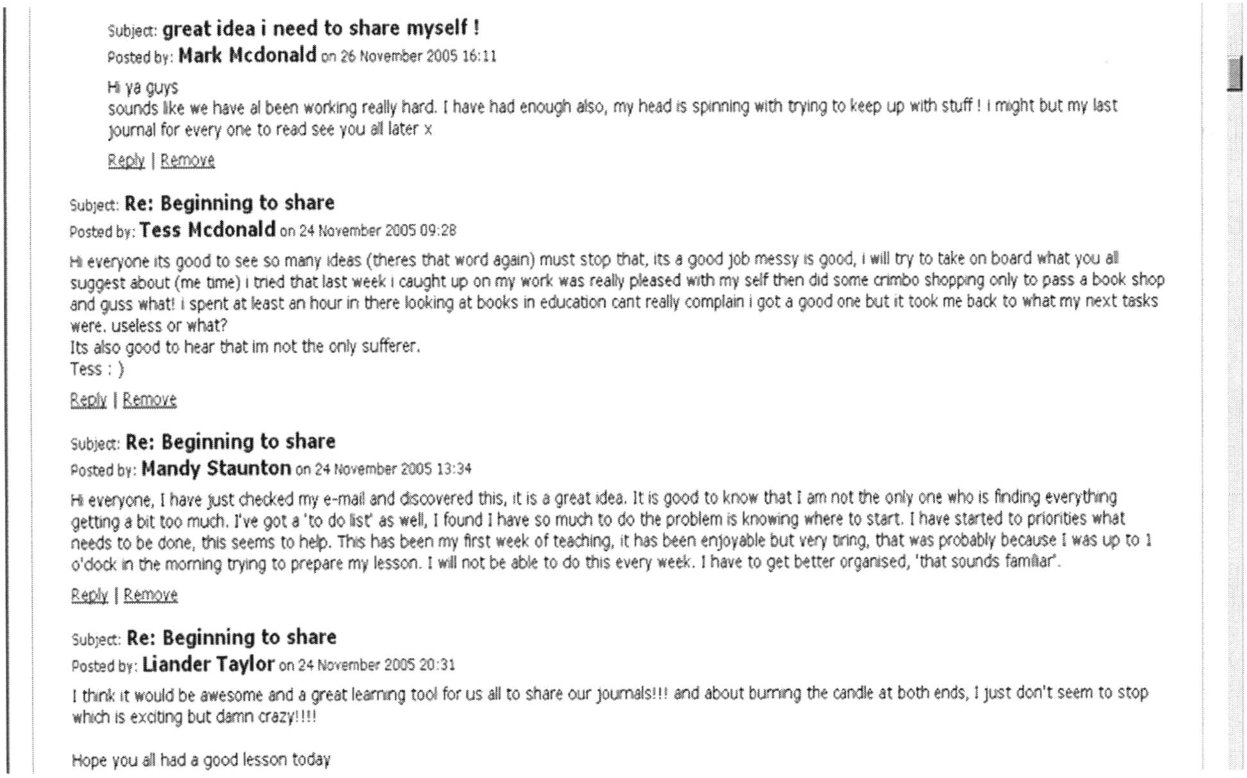

Subject: **great idea i need to share myself !**
Posted by: **Mark Mcdonald** on 26 November 2005 16:11

Hi ya guys
sounds like we have al been working really hard. I have had enough also, my head is spinning with trying to keep up with stuff ! i might but my last journal for every one to read see you all later x

Reply | Remove

Subject: **Re: Beginning to share**
Posted by: **Tess Mcdonald** on 24 November 2005 09:28

Hi everyone its good to see so many ideas (theres that word again) must stop that, its a good job messy is good, i will try to take on board what you all suggest about (me time) i tried that last week i caught up on my work was really pleased with my self then did some crimbo shopping only to pass a book shop and guss what! i spent at least an hour in there looking at books in education cant really complain i got a good one but it took me back to what my next tasks were. useless or what?
Its also good to hear that im not the only sufferer.
Tess :)

Reply | Remove

Subject: **Re: Beginning to share**
Posted by: **Mandy Staunton** on 24 November 2005 13:34

Hi everyone, I have just checked my e-mail and discovered this, it is a great idea. It is good to know that I am not the only one who is finding everything getting a bit too much. I've got a 'to do list' as well, I found I have so much to do the problem is knowing where to start. I have started to priorities what needs to be done, this seems to help. This has been my first week of teaching, it has been enjoyable but very tiring, that was probably because I was up to 1 o'clock in the morning trying to prepare my lesson. I will not be able to do this every week. I have to get better organised, 'that sounds familiar'.

Reply | Remove

Subject: **Re: Beginning to share**
Posted by: **Liander Taylor** on 24 November 2005 20:31

I think it would be awesome and a great learning tool for us all to share our journals!!! and about burning the candle at both ends, I just don't seem to stop which is exciting but damn crazy!!!!

Hope you all had a good lesson today

May. In May 2006, the professional program finished, and only 40 posts appear on our community blog. After that time, however, the levels of reflection upon professional practice have remained high during the postqualification year with extensive group support evident despite the substantial geographic dislocation. Put differently, although the tutor input is decreasing, this eportfolio community continues to sustain itself. This pattern of communication suggests that the engagement with an eportfolio blog community may act as a vital support and transition tool for new professionals in this sector.

Unpacking the dialogue within the blog space and the published writing that followed offers fascinating insights into learning within this community. Group members describe the blog space as "a big part of our growth as reflective writers" (Karim-Akhtar, et al., 2006), noting that it functioned as both "gateway" and "picture frame" allowing for the telling and retelling of stories from their teaching and personal lives. Also important were the ways that the eportfolio seemed to expand time. One student, for example, commented that "the flexibility of the eportfolio meant that we had the luxury of time for our reflections" (Karim-Akhtar), a concept of time somewhat at odds with the time designed into a teacher education curriculum driven by standards and performativity. Time was also described as a doubled entity: This dialogue community space gave learners "time to think" and importantly time to listen, the latter important because "sharing the reflections of others has enabled us to look at ourselves differently" (Karim-Akhtar). Situating and framing the learning in this way allows us to view eportfolios as "an integral part of generative social practice in the lived-in world . . . (whose) constituents contribute inseparable aspects whose combinations create a landscape—shapes, degrees, textures—of community membership" (Lave & Wenger, 1991).

Another theme in the student discussion was the role of the eportfolio in creating a safe space. Students perceived this space as both "safe" in terms of its academic closed membership and as a place "safe from ridicule and criticism" (Karim-Akhtar,

2006). This point is a vital one. If the community is to take on a life independent of the tutor and the course, the conditions for reciprocity and respect must be created and fostered. Being a student, being a writer, isn't fluid or unproblematic. Moreover, an approach to the writing out of self in a weblog can make visible previously invisible hierarchies and tensions. In fact, the leaky seams are often the most interesting border work and a rich source of meta-analysis as a transitional space. Unlike the ordered linear spaces on the PGCE course, the blog was a messy space. Its ownership and authorship were fluid and changing, and its internal hierarchies shifted as comments were addressed to peers rather than to the tutor, a situation that can highlight student vulnerability, as Mark notes:

> Others have made this journey before but I was prepared to travel uncomfortably and prepared to go the distance with the risk taking. I was going to make the journey of self reflection an opportunity that I have always been looking for and have now given another chance to explore and take those leaps into the unknown I was going to grab it with both hands, if I was complacent then others should know, let's make the voyage an experience and something to be shared and I did agonise whether to put myself out there all open and vulnerable, but share I did, making a dreadfully painful experience into something which changed me and maybe others. My shared reflective journal was such a rewarding experience for me personally, I grew in confidence and as a practitioner.

The iterative nature of the conversations within the blog format encouraged the "passing of the baton" within the performance as no comment was ever fixed or completed. The dialogic, rather than monologic, practices encouraged within this space offered the group members "each of us a different way in" such that "without the eportfolio and dialogue with peers and tutor the journey to becoming reflective writers would have been much harder and definitely much lonelier" (Karim-Akhtar, 2006).

Figure 5.5. Emma's hypertext/symphonic eportfolio

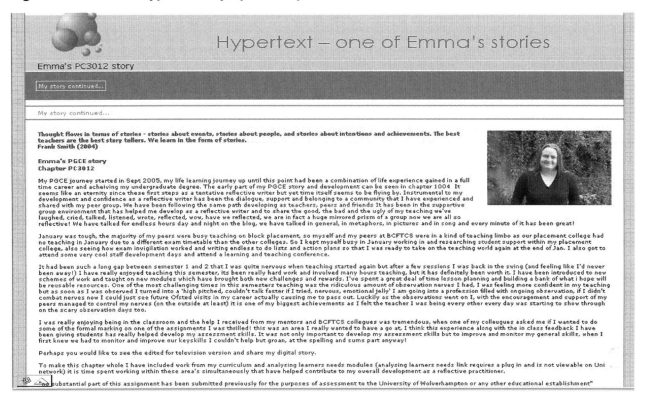

RECOMMENDATIONS

1. Encourage an eportfolio as a space for community-based learning. Research undertaken with the cohorts suggests that adopting an eportfolio as a dialogic learning and teaching tool from induction and as a forum for creative multimedia expression, as Emma's webfolio (Figure 5.5) demonstrates, may provide a powerful learning landscape for the development of reflective practitioners who integrate disciplinary and experiential knowledge. The stories generated within this environment suggest that the community element of the learning and the ongoing construction and questioning of professional knowledges and identities are key.

2. Structure eportfolio activities to encourage students to integrate professional identities into their repertoire of identities. Members of our cohorts have demonstrated knowingness in their community roles and an ac-

knowledgment of the shift from student teacher to teacher. The research suggests that being an eportfolio learner not only supports transitions and identity shifts but also creates a predisposition to the continuation of engaged and meaningful reflective practice and to a culture of lifelong learning.

REFERENCES

Creanor, L., Trinder, K., Gowan, D., & Howells, C. et al. (2006). *LEX: The learner experience of e-learning.* Retrieved January 5, 2007, from http://www.jisc.ac.uk/uploaded_documents/ LEX%20Final%20Report_August06.pdf

Dalziel, C., Challen, R., & Sutherland, S. (2006). ePortfolio in the UK: Emerging practice. In A. Jafari & C. Kaufman (Eds.), *Handbook of research on ePortfolios* (pp. 370–377). Hershey, PA: Idea Group Reference.

Duncan-Pitt, L., & Sutherland, S. (2006). An introduction to the use of eportfolios in professional practice. *The Journal of Radiotherapy in Practice, 1,* 1–7.

Hulme, M., & Hughes, J. (2006). E-learning dialogues in the process of becoming reflective practitioners. In J. O'Donoghue (Ed.), *Technology supported learning and teaching: A staff perspective.* Hershey, PA: Idea Group Reference.

Karim-Akhtar, Y., Mahmood, K., McDonald, M., McDonald, T., McGuinness, S., Staunton, M., et al. (2006, Summer). Pebble power. *ESCalate, 5.* Retrieved July 1, 2006, from http://escalate.ac.uk/2593

Kincheloe, J., & Berry, K. (2004). *Rigour and complexity in educational research (conducting educational research).* Maidenhead: Open University Press.

Lave, J., & Wenger, E. (1991). *Situated learning. Legitimate peripheral participation.* Cambridge: University of Cambridge Press.

Maiden, B., Penfold, B., McCoy, T., Duncan-Pitt, L., & Hughes, J. (2007). Supporting learning and teaching innovation and building research capacity using an e-portfolio at the University of Wolverhampton. *Educational Developments, 8,* 1.

Sutherland, S. (2005). e-Portfolios: A space for learning and the learner voice. In S. de Freitas & C. Yapp (Eds.), *Personalizing learning in the 21st century.* Stafford: Network Educational Press.

Yancey, K., & Weiser, I. (1997). *Situating portfolios. Four perspectives.* Logan, UT: Utah State University.

6

MAKING CONNECTIONS
The LaGuardia ePortfolio

BRET EYNON
LaGuardia Community College

The students of New York City's LaGuardia Community College are boundary crossers. Nearly two thirds of our 13,000 students are immigrants, coming from more than 160 different countries. Seventy percent are female, and most are low-income and first-generation college-goers. Eighty percent are "minorities," traditionally underrepresented in higher education. Ninety percent require developmental skills courses to prepare them to do college-level work. Our students are constantly navigating intersecting boundaries of nationality, race, gender roles and expectations, language, religion, economic class, and educational background.

For the past 5 years, LaGuardia has actively explored the use of eportfolio as a tool for helping students to more successfully make these transitions, overcoming fragmentation and building integrated new identities as learners, adults, and citizens. Building student engagement in the learning process, the LaGuardia ePortfolio also supports our holistic college-wide program assessment process. Our Inter/National Coalition for Electronic Research work has focused on the viability of eportfolios in this challenging context and the value of eportfolios for integrative learning. Our experi-

ence has suggested some of the challenges of undertaking eportfolios in a large, urban community college and with high-risk students. Meanwhile, our successes demonstrate, in a preliminary way, eportfolios' viability as an integrative tool.[1]

FINDING 1—LARGE-SCALE EPORTFOLIO IMPLEMENTATION

Large-scale eportfolio implementation *can* be successfully undertaken in a big urban community college and with high-risk students.

Drawing upon grant funding and institutional support, LaGuardia has succeeded in building a major eportfolio initiative. The number of students building eportfolios at LaGuardia has grown steadily (see Figure 6.1). In the 2003–4 academic year, a total of 370 LaGuardia students actively worked on their eportfolios. In the 2005–6 academic year, a total of 5,024 LaGuardia students worked on their eportfolios in courses from introductory ESL and mathematics courses to mid-level courses in humanities, health sciences, and business. And in 2006–7 that number approached 6,500. We are well on

Figure 6.1

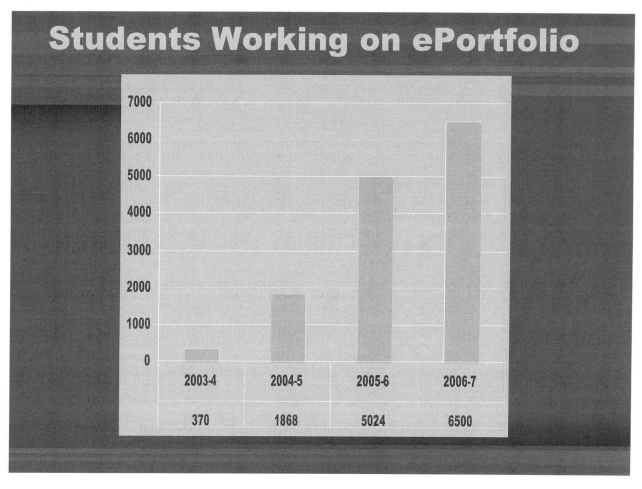

Students Working on ePortfolio

	2003-4	2004-5	2005-6	2006-7
	370	1868	5024	6500

our way toward our goal of offering ePortfolio to all LaGuardia students.[2]

LaGuardia eportfolios have many of the same features as eportfolios across higher education. The center of LaGuardia ePortfolio is a collection of coursework, drawn from a range of disciplines, assembled across semesters. Work includes papers, poetry, spreadsheets, lab reports, PowerPoint presentations, and artwork, as well as video- and audio-recorded speeches and performances. Students are prompted to attach written reflections to their coursework. They also write personal statements in two sections of the eportfolio: the About Me section, in which students create a self-directed life narrative; and the Educational Goals section, which focuses particularly on education and the future. A resume can be integrated into the eportfolio and hotlinked to

coursework and internship experiences. As discussed below, many students choose to use photographs and visual art throughout their eportfolios; some also utilize background music. Students create their eportfolio using one of three technology choices:

- Basic eportfolios, created with a form-based data management system, allow anyone to quickly create a simple Web-based presentation portfolio.
- Intermediate eportfolios, where students select and edit a template using Netscape Composer, are for students with some skills, who want to put in more time and work.
- Advanced eportfolios, created from scratch with Dreamweaver or other authoring software, and often integrating work with Flash

and other more sophisticated software, demand that students bring to the project a relatively high level of commitment as well as a preexisting foundation of technical skill.

Sample LaGuardia eportfolios that demonstrate the work students do at each level are available at http://www.eportfolio.lagcc.cuny.edu/basic_gallery.html, as well as at https://www.lagcc.cuny.edu/eportfolio/lab/scholars/default.htm.

FINDING 2—AN INTEGRATIVE APPROACH

An integrative approach to eportfolios can help combine different elements of students' learning experience and help students explore and express new identities as learners.

When LaGuardia began planning its eportfolio project in 2001, we found there were many different kinds of eportfolios, including career eportfolios, learning eportfolios, and advisement eportfolios. As we attended conferences and visited campuses from Kalamazoo to Wesleyan University, we heard that we should focus on one type of eportfolio. While respecting this perspective and the wisdom derived from experience, we persisted in creating a project incorporating a combination of approaches. LaGuardia's initial goals for the eportfolio were academic: strengthening learning and assessment. However, given the economic needs of our students, we felt that incorporating career development was important. Meanwhile, our research suggested that an approach that allowed for student creativity, reflection, and expression would be crucial to integrative learning and to generating student "ownership" of their eportfolios. So we decided to pursue a multipronged eportfolio strategy.[3]

Guided in part by LaGuardia's participation in the national Integrative Learning Project (sponsored by the Carnegie Foundation for the Advancement of Teaching and the Association of American Colleges & Universities), we have intentionally structured our eportfolio to address the goal of in-

tegration. LaGuardia's eportfolio is both longitudinal and interdisciplinary: students build their eportfolios over the entire course of their careers at LaGuardia, and they integrate work from many different classes. Many eportfolios are launched in interdisciplinary learning communities, where faculty jointly design activities aimed at helping students make connections across disciplinary ways of thinking. The learning performances students create through such interdisciplinary activities—for example, papers and presentations that reflect the guidance and joint assignments of English and business faculty or ESL and sociology faculty—become ideal components for an eportfolio. Meanwhile, particular courses and faculty (most notably faculty from our counseling and cooperative education departments) take responsibility for advancing the career and personal development elements of eportfolio. Throughout, the La-Guardia ePortfolio explicitly encourages reflection and the consideration of personal growth and change. And it allows for considerable visual creativity and expression. All these facets of La-Guardia's eportfolio strategy are designed to support integrative learning. (For information on the Integrative Learning Project and LaGuardia's report on eportfolios and learning communities, see Huber et al., 2007).

This integrative strategy has had a tangible impact on the experiences of LaGuardia students. Quantitative data collected over 3 years reveal that students value each element of the eportfolio and the combination of diverse elements into a single, integrated whole. Qualitative data give voice to this point. For example, Aaron Hudson, a working-class LaGuardia student who hopes to graduate and go on to Baruch College for a business degree, articulated the attractions of the career development side of eportfolios:

> Having your e-portfolio may place you a step ahead of the rest. You never know, employers may want to see more than just a resume, they will want to see some work that you have done, and they may want to see something that shows what kind of person you are. Before long, the standard

face-to-face interview will be a thing of the past and the sending of an e-portfolio to a possible employer will have taken over as the deciding factor of employment.[4]

Other students report that they value the process of making their learning public. Surveys have consistently shown that students respond enthusiastically to the possibility of "showing my e-portfolio to my family," giving this potential audience the highest ranking of all. Angelica Serrano, a human services major born in Mexico, described the impact of publishing an eportfolio that incorporated her work and her evolving vision of her life in America:

Publishing my work and my reflections on my e-portfolio changed the way I think about my writing. I wrote a reflective essay for my e-portfolio. I knew that my essay would be read not only by my professor, but by a much broader audience. I couldn't be so facile; now my life, my self-perception and my goals would be revealed to everyone. (Angelica Serrano, presentation to Queens Borough President Helen Marshall, May 16, 2005)

Looking at LaGuardia portfolios (see http://www.eportfolio.lagcc.cuny.edu/advanced_gallery.html), many viewers remark upon the tremendous energy that LaGuardia students put into the creative side of eportfolios. LaGuardia eportfolios are visually dramatic, rich with color and design. (See Figure 6.2.) LaGuardia English professor J. Elizabeth Clark has suggested that LaGuardia students are engaged in inventing "a new digital rhetoric," creating striking statements that draw on their rich cultural traditions and new urban experiences to express evolving identities through text, images,

Figure 6.2

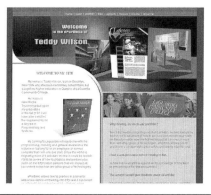

LaGuardia Community College ePortfolio

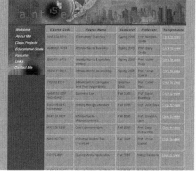

music, and video—hypermedia contributions to a new global literature. LaGuardia fine arts professor Michael Rodriguez has argued that the combination of written and visual reflections helps students take themselves and their eportfolios more seriously. Rodriguez suggests that faculty encourage students to synthesize the written and the visual. "The e-portfolio prompts my students to move forward in expressing their creativity across different media, in art and language," he explains. And this cognitive and affective synthesis leads to new discoveries: educational, artistic, intellectual, and personal.[5]

Student description of the eportfolio process underscores the ways that eportfolios help students become more aware of themselves as learners, developing new and more integrated identities. "From my first ESL class, when I was introduced to ePortfolio, I have grown a lot," wrote Sandra Rios, a Colombia-born student who started at LaGuardia in ESL and is now studying psychology at Hunter College.

Not only did I gain technical skills, but I learned how to express myself as a student. The different sections of my ePortfolio made me realize important things about how I see myself starting at La-Guardia, how I see myself now and in my future. My experience with ePortfolio at LaGuardia has made me see more of who I want to be.[6]

This integrative strategy has not been without cost. LaGuardia's approach to eportfolio puts additional demands on faculty and staff and on the eportfolio system itself. However, as the data summary below suggests, it appears to be paying off in helping both students and the college reach key eportfolio-related goals.

Figure 6.3

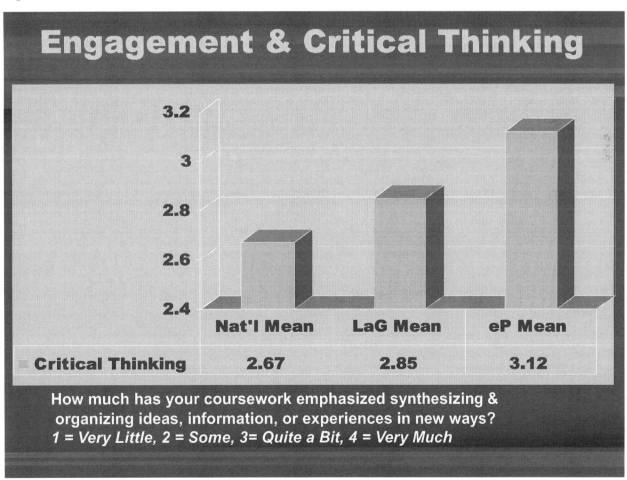

Engagement & Critical Thinking

	Nat'l Mean	LaG Mean	eP Mean
Critical Thinking	2.67	2.85	3.12

How much has your coursework emphasized synthesizing & organizing ideas, information, or experiences in new ways?
1 = Very Little, 2 = Some, 3= Quite a Bit, 4 = Very Much

FINDING 3

LaGuardia's experience demonstrates that eportfolios, implemented with institutional and pedagogical strategies that value integrative learning, help high-risk students engage more deeply in the learning process, leading to measurable improvement in student learning.

LaGuardia has been examining the impact of our integrative approach to eportfolios, using the Community College Survey of Student Engagement (CCSSE), student and faculty feedback, and institutionally generated outcomes data on pass rates and retention. Findings are still preliminary, and a full discussion of the data is well beyond the scope of this chapter, but a sample of findings is suggestive.

To determine whether student construction of eportfolios correlated with increased student engagement, LaGuardia compared 2005–6 CCSSE data, looking at questions drawn from Academic Challenge and Active Learning areas, illuminating a range of issues, including critical thinking, writing, technology, and collaborative learning. Targeting classes where students constructed eportfolios as a required element of the course curriculum, we included selected CCSSE questions in their end-of-semester feedback questionnaires. Then we compared the mean score from these eportfolio classes to college-wide means on the same questions.[7]

On virtually every question, students in these eportfolio-intensive courses tended to score higher in engagement than the college-wide sample reported by the LaGuardia Office of Institutional Research. For example, on one critical thinking–related

Figure 6.4

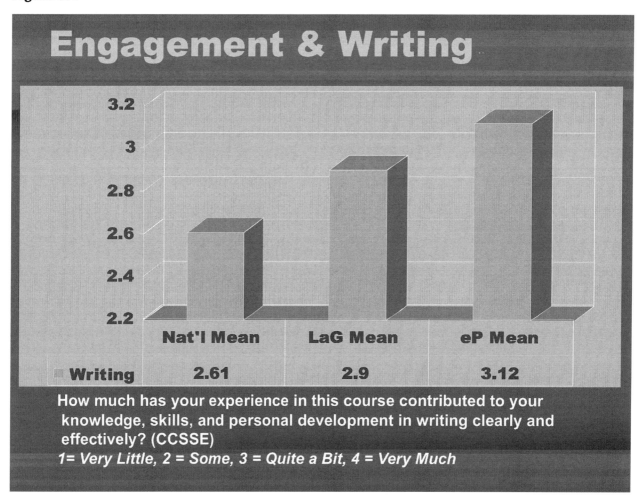

Engagement & Writing

	Nat'l Mean	LaG Mean	eP Mean
Writing	2.61	2.9	3.12

How much has your experience in this course contributed to your knowledge, skills, and personal development in writing clearly and effectively? (CCSSE)
1= Very Little, 2 = Some, 3 = Quite a Bit, 4 = Very Much

question (Question 5a from the 2005–6 survey: "How much has your coursework emphasized synthesizing and organizing ideas, information, and/or experiences in new ways?") the college-wide mean is 2.85 (a substantial .18 points above the national mean of 2.67). The mean for students in eportfolio courses was 3.12, an additional .27 points higher than the already positive college mean. The pattern was similar for questions about writing, effort, technology, and classroom collaboration. (See Figures 6.3 and 6.4.) Outcomes data, particularly data on failure and dropout rates, provide further evidence of the integrative eportfolio's positive relationship to student engagement and learning. For example, looking at two semesters of institutional data from the 2005–6 academic year, based on a sample of more than 2,500 eportfolio students, we compared the pass rate in eportfolio courses and non-eportfolio sections of the same courses. We found that the average pass rate in the comparison classes was 70.6

percent. The average pass rate in the eportfolio sections of the same courses was 76.0 percent. The pass rate in eportfolio courses, in other words, was 5.4 percentage points higher, a significant difference in a key academic area of need (see Figure 6.5).[8]

Retention data are similarly positive. For example, analysis of the transcripts of a sample of nearly 2,000 students in eportfolio-intensive courses in 2005–6 showed an average one-semester return rate that is 5.6 percentage points higher than the college average. Here, too, the use of eportfolio in an integrative manner correlates with better outcomes in an area that has stubbornly resisted improvement, despite years of effort across higher education (see Figure 6.6).[9]

These data on key academic outcomes triangulate with the indications of increased engagement evidenced by CCSSE and with the extensive qualitative and quantitative feedback generated by both students and faculty. Taken together, this evidence

Figure 6.5

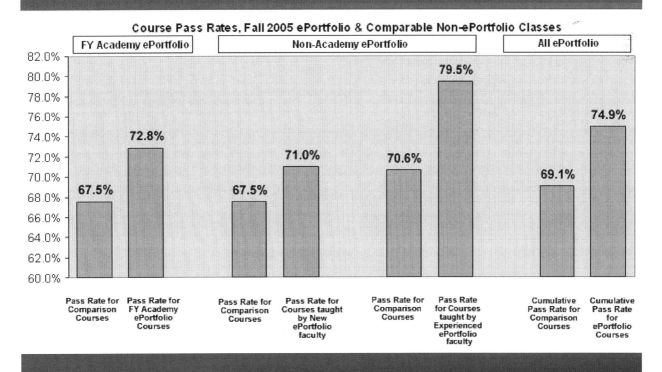

Course Pass Rates, Fall 2005 ePortfolio & Comparable Non-ePortfolio Classes

Figure 6.6

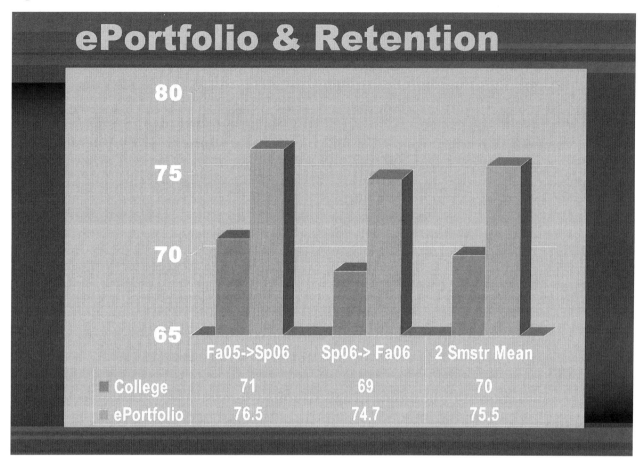

	Fa05->Sp06	Sp06-> Fa06	2 Smstr Mean
College	71	69	70
ePortfolio	76.5	74.7	75.5

suggests the positive impact of our integrative eportfolio strategy on student learning at La-Guardia. Moreover, it has helped to persuade outside agencies to recognize our work; in 2006 LaGuardia was awarded the MetLife Foundation Community College Excellence Award for successfully helping underserved students meet their academic and career goals. In 2007 the Community College Futures Assembly honored LaGuardia with the prestigious Bellwether Award for instructional innovation. In both cases, eportfolios and the evidence of their impact figured significantly in the award decision.

IMPLICATIONS AND RECOMMENDATIONS

1. Go for what you want. Against the odds, LaGuardia has pursued an integrated, multifaceted eportfolio strategy. Working in the most challenging of academic contexts, we have pursued a rich but demanding vision of eportfolios' potential. Although we have not finished our work (if such a thing is possible), we have made dramatic progress. We hope this record encourages others to aim high in their vision of what is possible for eportfolios.

2. Be intentional about integration. If we want eportfolios to support integrative learning, we must pay attention to the elements that support connection and synthesis. This goal requires careful thinking about pedagogy and structure, as well as software. In our experience, visual creativity is key, as are interdisciplinary linkages. Other approaches to integration may emphasize other elements. Whatever your emphasis, integration will happen only if you make it an important goal in your plans and your processes.

3. Build sturdy support structures. Implementing eportfolios takes work on the part of faculty and students. They need recursive assistance with this process. LaGuardia has created multifaceted support structures coordinated by the LaGuardia Center for Teaching and Learning, including faculty development seminars, dedicated eportfolio labs or "studios," IT infrastructure management, and specially trained student assistants called eportfolio consultants. Starting small, these supports have grown as the program has expanded. Without them, our expansion and our success would have been impossible.

4. Be patient—this is a long-term process. We've been working on eportfolios for 5 years, and although we have made progress, we are not finished. Eportfolio is an institutionally transformative project, requiring broad effort. Such transformations take time.

5. Gather multiple sources of data appropriate to your goals. To sustain such an effort, we must pay serious attention to the issues of data and evaluation. For LaGuardia, the data on engagement (gathered through CCSSE) have been very helpful. They connect to a range of other data elements, including self-designed survey data, qualitative feedback, and data on key student outcomes such as pass rates and retention. Together this combination helps us to understand the impact of eportfolio and to sustain our broad, college-wide effort.

NOTES

1. The growing discussion about integrative learning in higher education is most easily accessed through the work of the Integrative Learning Project, made public at a Web site hosted by the Carnegie Foundation (at http://www.carnegie foundation.org/files/elibrary/integrativelearning/index.htm) and summarized by Mary Taylor Huber et al. in "Leading Initiatives for Integrative Learning," *Liberal Education,* Spring 2007.

2. In 2006–7, just over half of the students working on their eportfolios were primarily focused on depositing coursework in their eportfolio folders. The other half went substantially further, assembling coursework, reflections, and personal statements into a more comprehensive Web-based presentation.

3. The categorization of different types of eportfolio has been done in many different ways. The AAHE Electronic Portfolio Clearinghouse identified six different primary functions for eportfolio: educational planning; documenting knowledge, skills, and abilities; tracking development; finding a job; evaluation within a course; and performance monitoring in the workplace. Helen C. Barrett and Judy Wilkerson discuss the issues confronting universities as they "make decisions about an electronic portfolio strategy" in "Conflicting Paradigms in Electronic Portfolio Approaches," 2005, available on Helen C. Barrett's Web site at http://electronicportfolios.org/systems/paradigms.html. In his 2005 report, "eFolio Minnesota for Lifewide and Lifelong Learning: Research Results," Darren Cambridge examines the ways Minnesota users combined and moved across different types of eportfolios.

4. One of Aaron Hudson's early ePortfolios is available on the LaGuardia eportfolio site at http://www.eportfolio.lagcc.cuny.edu/ePortfolios/intermediate/Aaron.Hudsonrev/ index.html. Quotation from interview with Aaron Hudson (December 4, 2006).

5. Clark's and Rodriguez's remarks were made during discussion of visual creativity in LaGuardia's ePortfolio Leadership Colloquium, November 12, 2006.

6. Sandra Rios' eportfolio is available on LaGuardia's ePortfolio Web site at http://www.eportfolio.lagcc.cuny.edu/ePortfolios/Advanced/Sandra.Rios/Spring/2005/index.html; statements from page 2 of the Welcome to my ePortfolio section.

7. Additional information on CCSSE is available at http://www.ccsse.org. LaGuardia's use of the CCSSE data around eportfolio has been commended in two recent (2005 and 2006) CCSSE annual reports, available at this site. LaGuardia's

overall CCSSE scores are collected by the Office of Institutional Research and made available at http://www.lagcc.cuny.edu/facts/inst_research.aspx.

8. Data on attrition were provided and analyzed by the LaGuardia Office of Institutional Research in response to queries from the LaGuardia Center for Teaching and Learning.

9. As with the course attrition data, the data on retention were provided and analyzed by the LaGuardia Office of Institutional Research in response to queries from the LaGuardia Center for Teaching and Learning.

REFERENCE

Huber, M. T., Brown, C., Hutchings, P., Gale, R., Miller, R., & Breen, M. (Eds.). (2007, January). *Integrative learning: Opportunities to connect.* Public report of the Integrative Learning Project sponsored by the Association of American Colleges and Universities and The Carnegie Foundation for the Advancement of Teaching, Stanford, CA. Retrieved from http://www.carnegie foundation.org/files/elibrary/integrativelearning/index.htm

7

CONNECTING CONTEXTS AND COMPETENCIES

Using Eportfolios for Integrative Learning

TRACY PENNY LIGHT, BOB SPROULE, and KATHERINE LITHGOW

University of Waterloo

The University of Waterloo's Competency Portfolio project helps students to connect their learning experiences in a variety of different contexts—academic, workplace, and community—to demonstrate competency in a given domain or set of domains (Figure 7.1).

Although we know that students learn skills in these different contexts, university education often focuses on the academic setting only, encouraging students to limit their thinking to a specific course without connecting between courses, much less beyond them. Such connections would seem to be especially important at the University of Waterloo, where, as a large cooperative education provider, over 60 percent of students are enrolled in co-op programs. Our study of our co-op programs, however, has revealed a large gap between what students learn in academic settings and what they learn in workplace settings. In brief, there is very little, if any, integration of learning on the part of either students or faculty (Co-op Review, 2005). Electronic portfolios (eportfolios), we believe, can provide that opportunity for integration through a site where learners articulate and make connections between their experiences at university in many dif-

ferent ways. Most importantly, eportfolios allow students to not only "show" but also to demonstrate concretely what they know to the world. And as this chapter reports, in terms of professional practice—specifically, in the professional practice of accounting—eportfolios provide students with a way to document and demonstrate their competency in knowledge and skills that their profession has deemed to be important (Colman, 2005/2006).[1]

Increasingly, universities are reviewing their programs for relevance and the provision of skills to ensure that their curricula align with the competencies outlined by professional societies. In the case of accounting, a broadening of the accounting skill set is necessary. Beyond changing curricula to better address the professional competencies requiring a breadth and depth of critical strategic knowledge, including a strong foundation of accounting knowledge, we need evidence that such curricular change is actually producing graduates with the desired competencies and qualities. In the past, students indicated on their résumés that they possessed certain skills. However, saying or writing that skills have been acquired is different from documenting those abilities; electronic portfolios allow

Figure 7.1. University of Waterloo Competency Portfolio Project.

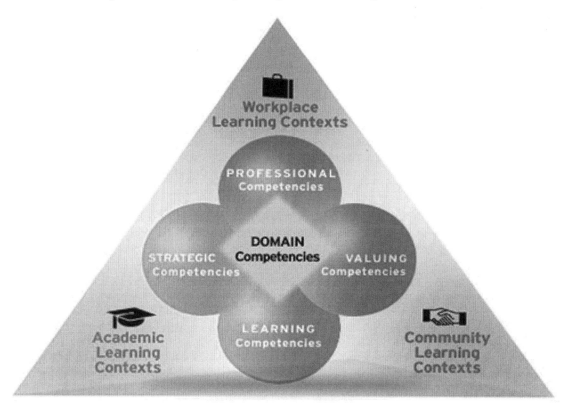

students to provide the documentation demonstrating their competencies. In addition, as we explain below, the act of articulating connections in learning, encouraged by eportfolios, is powerful in and of itself.

In fall 2004, we initiated two pilot projects introducing students to eportfolios and studying the learning impact of creating eportfolios. Here we report some of our early findings of eportfolios in two domains—accounting and financial management (AFM) and history—and explore the ways these findings are leading us to develop further eportfolio projects. In all of our projects, we follow students between contexts (i.e., from their academic courses to their work terms and back) to track how their eportfolios evolve over time. We are particularly interested in how students' thinking develops in both of these domains as well as where and when that development occurs.

In Chapter 4, Darren Cambridge discusses the role of eportfolios in developing the networked and symphonic selves. The distinction between these two selves is particularly useful for us. In our case, the goal is to develop the symphonic self; we want students to develop their "whole person" rather than learn only to make strategic connections.[2] However, that said, the ability to make connections strategically (perhaps even entrepreneurially) is important. We see this, though, as a developmental stage.[3] Indeed, we are most interested in learning whether eportfolios assist in or facilitate changes in student behavior around the development of the competencies we are trying to cultivate. The theoretical framework for this question is outlined below. Early evidence suggests that this approach is beneficial to students as it assists them to better integrate their various learning experiences.[4] A by-product of this activity may be, particularly in professional programs, students who are more competitive on the job market. We then conclude with some suggestions for future work, both in our own context and for others considering using eportfolios as a way to promote integrative learning.

INTEGRATIVE LEARNING AND OUR EARLY PILOTS

As noted, our thinking about integrative learning stemmed from the recognition that students were not connecting their academic and workplace learning experiences. We were also influenced by the work on integrative learning from Mary Taylor Huber and Pat Hutchings of The Carnegie Foundation for the Advancement of Teaching. As Huber and Hutchings (2004) note, "students today would benefit from taking a more intentional, deliberative, and reflexive stance toward vocation." The need for this, they point out, stems from changes to our world as a result of technology and globalization; the sheer amount of information that we all have access to requires that we are able to effectively "connect" the pieces that matter (Huber & Hutchings, 2004). Agreeing with this position and also that "integrative learning does not just happen" (Huber & Hutchings), we set out to explore how eportfolios as a teaching, learning, and assessment tool could assist in achieving this goal. This is an important point. It was clear early on, especially given the changes to the world outlined above, that we could not just "add on" eportfolio tasks to those assignments that students have traditionally completed in different contexts. Rather, we needed to integrate the eportfolio as a teaching, learning, or assessment tool as a means to achieve a particular outcome. We wanted to ensure that the eportfolio was in alignment with the other outcomes for a particular learning experience. What follows are two examples of how this integration occurred.

ACCOUNTING AND FINANCIAL MANAGEMENT (AFM)

Professional societies and institutes have determined that technical knowledge alone is not adequate preparation for a career as an accountant and financial manager. As a result, an increasing emphasis has been placed on "nontechnical" skills such as written and oral communication, analysis skills, professional ethics, and interpersonal skills of leading and partic-

ipating in groups. Our students in the professional AFM program are highly motivated and focused, quickly determining what the performance measurement criteria are and working to meet them. The shift from the traditional demonstration of technical skills through examination to a new program focus on small group, project, and presentation type of educational experience requires a new way to integrate the program and track the development of students' progress in these "soft" skills. In addition, traditional work term reports, completed at the end of co-op work terms, have failed to achieve the objective of having students connect the academic concepts with experiences in the workplace. In our AFM program, then, eportfolios, which are connected to developing professional soft skills or competencies such as teamwork, communication (oral and written), and leadership, provide a mechanism for tracking such development in and between learning contexts.

The eportfolio acts as a tool of integration, an area where students can make connections and reflect upon them and plan for the future.

For example, students in a second-year accounting course were asked to outline where they viewed connections between the concepts studied inside a concept map. As Brooke noted, "The biggest challenge I faced when creating my concept map was trying to identify relationships. It was very easy to name accounting concepts, but developing relationships between the concepts was a challenge" (see Figures 7.2 and 7.3).

In addition to supporting integration, this eportfolio has as a key feature the ability to share the eportfolio and receive feedback from peers, instructors, and mentors, responses that will help students plan for future growth and development.[5] Rather than regarding their university experience as a series of unrelated courses that they must complete in order to graduate, students can use the eportfolio to think about all aspects of their university experience.

Similarly, at a course and program level, course instructors and administrators are able to see the connections students are making between various learning experiences and the lessons students are learning as they progress through a program.[6]

Figure 7.2. Brooke Hancock reflection.

| Who Am I? |
| Teamwork |
| Leadership |

Brooke Hancock

"Mission Statement"

My goal has been, since the age of 6, to become an Accountant with her ARCT in piano performance. Someday I hope to be the Accountant for a music related company such as Virgin Records.

"Vision Statement"

To achieve my mission I will graduate from the University of Waterloo with my Bachelor of Accounting and Financial Management (BAFM) with a minor in Music and my Master of Accounting (MAcc);I will learn as much as possible along the way by volunteering and working in Accounting related jobs and practicing and performing the piano during every spare moment. I will then work toward getting both my CMA and CA designation and work ~~towards getting my ARCT in piano. It~~

Resume (Microsoft Word document)

"Value Statement"

Something I value greatly in life is balance. It is very important to me to learn a variety of things and participate in a variety of activities. My mission is always in mind but I try to balance my activities to stay healthy and happy...like the fundamental accounting equation, "Assets = Liabilities plus Owners' Equity." My assets are a variety of things I value in life such as satisfaction and pride, knowledge, independence, realationships, faith, ~~involvement in my community, and~~

Figure 7.3. Brook Hancock concept map.

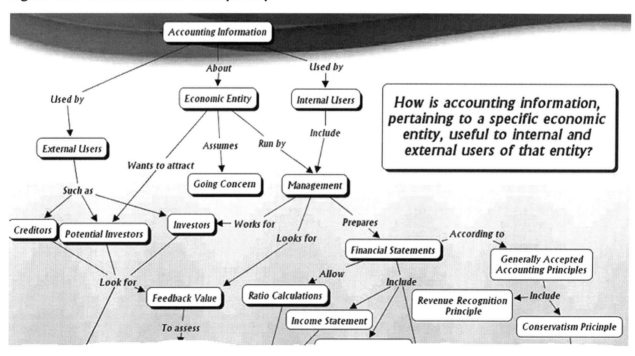

Students have reported, for instance, on the connections they are making between academic content learned in the program and practical applications of that content in the workplace. As one student noted,

> I would just like to say that I never knew just how important the team reflections from AFM 131 would be, until I began preparing for interviews for summer internships at accounting firms. I figured they would ask about teamming [sic] experience (which they did) and I was fully prepared to answer their questions because I referred to what I had wrote [sic] in my team reflections.
>
> On a side note, I have received an offer . . . and I owe a lot of that to the reflections! Virtually all of their questions were about experiences in teams. (student e-mail to professor, February 25, 2007)

Just as students are able to use the feedback to create a plan for further development, instructors and administrators have the potential to use this information to guide plans for improving courses and programs based on the reflections and documented experiences of our students.

Ultimately, eportfolios provide students with a place where they can present evidence of the distinguishing characteristics of a University of Waterloo education—evidence of well-honed problem-solving and critical thinking skills and examples showing their ability to build relationships and work effectively in teams. The focus on team skills illustrates how the eportfolio interfaces with both curriculum and experience. Students are introduced to team skills in their first-year AFM 131 class,[7] where they reflect on their teamwork abilities as they work on a team project. Students continue to reflect on their teamwork skills as they move into the second year of the program and then into their co-op work terms (see Appendix A). Commitment to continuous improvement and assessment can be evidenced by the plans they have created for personal growth and development and the ways they have acted upon the feedback from peers, mentors, and instructors. By encouraging students to use their eportfolios as places to document and reflect upon the lessons they have learned and the feedback they have received, and to consider how these will affect their future actions and reactions, students benefit from a more holistic approach to their university education and a deeper level of understanding.

HISTORY

By way of contrast, we have used eportfolios for a very specific purpose in one undergraduate elective history course. Students from across the disciplines and in different stages of their university career—from first to final year—use the eportfolios to document their ability to "think historically."

Students are introduced to this concept at the beginning of the course using the concept map shown in Figure 7.4. Most important for the students' learning in this particular course is to develop an understanding of the process of "doing history"—the critical thinking and analysis that arise from the study of documents and that lead to the development of an interpretation of the past.[8] Because the majority of students in the course are not history majors, the goal is to develop this competency so that it can be "reused" in other learning contexts. Students reflect on their understanding of and ability to "do history" throughout the course; they create an eportfolio as the culminating activity. They "make connections" between the course content and process and other experiences they have had, whether they are in the academic, workplace, or community context. Students not only think critically about what it means to "do" history and to come up with their own "take" on the process but also to explore how their own experiences shape that process for them individually.

Thus, for example, a student in the course, Chris Moffatt, concluded that history was "more than just books"; Chris had also traveled to Europe and so incorporated images and thoughts of that trip into his thinking about the course and the connections he made. He also linked the content and process of HIST 200 to other history courses that he had taken.

Figure 7.4. "Doing History" concept map from HIST 200.

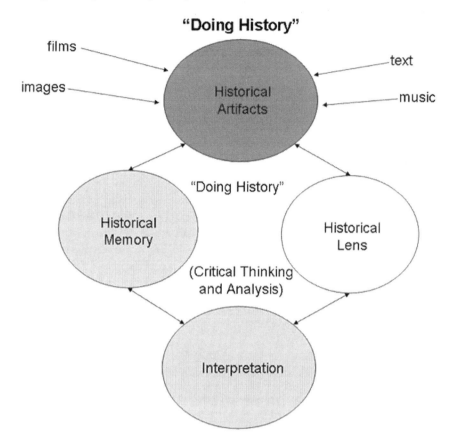

MAKING CONNECTIONS IN THE FUTURE

Although we are still in the early stages of our longitudinal work exploring the use of eportfolios to promote and develop integrative learning, it is clear that eportfolios, when integrated into a learning context in order to achieve a specific goal or outcome, are effective tools. We realize now more than ever, though, that this is a developmental process. Making connections by reflecting on one's experience is a learned skill, one that students need time to develop. Our current research is exploring this change over time. Early results indicate that students often do not understand "why" they are developing their eportfolios until they have an opportunity in another learning context to make a connection, as was the case with the student who was searching for an internship and participating in interviews. Before this "connecting" happens, reflections are often superficial and descriptive. As

students' awareness of their experiences develops and as they are able to provide evidence and examples of their learning, their reflections also deepen.[9] Therefore, in one-time contexts—for instance, one course—we need to be careful to scaffold this learning for students and help them early on to build a framework for integrating their learning so that they take that skill to other learning contexts—and as they move from and integrate the networked and the symphonic selves (Cambridge, Chapter 4). Our experience has shown that this scaffolding, linked closely with the outcomes we have for our learners, is crucial. Electronic portfolios can be powerful tools; making clear the goals and outcomes that they address both for the teachers and for the learners helps their potential to be fully realized. Clearly defining outcomes and ensuring scaffolding for the learning experience, either within one course or in an entire program, is essential in helping students to change how they think.

APPENDIX A

This is an example of a student's reflections on his or her teamwork skills. The Individual Skills worksheet was first used in the AFM 131 class in first-year. Students were then encouraged to continue to reflect on their skills into their first co-op work term.

STUDENT REFLECTIONS ON LEARNING

Areas of Growth

Overall, since starting this program, the key improvements I have made include adapting to cultural norms and taking initiative when starting the lines of communications. Since the midterm evaluation, the co-op students in my department decided to regularly meet for lunch, often at restaurants from a variety of cultures. For example, one coworker is Tamil, so for lunch we went to an Indian buffet where she explained the different foods and etiquettes found in the Indian culture. These social events opened up others to disclose their backgrounds and views, helping me understand their working habits back at the firm. I now realized the importance to some cultures of being highly formal in communication, while others respect being laid-back and more personal in work discussions.

When I started working on personal tax returns for the first time, I continued to develop my communication initiative. Often I was to call brokers in order to confirm book values or transaction costs in order to calculate capital gains. This required me to look up a broker's information, call them, and establish a relationship by constantly working with them via phone or fax to determine the necessary numbers for the returns. After a few months of this practice, I feel much more confident in starting new business, school, and personal relationships.

The other areas I felt developed were my coaching skills and adapting to different work styles. My teaching skills were often challenged when new hires entered our department and needed guidance on certain firm processes, even how to complete T1 returns. Surprisingly, some of them were full

INDIVIDUAL SKILLS WORKSHEET

Please indicate the extent to which you agree or disagree with each of the following statements about your team-related skills. Rate the items using the following scale:

1 = Strongly Disagree   4 = Strongly Agree

Highlight areas of growth in the past year and a half. How do I know that I am improving in the indicated area?

I need to improve my . . .	1	2	3	4
Listening skills				x
Skills to evaluate the performance of other team members		X		
Skills to provide constructive feedback to team members			X	
Skills to receive feedback from team members				x
Coaching skills				x
Negotiating skills				x
Skills to communicate with other team members				x
Skills to manage a team project				x
Skills to be a team leader				x
Skills to adapt to differences in team members' work styles				x
Skills to adapt to different cultural norms of team members				X

CAs and one of my new managers! Either way, I would take the time to understand their issue by clarifying what they were asking and then show them step by step how to accomplish it. Furthermore, I would help them adapt to the work styles of the two specific managers for the T1 pool. Through my experiences with both of them, I created a list of how each manager preferred the returns to be presented. For example, one manager preferred the client letter to include the tax installments, while the other requested it on a separate schedule. These were some of the little things that I luckily managed to quickly adapt to.

Employer Evaluation vs. Self

When I look back at the employer evaluation, I can be confident in saying that I agree with the way others see my work habits. For example, I felt I had improved greatly in communication since the beginning of my program via AFM 131 and the work term. My councilor picked up on this too, stating I have "very good oral and written communication skills." To add, I concur that I am a self starter (show initiative) and quick to learn. As I have said all term, I believe my co-op experience has prepared me from university this summer, as all my tax knowledge, such as capital tax and personal tax return preparation, has been learned via this term rather than through specific classes such as AFM 201. Moreover, this point agrees with the fact that I do need to gain more job-related knowledge, again noted by my employer. For a line-by-line comparison, please refer to my midterm reflection.

Work Term Summary Form

I. Identify two things you considered positive about the experience.

The two most positive experiences I have had this term were the opportunity to meet and team with amazing people, and gain the skills to learn independently. Firstly, I worked alongside five other co-op students: two from third year, two from fourth year, and a Masters of Tax student originally educated as a lawyer. Although we all came from different backgrounds and worked differently from each other, these were the people I could go to for help, such as how to use TaxPrep software or simply for support when we were going through a busy season. In addition, I learned about their backgrounds, programs they were in, and where they wanted to go with their careers. It was these coworkers that made me realize that the difficulty and tears of the 2A term were worth it.

On the other end of the spectrum, this term gave me the skills to work independently. While I was able to ask others for help at the beginning of the term, I somehow learned that if I put my mind to it, I could figure out some the tax practices and regulations on my own. To illustrate, I ordered the firm's tax guides, the Income Tax Act and went to the CRA Web site to read up on policies, such as the different classes of assets for capital cost allowance calculations. I also learned how to network within the firm to find the right people to answer specific questions. The latest example would have been how to eFile personal tax returns. All in all, every experience this term contributed something positive to my collection of skills.

II. Identify two things you could have improved on or done differently.

One thing I wish I had handled differently would have been the conflict over time off for vacation. As discussed with our firm's human resources department, co-op students are allowed paid vacation; however, when I tried to book off this time, I was met with much disapproval from managers and even firm partners. Personally, I am not used to dealing with conflict at work, as throughout my courses such as AFM 131 or CS 100 I have never worked in a group that had major disagreements. In this specific situation, my scheduler was the one discussing the issue among those in disagreement, whereas it should have been me. In the future if something similar was to arise, I plan to ask which parties are involved, ask for a brief moment to discuss the issue with them, and try to coordinate a reasonable solution myself.

The second improvement I wish I had made this past term would have been time management. As noted before in the midterm evaluation, I would be on either end of the spectrum: sometimes without work, other times working 12-hour days to complete a specific engagement. While I believe this is partly the nature of the work environment, I would have liked to be able to coordinate assignments better to reduce stress and meet deadlines without having to rush at the last minute. In order to achieve this in the next work term, I will try to meet with my scheduler on a regular basis to ensure my engagement list is accurate and appropriate. Additionally, instead of calling or e-mailing managers to check on the status and length of assignments, as many don't respond, I hope to meet them in person. This would make certain I don't take on too much work at one point and be left with nothing later in the week or vice versa.

III. Identify two things you have learned from this team experience.

As discussed in AFM 131 and at the True Colours Workshop, part of teamwork is listening. It is one thing to contribute to a team but another thing to hear a colleague, clarify their viewpoint, and make appropriate decisions with information or instructions evidently laid out. Working with a variety of managers, all with their own preferences and work styles, I've learned a couple key strategies to saving time doing my own work. First, when first discussing an engagement, bring paper and a pen, listing exactly what is to be done and how it is to be completed. Second, when in doubt, ask. There is nothing more time-consuming and wasteful, assuming you know a tax treatment only based on last year's numbers. When you ask, you know exactly how to tax something for one client but can apply it to others, making those assignments run smoother too. Finally, listen to deadlines and never assume something is to be done ASAP when, in fact, not all information is yet available and the client only needs it a couple months down the road. This is a major time saving and the quickest way to prioritize work so you do not burn out before the week's end.

A skill that I have developed but still need to continue to improve is the ability to say no to being overworked/overassigned. As per AMF 131, leaders are not there to control but to help adapt. In order for me to become a better leader, I have tried to understand when I have too much work and even been able to delegate others to it when they have little or no work. For instance, at the end of term, some clients required repetitive tasks such as inputting medical receipts into personal tax returns. When I felt overloaded, I was able to delegate this task to another co-op who gladly took on the work to fill their empty schedule. Moreover, in terms of saying no, I am now better able to determine when I have too much on my schedule and to kindly decline additional engagements when it is appropriate. As per the feedback on my midterm evaluation, managers do in fact respect work-life balance, as it could interfere with the quality of the work you produce.

IV. Referring back to your Individual Skills Worksheet, would you change any of the ratings if you were to redo the form today?

For this self-evaluation, I did include updated ratings as per above with explanations listed in the *Areas of Growth* section. I feel that the main areas that have developed over the past year and a half have definitely been adapting to different work styles and cultures and, of course, communicating with other team members. The co-op experience has provided me with multiple teams, distinct from any I have worked with during my university classes. Diverse backgrounds, work ethics, and position levels have all contributed to forming my current skill set within the leadership and teaming environment.

NOTES

1. In Canada, the Certified Management Accountants have recently completed a new competency map for their profession. The map consists of three pillars: accounting, management, and strategy. There are six functional competencies that bridge the pillars (strategic management, risk management and governance, performance management, performance measurement, financial resource management, and financial reporting) with an additional four competencies that are considered to be "soft-skills" (problem solving and decision making; leadership and group dynamics; professionalism and ethical behavior; communication).

2. What we have seen in the past is students who focus on what they need to do to complete their degree (the networked self), and what we would like to see is students who view their degree as an opportunity to find out about themselves and to develop their abilities (symphonic self). The School of Accountancy at the University of Waterloo is currently engaged in a curriculum redesign project where all the programs will be revised to meet a set of learning outcomes meant to address the development of the whole person, not just the "professional accountant."

3. Many of the kinds of thinking attributed by Cambridge to the networked self seem congruent with lower-order thinking on Bloom's taxonomy of the cognitive domain. In contrast, the thinking associated with the symphonic self (i.e., synthesizing insights and evidence) match Bloom's higher-order thinking (evaluation and synthesis).

4. Although this is important, in our view, in all disciplines and programs, it is particularly so for students enrolled in the co-op stream. The research has shown that "academically, internships (cooperative education) can significantly and positively enhance the knowledge base and motivational level of aspiring accountants. These experiences can make subsequent study more meaningful and develop the student professionally before entry into the marketplace" (Beard, 1998; English & Koeppen, 1993).

5. In this program, students receive feedback from professors on their reflections, from their peers as they evaluate each other's teamwork skills, and from mentors who are members of the profession. We recognize that it is crucial to provide feedback to the students early and often so that they can continuously revisit their learning. In our planned curriculum redesign, we envision building in more explicit opportunities for reflection and feedback than are currently available so that students' learning is better supported.

6. For instance, we are currently using our eportfolio work in this program for curriculum redesign.

7. AFM 131 is Introduction to Management. In this course, students participate in a business strategy game in teams to use the concepts presented in class. Students are asked to inventory their own teamwork skills and then receive feedback from their peers regarding areas of strength and areas to improve. Students then continue to develop those skills as they work through the program.

8. The research has shown that thinking historically is an "unnatural act" that students need to develop over time (see Wineburg, 2001; Sandwell, 2006; Stearns, Seixas, & Wineburg, 2000). This course introduces students to this kind of thinking as they interpret the past through a wide variety of documents—text, films, images, music—guided by the professor.

9. We are seeing this as we code the data for our accounting project. Students early on in their university careers are completing the reflections but, for the most part, only as they are required. In other words, they are going through the motions for the credit but do not seem to be internalizing the process at the higher-order thinking levels (evaluation and synthesis) that we would like to see. However, data from their first co-op work terms (which happens at the end of the second year or beginning of the third year) suggest that their reflections are much deeper and focused than they were early on.

REFERENCES

Beard, D. F. (1998). The status of internships/co-operative education experiences in accounting education. *Journal of Accounting Education, 16*(3 & 4), 508.

Colman, R. (2005/2006). Bridging academia and application. *CMA Management, 79*(8), 22–28.

Co-op review. (2005). Learning from experience: Enhancing co-operative education at the University of Waterloo. Retrieved July 15, 2008 from http://secretariat.uwaterloo.ca/OfficialDocuments/CECSReport.pdf

English, D. M., & Koeppen, D. R. (1993, Fall). The relationship of accounting internships and subsequent academic performance. *Issues in Accounting Education,* 292–299.

Huber, M. T., & Hutchings, P. (2004). *Integrative learning: Mapping the terrain.* Washington, DC: AAC&U.

Sandwell, R. (Ed.). (2006). *To the past: History education, public memory, & citizenship in Canada.* Toronto: University of Toronto Press.

Stearns, P., Seixas, P., & Wineburg, S. (Eds.). (2000). *Knowing, teaching & learning history: National and international perspectives.* New York: New York University Press.

Wineburg, S. (2001). *Historical thinking and other unnatural acts: Charting the future of teaching the past.* Philadelphia: Temple University Press.

SECTION THREE

Establishing Identities: Roles, Competencies, Values, and Outcomes

Faculty members are often eager to innovate. In the classroom-based eportfolio practices within *Electronic Portfolios: Emerging Practices in Student, Faculty, and Institutional Learning* (Cambridge, 2001), faculty in a range of disciplines, from humanities and writing to business and nursing, articulated both the why and the how of eportfolios in their classroom contexts. They often focused on a single portfolio or limited set of individual eportfolios to show what learning looks like inside this new space. One student model in that volume, however, was keyed to programs, to outcomes, and to the ways that student development and achievement can be plotted for review of the individual student and, at the same time, for review of program goals. This model forecasts an important new purpose of eportfolios, one focused on context and outcomes, that is documented in the following chapters.

For many years, faculty members, programs, departments, and even institutions focused on objectives, typically thought of as discrete items—for example, the ability to use a semicolon correctly, to name the capital of Estonia, or to know the components of an engine. During the last 20 years, however, higher education has shifted from objectives to outcomes located in higher-order thinking. These learning outcomes include what students know, what they can do, and often, through reflec-

tion, how well they can guide their own next steps. Outcomes, of course, imply standards, but the question about which standards are appropriate for a given set of outcomes is precisely the question that institutions want to address.

The question is taken up in many interesting ways in this section of reports. As Michael Day explains in Chapter 8, the eportfolios in this section profile an interesting range of outcomes-based eportfolio models. In the case of Kapi`olani Community College (Chapter 11), for example, the outcomes provide a *culturally based* intellectual framework for student work, whereas in the case of Clemson University (Chapter 12) and University of Nebraska–Omaha (UNO; Chapter 13), the outcomes are *preprofessional*. The institutionally specific outcomes for Indiana University Purdue University Indianapolis (IUPUI; Chapter 10) are *general education* outcomes, whereas at Thomas College (Chapter 9) students locate their work inside institutionally specific *graduation* outcomes. Working in still another way, Northern Illinois University (Chapter 8) intentionally adopted a national outcomes statement in designing its *writing* outcomes. Looking at these diverse outcomes as a set, we see that outcomes can take a diversity of forms—fostering foundational knowledge, mission-specific knowledge, cultural knowledge, or preprofessional knowledge—and thus can and will exert different effects.

At the same time, a review of these models shows that they are similar in some ways. In one similarity, they rely on multiplicity—in materials, in reviewers, or in both. At Clemson University, for example, multiple reviewers—students, peers, and faculty members—are at the heart of the model: Learning-as-a-social-activity, built into the model, therefore serves as a de facto learning outcome. Likewise, the Thomas College model builds multiple reviewing into its model by including an "adjudication process" whose successful completion permits a student to post his or her eportfolio on the college's website. The materials in these models increasingly include multimedia artifacts, such that when one University of Nebraska student reviews her eportfolio, she comments that she can literally *see* herself learning.

In another similarity, the outcomes offered are not static fill-in-the-blank exercises; rather, they function as dynamic frameworks for student artifacts and commentary. In the Kapi'olani model, for example, students use the concepts of one framework—native culture and language—to locate and explain their academic learning that comes with its own framework. In a similar process, the IUPUI model invites students into matrix thinking, where students are asked to think quite literally *outside the outcome box* as they consider how an artifact might demonstrate their learning. Not only do students use these outcome frameworks, but the frameworks function as opportunities for *translation,* with one set of understandings being translated into another. For instance, academic learning is translated into the local culture in the Kapi'olani model. This opportunity to see multiple frameworks and to translate, in fact, may be a chief value of outcomes-based eportfolios.

Curricular changes accompanying these eportfolios are also important. In some cases, the change may be small: The students at UNO recommend including the eportfolio inside their coursework. In other cases, the changes may be large: Kapi'olani has a new curriculum; Clemson has a new set of practices connected to peer review; reflection is receiving new attention across all the campuses, with Northern Illinois building a new emphasis on reflection into faculty development and Thomas College generating a set of benchmarks to guide that new reflective thinking both for students and for their faculty reviewers.

In these chapters you can observe the different kinds of outcomes important at different institutions. Which is closer to the intent of your program—a set of outcomes keyed to local institutional culture or mission, or perhaps preprofessional outcomes? You can also consider how the articulated outcomes in these institutions are located in curricula: Do you have curricular components in place supporting outcomes, or will those need to be designed and developed? In addition, you can see the effects of each kind of outcome, from helping students engage in "translation" activities keyed to learning to assisting students to make their place in the world outside the academy. Which effects are most important for your program?

8

INFLUENCING LEARNING THROUGH FACULTY- AND STUDENT-GENERATED OUTCOME ASSESSMENT

MICHAEL DAY
Northern Illinois University

Electronic portfolios have a range of purposes, often multiple and always depending on local needs and contexts. This chapter examines practices on multiple campuses as they describe traditional uses of eportfolios for assessment of outcomes-based learning and then investigates wider circles of eportfolio influence on colleges and universities. The move is from an eportfolio as a set of data to be assessed to the eportfolio as a network of practices that affect all stakeholders in higher education—students, teachers, administrators—in ways that cannot easily be quantified. In fact, the interplay among outcomes, reflection, and audience in electronic portfolios can serve as a lens through which students, teaching assistants, faculty members, and administrators can generate and maintain multiple identities: personal, social, and professional.

Programs or institutions interested in using eportfolio assessment typically create or revisit learning outcomes before designing an eportfolio system. Some programs, such as Northern Illinois University's first-year composition program, have effectively used disciplinary guidelines, like the Council of Writing Program Administrators (WPA)

Outcomes Statement, as a starting place for discussions that lead to a set of local outcomes. WPA's *The Outcomes Book* (Harrington, Rhodes, Fischer, & Malenczyk, 2005) provides examples of ways in which a global statement can help a program or department focus on what college students should learn and do in a class or a sequence of classes in any discipline or program. Although initially it may seem that for some programs the technology and faculty development support needed for an electronic portfolio assessment are more than they can manage, those programs may have an institutional charge for some level of mastery of computer and Internet technologies by students in a class, sequence of classes, or program. For example, because of an institutional charge, all first-year composition classes at Northern Illinois University are taught partially in lab spaces, and some class discussion and activities take place online. In such a situation, it made perfect sense to develop a set of technology outcomes in addition to writing outcomes. Because computer and Internet-based outcomes cannot easily be demonstrated in a print portfolio, the electronic portfolio was the best choice. Of course, programs with enough technology and faculty development may decide to use electronic portfolio assessment for other reasons, such as storage space, ease of duplication and transmission, and the new intellectual and social associations afforded by hypertext linking.

Outcomes related to writing, technology, and many other domains are often developed from the top down and then tweaked as the assessment data come in and suggest changes. However, faculty and administrator decision making is not the only way to develop outcomes. For Alverno College's Digital Diagnostic Portfolios (DDP), students analyzed patterns in their own learning (Chapter 2). Then researchers in the Office of Research and Evaluation mined student eportfolio reflections for categories of experience and learning that led to organic discovery of traits relating to students' ability to self-assess, use self-assessment to improve learning, and situate particular learning experiences within a context of lifelong learning. In this case, students tell faculty and administrators what they learned in their classes and describe the skills and patterns of development they see in those learning experiences. Where most institutions develop outcomes from the top down, Alverno used a kind of grounded theory to develop outcomes from the bottom up. Alverno's practice provides a clear illustration of the ways in which student input and involvement are crucial to eportfolio assessment. As students work with peers and instructors to determine which documents best demonstrate outcomes and make reflective arguments about their learning based on those documents and outcomes, they discover and share much more than data that can be reduced to numbers and sorted into discreet categories. And, because reflection "makes thinking visible" (Yancey, 2001, p. 17), programs that tune into what students are saying can get a fuller picture of what their outcomes mean within a variety of local contexts.

Programs described in the following chapters illustrate the importance of outcomes influenced by local context and by student voices. Each institution generated a set of outcomes based on local needs and contexts for learning. For example, because of its need to demonstrate that preservice teachers met official standards, the College of Education at the University of Nebraska–Omaha selected outcomes based on Interstate New Teacher Assessment and Support Consortium (INTASC) principles (Chapter 13). In a different direction, Kapi`olani Community College in Hawaii decided to use outcomes based on the native Hawaiian value system, *Nā Wa`a*, which uses the metaphor of preparing, planning, and building a canoe for a journey (Chapter 11). In applied psychology at Clemson University, stakeholders were most concerned about guiding students toward graduate research, so they designed outcomes based on student interest and involvement, including their ability to project themselves into the future in the role of researchers (Chapter 12). At Indiana University Purdue University Indianapolis, assessment architects keyed their developmental eportfolio model to the university's six Principles of Undergraduate Learning (PULs) (Chapter 10). A much smaller institution, Thomas College, took a similar approach in designing outcomes that measure the school's four core competencies through course work and through connections to the outside world (Chapter 9). In all the models, outcomes not only answer the question "What do we want to measure in the eportfolio?" but also provide a heuristic that allows students to generate *their own* interpretations and responses to the outcomes.

Another feature highlighted in these eportfolios is that thinking about learning and outcomes is made visible. At Thomas College, students use reflection in electronic portfolios to show connections among their learning, the school's four core competencies (outcomes), and their experiences outside the classroom. In Chapter 9, "The Promise of Eportfolios for Institutional Assessment," Tom Edwards and Colleen Burnham borrow a term from mathematics, "showing our work," to characterize the importance of making thinking visible through reflection. Models like this one cast a wide net to capture unexpected discoveries in learning. Students move beyond listing documents according to the learning outcome being demonstrated by showing the process (the set of logical steps they followed in connecting evidence to outcome), in demonstrating higher-level thinking by synthesizing artifacts and outcomes, and in applying their discoveries to personal growth and social problems. Taking the metaphor of showing our work even further, Thomas College makes electronic portfolios public on the Web after the eportfolio has been judged to be "proficient" or "exemplary." Edwards and Burnham claim that showing our work in this way allows students to demonstrate lifelong learning and allows the college to demonstrate, through examples on the Web, how students at Thomas participate in an integrated educational experience in pursuit of principles of the college's mission. In an accountability climate in which the U.S. Department of Education seeks evidence of value added at higher education institutions through one-size-fits-all comparative measures, showing our work allows institutions like Thomas to honor the missions that make our schools unique and to give the public "a far richer, more compelling picture of who we are and what we do." Thomas' public eportfolios exemplify the ways in which portfolios are crafted for a specific audience and purpose; they remind us that when we make thinking visible, we must always ask, "Visible to whom, and for what purpose?"

Sometimes purposes and audiences change. In Chapter 10, IUPUI researchers Susan Kahn and Sharon Hamilton use the university's principles of undergraduate learning-based outcomes to challenge students to do "matrix thinking": "the kind of reflective thinking that results when students combine the elements of a matrix and use the resulting conceptual construct as a lens through which to revisit work initially created in a different context for a different reason" (p. 94). For example, one student makes a connection between a principle, critical thinking, and the student's chosen career of editor, so that the student reflects upon the critical thinking skills needed by an editor. Instead of linking artifacts and learning experiences to a single outcome, students must articulate *relationships* among principles so that the matrix, instead of providing only fixed categories of experience, provides a generative lens through which students can view their work, make their thinking visible, and make new meaning through connection

in a manner similar to hypertext linking. Indeed, in matrix thinking, students find the logic of an unexplored connection and make it explicit.

Kapi'olani Community College's approach to making thinking visible in electronic portfolios (Chapter 11) recognizes a local context and value system different from the outcomes and core competencies envisioned by the other institutions showcased in this section: the native Hawaiian values of *Nā Wa'a* (literally, "the canoes"), "a voyaging metaphor for students to use to record their learning, connect their academic, career, and personal work to Hawaiian values, and position these works within a stage or level, the four *Pae* stages in the matrix." For some students who have been conditioned by years of conformity to European-based North American rules and values, using a different metaphor for the educational journey is a refreshing change as well as an affirmation of the importance of local context and history. Unlike many rubrics for assessment, the *pae* stages are not conventional "levels of achievement" but instead provide alternative lenses through which to view and articulate educational growth. The *pae* are generative because students interpret the meaning of the *pae* based on the interplay among the artifacts, personal reflection on learning, institutional values, and the larger, "lifelong learning" trajectory of educational and career development. According to researchers Renner, Kirkpatrick, Kanae, and Goya, instead of being punitive or directive like many forms of assessment, the *Nā Wa'a* electronic portfolio is encouraging, giving students ownership of artifact, experience, and learning in a way that values their cultural intelligence.

According to Stephens (Chapter 12), as students in applied psychology internships at Clemson University made their knowledge visible in eportfolios, they became acutely aware of audience. Although the objectives of the internships are "to increase talented students' interest, understanding, and commitment to research, science, and scientific careers," Stephens and his colleagues, like IUPUI and Thomas College researchers, have found that students demonstrated types of social awareness and made connections beyond what could be described in program outcomes. The students were "keenly aware of the various audiences implied from the public nature of their presentations." Those audiences ranged from instructors, mentors, and peers all the way to National Science Foundation scientists and reviewers of graduate school applications who might see the students' work. This keen awareness of audience, according to Stephens, "fostered professional impression management goals"; in other words, it taught students how to view themselves in multiple identities and to create and maintain those identities through the hierarchical structure of a Web site. In comparing the "concept maps" of first-year and senior eportfolios, Stephens observes that the more experienced students use a much more elaborate hierarchical hypertext linking structure than the less experienced ones, and he attributes the difference to the seniors' more sophisticated thinking about identity in terms of social contexts and audiences outside the university.

Based on the success of an electronic portfolio assessment project in the College of Education at the University of Nebraska–Omaha, the institution is moving to an electronic portfolio initiative called myMAPP—Mapping Academic Performance Through Eportfolios. Faculty and administrators are encouraged about the potential of this campus-wide eportfolio, in part, based on results from research done by Neal Topp and Bob Goeman (Chapter 13). Their study shows that for students in teacher education whose eportfolios were inte-grated into their curriculum, the process of creating and reflecting in the eportfolio had a positive impact on learning. In addition, showing their work in a reflective eportfolio helped students demonstrate their understanding of the INTASC principles for teachers better than they could in the context of more traditional assessments. Important for future development, students recommended that more integration of the eportfolio into the curriculum is critical for its success.

In all these models, students key their accomplishments to outcomes while concurrently showing the value of different kinds of relationships. In those processes, they make thinking visible and demonstrate the value of eportfolios in generating and assessing learning.

REFERENCES

Harrington, S., Rhodes, K., Fischer, R., & Malenczyk, R. (Eds.) (2005). *The outcomes book: Debate and consensus after the WPA Outcomes Statement.* Logan, UT: Utah State Press.

Yancey, K. B. (2001). Introduction: Digitized student portfolios. In B. L. Cambridge (Ed.), *Electronic portfolios: Emerging practices in student, faculty, and institutional learning* (pp. 15–30). Sterling, VA: Stylus (originally published by American Association for Higher Education).

9

THE PROMISE OF EPORTFOLIOS FOR INSTITUTIONAL ASSESSMENT

THOMAS S. EDWARDS and COLLEEN BURNHAM
Thomas College

Einstein: $E = mc^2$
Teacher: B+ Good answer, but next time, please show your work.

In his book *Making the Most of College: Students Speak Their Minds*, Harvard professor Richard Light (2001) reports that when he "asked students to think of a specific, critical incident or moment that had changed them profoundly, four-fifths of them chose a situation or incident outside the classroom." Until now, however, colleges have been unable to measure this opportunity for learning that has such a powerful and profound impact on our students' lives.

Similarly, we have proven inadequate to the task of making explicit the links between the learning that takes place across unique courses, especially between the liberal arts (or humanities) and discipline-specific courses. Although college mission statements often reference lifelong learning or critical thinking, we generally fail to provide students with a structure or design that inspires them to make the connections between the writing, thinking, and analytic skills that make such learning possible.

The experience of Thomas College, a small liberal arts college in central Maine, shows that eportfolios represent a potentially powerful tool that can create those explicit, practical connections. Additionally, eportfolios demonstrate great promise for assessment at the institutional level.

CENTRAL RESEARCH QUESTION

The mission of Thomas College is "to prepare students for success in their personal and professional lives, and for leadership and service in their communities." Committed to that mission, the college offers guaranteed job placement for its graduates. Before the implementation of an eportfolio program, there was no effective process in place to document how distinct parts of the curriculum at Thomas provided the comprehensive experience that makes such a guarantee possible.

A first positive step was the creation of a faculty-defined set of four core competencies, categorized as communications, leadership and service, critical thinking, and community and interpersonal relations. However, the college lacked a vehicle whereby students could demonstrate how those skills were developed and applied throughout their college career. For their part, faculty lacked a common method for relating specific course materials either to the overall college mission or to the more general core competencies. The solution came in the form of an eportfolio model developed with the assistance of the Inter/National Coalition for Electronic Portfolio Research.

As a result of the incorporation of an eportfolio model, Thomas College has seen changes: (a) Students are now introduced to the concept and the process of creating eportfolios in their first year; (b) faculty have adopted a common requirement to link each course offered at Thomas to one of the core competencies; and (c) a growing number of senior capstone courses include the requirement that the students complete an eportfolio. Moreover, the evaluation of a set of student eportfolios in the spring of 2007 demonstrated that eportfolios provide a powerful tool for students to integrate their learning across course boundaries and to showcase their skills. As students go through the process of collection, selection, and reflection, they show the ability to identify the larger design that informs their college experience.

THE MODEL

Students in the college's first-year experience course are introduced to eportfolios and to the college's core competencies. They receive instruction and assistance in creating individualized folders for each core competency, and they are encouraged to store examples of their personal and academic work as they progress through their academic career.

A list of sample artifacts that students can use to demonstrate achievement is provided to students for each competency area. The identification on each syllabus at the college of course assignments that are relevant to specific core competencies reinforces the concept that all courses—both liberal arts and major discipline requirements—are part of a larger design. For example, the development of an Excel spreadsheet in a math or an accounting course could qualify as a contribution to the category of "analytic reasoning." For the core competency in leadership and service—"Thomas students

exhibit a command of interpersonal, leadership, and teamwork skills, and demonstrate a commitment to community service"—students are encouraged to provide evidence ranging from their work as a resident assistant or a tutor to their participation in community service.

The gradual implementation and current voluntary nature of the program, combined with the brief introduction to eportfolio use that students receive as they begin their academic career, predicted the relatively low numbers of active (and useful) junior and senior student eportfolios available for review in the spring of 2007. Nevertheless, those students who did produce an eportfolio grasped the value of the exercise, demonstrating a keen awareness of the link between the core competencies and their work from various courses and experiences inside and outside the classroom. Students seemed to easily grasp both the developmental and integrative power of eportfolio documentation of their academic work, as evidenced in the artifacts they selected and in the reflections they composed.

In the spring of 2007, to test the effectiveness of the eportfolio model as a measure of student learning as identified by the core competencies, students in two senior seminar courses were asked to submit an eportfolio for review by a committee of faculty and staff.

Students were provided with a rubric that had originally been drafted for adjudicating eportfolios residing on the college intranet. Students wishing to post their eportfolios publicly on the college's Career Services Web page need to pass this adjudicating process. The design of the rubric was not intended to assess *quality* of individual artifacts but to determine how appropriate the selected examples were in meeting the goals of the eportfolio overall. The committee reviewed a set of 10 student eportfolios, using the rubric to assign a score to each of the four competency folders, as well as to a separate folder for reflection.

STUDENT EPORTFOLIOS

Chelsea Reynolds, a junior accounting major, chose a wide range of documents from a variety of different courses for her folder on Critical and Analytic Thinking. Chelsea's selections included Excel spreadsheets from accounting classes, math projects from a statistics class, and a company analysis project from an economics course. Interestingly, Chelsea chose a project titled "Brand You" produced in a marketing course as a reflection piece. Chelsea's choices reveal a clear sense of how critical thinking skills transcend the boundaries of specific projects or courses.

For her folder on Communications, senior accounting major Krista Salvas chose a number of documents as artifacts, keyed to the process of developing her career. As Krista pointed out in her reflection, "The documents contained in this folder are professionally written and should give the employer a good impression when they see them." Interestingly, she hopes to exert a specific influence on her audience: "I want the company that I work for to feel confident that I can represent them successfully."

The Leadership and Service folder from senior accounting major Nicole Irish shows the power of an eportfolio to document a student's growth and development outside the classroom, areas that are often missing in the shorthand of a student's academic transcript. Nikki's folder contains examples of her study abroad experience and her participation at off-campus events; her choices reflect her wide-ranging responsibilities as a student leader on campus. In her reflection on this folder, Nicole writes, "I chose these documents . . . because to me these experiences and opportunities have formed the person that I am today and they show that I am a leader and I will work hard to be as involved as possible, because the only way to learn is to go above and beyond what is offered to you."

As the committee worked through the process of evaluating the student eportfolios, several interesting differences emerged. The most striking was the varied interpretations of the reflection requirement. Several students created a standard, separate "reflection folder"; a few included formal assignments for which they had been asked to write about themselves; and some wrote a reflection essay for each folder. The last group proved quite inventive with the use of *1*s and *0*s in the file names

to "float" the reflection pieces to the top of the folder list. Krista Salvas offered a unique approach to her reflection on her leadership abilities; she created a PowerPoint presentation that outlines how little work she has documented in her folder in her quest to become a successful leader. Krista explained her presentation with a reflection essay, in which she writes, "This folder is quite empty. All I have documented in it is a power point on what leadership is and what it takes to be a leader. This is because I don't feel like a leader yet. By putting this piece of work together, I have recognized where I need to begin to become a leader."

RECOMMENDATIONS

The calls for assessment of student learning outcomes challenge institutions to identify appropriate means for assessing their effectiveness related to their mission. When that mission includes lifelong learning, service, or learning outside the classroom, we must find creative and convincing ways to demonstrate student achievement. By using eportfolios to bridge the gap between mission and student achievement, we offer our students and the public a far richer, far more compelling picture of who we are and what we do.

Eportfolios provide colleges with a means for evaluating student achievement that can cut across disciplinary lines at an institutional level and that can include such crucial areas as leadership and service. The process at Thomas revealed that a single, holistic score for a student eportfolio will ultimately be preferable to the current rubric that derives a composite score from the ratings of each individual folder, a process that introduces too much variability across reviewers (though individual mean scores for communications or critical thinking will still be useful). In the future, a single rating system will be developed that will produce an overall evaluation of an eportfolio that identifies it as "proficient" or "exemplary," making it eligible for posting on the College's Career Services Web page, as has been requested by students.

The challenge for an eportfolio model on any campus is countering the power of the traditional measure of student learning in higher education, the stand-alone course. Only with significant reinforcement by faculty will students learn to view their eportfolios as an integrative tool for learning or as a representation of their accomplishments. The gradual adoption of eportfolio requirements in senior capstone courses at Thomas College will inherently reinforce the development aspect of eportfolios, which faculty and students already recognize as an important part of the process of an education. Communicating with students early and throughout their academic career about eportfolio design and development will help to reinforce the value of the model across the campus community. Additionally, the college has identified meaningful links between its core competencies and individual items on three measures—the National Survey of Student Engagement (NSSE), the Standardized Assessment of Information Literacy Skills (SAILS), and the standards of the college's regional accrediting association, the New England Association of Schools and Colleges (NEASC)—that indicate a realistic potential use of eportfolios as a practical assessment at the institutional level.

The students who responded to Richard Light's survey underscore what we have long believed to be true in American higher education: education takes place in many ways and in many places, and students are making connections to learning both inside and outside the classroom in ways that we cannot easily measure or demonstrate. What eportfolios provide is a means whereby, like Einstein, we can both make the grade and show our work.

REFERENCE

Light, R. (2001). *Making the most of college: Students speak their minds*. Cambridge: Harvard University Press.

10

DEMONSTRATING INTELLECTUAL GROWTH AND DEVELOPMENT

The IUPUI ePort

SHARON HAMILTON and SUSAN KAHN
Indiana University Purdue University Indianapolis (IUPUI)

The recent spate of national reports on improving undergraduate learning attests to wide recognition of the need to educate students who can address 21st-century global complexities. IUPUI's electronic portfolio (ePort) aims to develop and document the kinds of higher-order learning outcomes today's students need to achieve in school and in the world—for example, abilities to think critically, integrate and apply knowledge in a dynamic world, work within diverse cultural contexts, and solve problems innovatively. This chapter discusses how ePort and the ePort initiative at IUPUI are structured to carry out these aims, focusing on a specialized form of reflective thinking, "matrix thinking," that has emerged from our research. As this chapter explains, we believe that matrix thinking can serve as a powerful tool for helping students master the kinds of learning demanded by our changing society.

The conceptual core of IUPUI's ePort is a matrix that visually represents developing proficiency in the campus's six Principles of Undergraduate Learning (PULs) over an undergraduate career (see Figure 10.1). The PULs matrix gives visual form to the definition of ePort at IUPUI: "A selection of purposefully organized artifacts that support retrospective and prospective reflection and

that document, assess, and enhance student learning over time." This matrix is at the heart of both the learning and assessment functions of ePort, capturing the entire undergraduate learning experience on a single screen. Students create evidence of their intellectual growth as they place artifacts in matrix cells representing introductory, intermediate, and advanced levels of proficiency and write reflections that demonstrate and enhance their learning of these outcomes. Assessors draw on materials in the matrix to determine how well students at the course, program, and institutional levels are progressing in the PULs and to identify improvements needed to support increasing mastery as students move through the institution.

Assessment of matrix materials is guided by faculty-developed rubrics. Drafts of rubrics for the introductory and intermediate levels of the PULs have been developed by interdisciplinary faculty "Communities of Practice." For example, the description of the "Values and Ethics" PUL specifies that "students are able to make judgments with respect to individual conduct and citizenship." At the "introductory" level, after completing 26 credits, students demonstrate this ability by showing "an understanding of how one's values influence personal ethics and conduct." At the "intermedi-

Figure 10.1

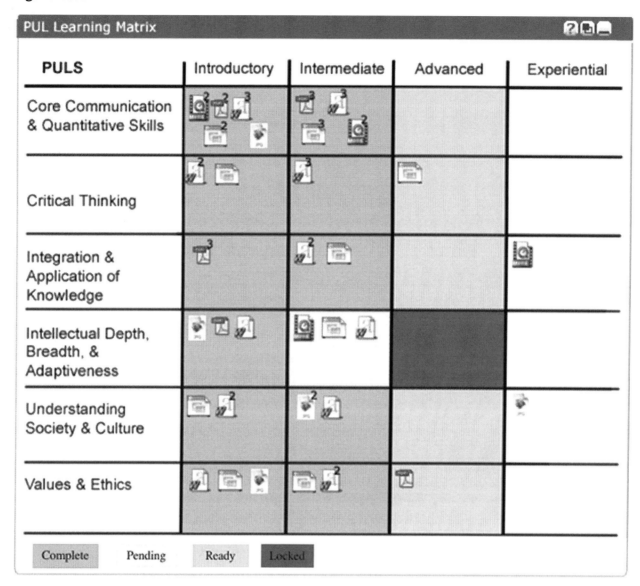

ate" level, after 56 credits, students demonstrate this ability by showing "an understanding of and respect for the values of others in contrast to their own" and "awareness of how decisions and conclusions may vary based on different perspectives."

In practice, at the current stage of IUPUI ePort implementation, most of this assessment occurs within departments adopting ePort as part of their curriculum. These departments design their own developmental matrices, using discipline-specific learning outcomes mapped to the university-wide PULs. The Department of Secondary Education, for instance, has created a matrix organized around

its "Principles of Teacher Education" or PTEs (see Figure 10.2). These map, in order, to the six PULs: PTE 1, Understanding of Core Knowledge, maps to PUL 1, Core Communication and Quantitative Skills; PTE 2, Reflective Practice, maps to PUL 2, Critical Thinking; and so on. These relationships are readily apparent when one reads the descriptions of each PTE that appear when one moves the cursor over them: Reflective Practice, for example, is described as "the ability of teachers to step outside the practices that make up teaching and to analyze and critique the impact of the experiences and contexts from multiple perspectives."

Figure 10.2

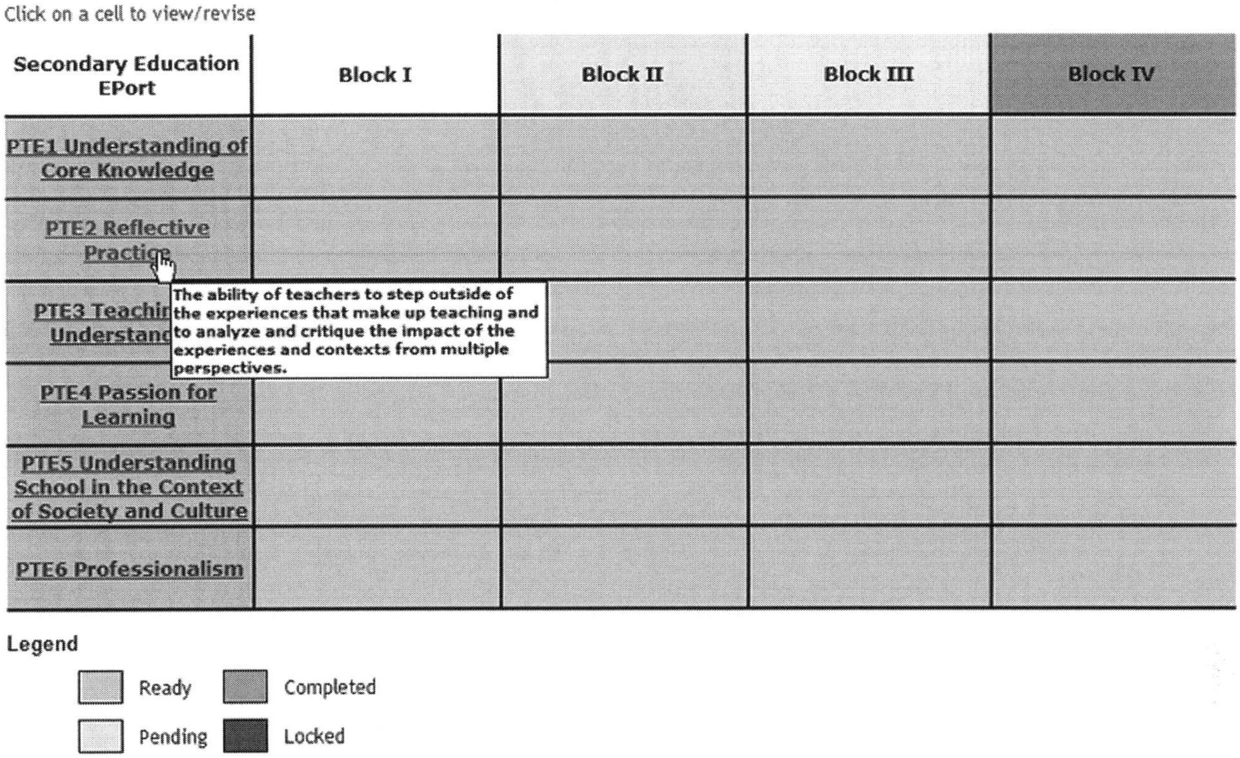

Click on a cell to view/revise

Secondary Education EPort	Block I	Block II	Block III	Block IV
PTE1 Understanding of Core Knowledge				
PTE2 Reflective Practice				
PTE3 Teaching Understanding				
PTE4 Passion for Learning				
PTE5 Understanding School in the Context of Society and Culture				
PTE6 Professionalism				

The ability of teachers to step outside of the experiences that make up teaching and to analyze and critique the impact of the experiences and contexts from multiple perspectives.

Legend

☐ Ready   ▨ Completed

☐ Pending   ■ Locked

The PTE matrix cells represent developmental stages of mastery that correspond roughly to the intermediate and advanced levels of proficiency in the PULs. Thus, when the Department of Secondary Education assesses student achievement of the PTEs, it simultaneously assesses achievement of the corresponding PULs at those levels. As more departments adopt ePort, develop program-specific learning outcomes, and map these to the PULs, the university as a whole will increase its ability to make assertions based on authentic work contained in ePort about students' achievement of the PULs campus-wide. Both individual programs and the whole university will have at their disposal a growing body of evidence for identifying strengths and weaknesses in curriculum and pedagogy and deciding where changes and improvements are most necessary.

This body of evidence includes a component of learning that has become increasingly significant with the evolution of student portfolios: reflective thinking. The metacognitive act of "thinking about thinking," while informally a part of all learning, is now formally integrated into the design of many electronic portfolios, including the IUPUI ePort, and it served as the focus of our project for the Inter/National Coalition for Electronic Portfolio Research. Our 2004–5 ePort pilot that focused on reflection included both first-year Themed Learning Communities and a senior capstone seminar in English. We gathered reflections from both sets of students, analyzing them with the help of a scheme for intellectual development in reflective thinking based on a template originated by Alverno College (Appendix). This template is organized around three major areas of intellectual development: ability to self-assess; ability to use these assessments to improve; and ability to situate particular learning experiences within a context of lifelong learning.

Our findings included the predictable discovery of more evidence of advanced reflective thinking in our seniors than in our first-year students, which also provided a level of confirmation for the construct of our developmental framework for reflection. Much more noteworthy, however, was our discovery of a phenomenon that we call "matrix thinking," the kind of reflective thinking that results when students combine the elements of a matrix and use the resulting conceptual construct as a lens through which to revisit work initially created in a different context for a different reason. For example, the portfolio matrix for our English capstone had the following conceptual framework:

	Lifelong learning	Career	Who I am as a citizen of the world
Most important PUL			
Reason for becoming an English major			

For each matrix cell, students were asked to upload at least two pieces of work from previous classes in any discipline that they felt met the two criteria for each cell. They were then asked to conceptualize the nexus between the two criteria. For example, if their most significant PUL was "critical thinking" and their chosen career was "editor," they were to articulate what aspects of critical thinking were most salient to a career in editing. They then were asked to reflect upon their two chosen artifacts in relation to that conceptualization. That requirement catapulted our students' thinking into connections that were more profound than either we or our students anticipated, prompting us to label this thinking "matrix thinking." The reflections of those who completed the assignment as directed were clearly moving into the realm of "advanced reflective thinking" as defined by the Alverno College Developmental Framework for Reflective Thinking, which was adapted for our study at IUPUI (see Chapter 2). The following example of "matrix thinking" from one student's reflection illustrates how she combines her understanding of the Critical Thinking PUL with her career aspirations:

Critical thinking is my most important PUL because, no matter what goal I am pursuing, critical thinking will be a necessary step before that goal will ever be reached [exemplifies the student's ability to see her "own identity as a learner, employing an internalized construction of effectiveness"]. . . . Thinking about working as an advocate of the law in a globalizing world is intimidating. The documents in this cell, however, have calmed my angst so that I feel as though I am capable of accomplishing my goals. Two of the papers in this cell are only one page in length. *I've come to learn that brevity and conciseness coupled with poignancy and clarity serve as valuable evidence that one has thought well and critically* [exemplifies her ability to "understand her own performance as a learner and transfer learning strategies to multiple contexts"]. To be brief is difficult if there is a lot to say. . . . longevity of thought is sometimes necessary before brevity of a statement can be made clear. . . . Islam.Y107.doc exemplifies my ability to be a critical thinker because I had to put forth significant effort to separate my emotions from the facts and research. I believe that objectivity and rationality are at the core of every serious student— this paper shows me that I can be a serious student. *Every class that I have taken in political science, English, and philosophy has emphasized the importance of looking past the surface of things* [an example of "using multiple and interdisciplinary frameworks to understand"]. Additionally, my education in the liberal arts has taught me that there is much more to things than what my emotions tell me there are. . . . My emotions are central only to my own experiences, and *my critical thinking skills allow me to leap outside of my own experiences* [shows the student "probing her own work and understanding"].

Based on the large percentage of students in the study whose reflections demonstrated three or more characteristics of advanced reflective thinking according to our Alverno-based rubric, we are continuing to pursue our inquiry into the "matrix thinking" that the IUPUI ePort matrix seems to engender.

Not coincidentally, "matrix thinking" or "advanced reflective thinking" also contributes to and demonstrates "advanced" proficiency in several, if not all, of our PULs: critical thinking, integration and application of knowledge, and intellectual depth, breadth, and adaptiveness come most immediately to mind. All of these are abilities that speak to the new century's need for lifelong learners and integrative, innovative thinkers. Indeed, in a survey of freshmen in IUPUI's Themed Learning Communities, another part of our 2004–5 research project, respondents who had worked with ePort reported more engagement and a greater sense of competence in most of the PULs than students who had not been exposed to ePort.

Our ePort is still very much under development. As successive departments and faculty members adapt and adopt the ePort, the IUPUI ePort initiative is striving to create a flexible tool that can meet the needs of teachers and learners across disciplines and throughout undergraduate careers. Ultimately, we hope that the developmental model that provides ePort's conceptual framework will prove its usefulness both for helping students build critical intellectual and personal capacities and for enabling departments, programs, and the entire institution to demonstrate these capacities.

On the basis of our experience, we include several recommendations for encouraging effective reflection and matrix thinking:

1. Create an intentional and meaningful context for reflection by explaining the goals of reflection to students and carefully designing prompts, questions, or matrices.
2. Share ideas about "advanced" vs. "introductory" reflection with students, so that they clearly understand the steps entailed in reaching the advanced level and the value of doing so. In our case, we distribute our document on "Development in Reflective Thinking" to our capstone students and devote a portion of a class session to discussing it.
3. Give students the opportunity to peer review first drafts of one another's reflections. Our students have found these opportunities extremely helpful in guiding their revisions, while the resulting class discussions further clarify what meaningful, advanced reflection "looks like."

APPENDIX

Development in Reflective Thinking

Areas of Development	Introductory	Intermediate	Advanced
Ability to self-assess • Observing own performance • Using feedback & evidence • Finding & analyzing patterns • Making judgments	Global judgments without evidence Sees performance same as assignment (did what was told) Repeats judgments of evaluators Sees feedback as affirmation and evidence Narrates process (did this; did that) Observes rather than infers	Applies disciplinary constructs Demonstrates deeper understanding of concept Uses feedback to expand understanding Recognizes connections, links, and relationships, such as cause & effect Makes inferences (relates judgments to evidence)	Observes intentional changes as a basis for higher learning Probes own work and understanding Uses multiple and interdisciplinary frameworks to understand Makes connections, applications, and uses to move forward
Awareness of how one learns • Concepts and misconceptions • Knowledge construction • Metacognition	Limits concept development to the terms given in the assignment Sees feedback as external and not subject to analysis Sees knowledge construction only within terms of the assignment Employs personal theories largely without explanation or analysis	Sees feedback as a means to understanding links between current and future performance Notes changes in own patterns of performance Sees knowledge construction as integrating current and new knowledge Applies theories or broader frameworks to discussion of learning	Integrates feedback and past performance to construct future learning plans Uses growing awareness of knowledge structures to envision future learning Understands own performance as a learner and transfers learning strategies to multiple contexts
Developing lifelong learning skills • Developing identity as a learner • Transferring learning to other contexts • Understanding learning as a lifelong process	Confuses performance and feedback with identity as a learner Uses generalized notions of success or effectiveness as basis for reflection Minimizes connections between performance and reflecting on performance in global self-evaluation	Self-identifies as a learner, constructing meaning within experience, now and in the future Questions personal assumptions and recognizes multiple perspectives Identifies challenges, demonstrating positive attitude and confidence, using self-assessment as a basis to improve	Sees own identify as a learner, employing internalized construction of effectiveness Questions assumptions to construct intellectual commitments, aware of multiple perspectives Situates personal narrative in larger intellectual/professional frameworks, transferring learning to new situations

Source: Derived from a model of "Developmental Perspectives on Reflective Learning," Alverno College 2004. Sharon J. Hamilton 2005.

11

A VALUES-DRIVEN
EPORTFOLIO JOURNEY

Nā Wa`a

JUDITH KIRKPATRICK, TANYA RENNER, LISA KANAE, and KELLI GOYA

Kapi`olani Community College

The electronic portfolio at Kapi`olani Community College focuses on assisting students to incorporate native cultural values with academic achievement, and our study uses several measures to assess the impact of this approach to learning, especially when connected to the eportfolios. Central to our project is a cultural framework central to the school's mission and to the eportfolio itself.

We begin with the eportfolio: The faculty from the Mālama Hawai`i Center, where Native Hawaiian programs, projects, and student services take place, titled the eportfolio model the *Nā Wa`a*, which literally means "the canoes." This voyaging metaphor provided a frame for three purposes: (a) to assist students in recording their learning; (b) to connect their academic, career, and personal work with various Hawaiian values; and (c) to position these works within a stage of growth. Regarding the latter, the student is challenged to place the work in one of four *pae* levels—growth, building, set sail/traveling, or landed—based on her interpretation of herself and her artifact. This nondirective, nonpunitive act gives the student ownership of her artifact, experience, and learning, while at the same time validating her cultural intelligence.

The result is a digital archive that provides evidence of what the student knows and a record of both academic and personal growth.

Nā Wa`a also asks for student self-reflection on the works within the values/*pae* matrix. Students write a reflective analysis of each artifact as it is placed in the eportfolio and submit their reflection and work for review to their Mālama Hawai`i faculty. The reflective analysis asks that students complete three analytic tasks in each reflection: (a) explain the origins of the works; (b) record how the selection and related experiences have challenged them to grow personally, academically, and professionally; and (c) speculate on how relevant activities over the next 10 years might further contribute to their learning in this area. The reflective analysis requires a sense of self-awareness and self-direction, which provides students with experience in assessing their strengths and weaknesses, as it inherently suggests that learners can reflect on how they think, learn, and monitor their progress in relation to cultural values. The reflections also display evidence of an emotional connection to academic assignments, demonstrating that cultural and emotional factors influence thinking and information processing. Later, feedback to students impacts learner-centered behaviors such as motivation, orientation toward learning, and a deeper understanding of the relationship of the subject matter to Hawaiian values and the canoe journey metaphor.

The Nā Wa`a research team hypothesized that the Nā Wa`a approach to eportfolios would promote students' abilities to pursue learning in college and stimulate a sense of empowerment for students by assisting them to take responsibility for their own education. The central research question of this pilot study is whether this approach is, indeed, learning centered. For purposes of this project, *learning centered* is defined as promoting the ability to pursue learning in college and throughout life and engendering a sense of empowerment for students by assisting them to take responsibility for their own education.

The Nā Wa`a eportfolio project team designated first-year composition and second-year Hawaiian language courses for the study, and for first-year composition, designated a control class taught by the same instructor but without the use of the Nā Wa`a eportfolio. The researchers administered two instruments, the Learning and Study Strategies Inventory (LASSI) and the Nā Wa`a ePortfolio Survey, in addition to analyzing the students' reflective learning analyses to explore whether the approach is truly learning-centered.

The Learning and Study Strategies Inventory (LASSI) (http://www.hhpublishing.com/_assessments/LASSI/index.html), electronically administered at the beginning and end of the semester, was chosen to assess the impact of the eportfolio as an educational intervention that improves student learning-centered behaviors and attitudes. LASSI is a 10-scale, 80-item assessment of students' knowledge and use of strategic learning strategies. The LASSI also gives students useful immediate feedback on where they need to improve their knowledge, attitudes, beliefs, and skills.

The Nā Wa`a ePortfolio Survey, electronically administered at the end of the semester, uses 12 questions based on the Community College Survey of Student Engagement (CCSSE; http://www.austincc.edu/oiepub/ext_rpts/ccsse.html), for which the college has local and national bench-marks, and three instructor-generated questions. The CCSSE questions were chosen because they measure levels of student engagement in their learning. (To view the survey, see http://moosurvey.kcc.hawaii.edu/nawaa.)

RESULTS: LEARNING AND STUDY STRATEGIES INVENTORY

The research team expected to see improvement for all groups on the LASSI scales between the pretest at the beginning of the semester and the posttest at the end, because participation in college courses may be expected to enhance the learning-centered behaviors and attitudes that the scales measure. Greater improvements for students in the eportfolio courses were expected for at least some of the scales such as greater motivation and attitude improvements, at least in part because the use of the Hawaiian values would help students understand the relevance of the academic work to their own lives. Another likelihood was that eportfolio students would show greater improvement in information processing and selecting main ideas because the reflections they wrote for the eportfolio selection of artifacts would prompt them to think critically about the meaning of their work.

The data were assessed with the *t* test for repeated measures. Before-and-after results in the fall 2006 semester of implementation showed real improvement after instructors made significant changes to their curriculum, integrated the eportfolio approach with other assignments, and created new assignments specifically for the eportfolio.

LASSI'S *Skill Component* examines students' Test Strategies, Information Processing, and Selecting Main Ideas scales. Table 11-1 shows the average scores for the Skill Component scales. This component appears to be where the eportfolio students may ultimately demonstrate a greater advantage, because they showed significant improvements in two of the three scales.

LASSI's two other components, the *Will Component* and the *Self-Regulation Component*, showed significant improvement in both the control group and the eportfolio group. The *Will Component*

Table 11-1. Average Scores for Skill Component Scales

Section	Fall 06 Control	Fall 06 Control	N = 9	Fall 06 Eportfolio	Fall 06 Eportfolio	N = 20
Scale	Pretest	Posttest		Pretest	Posttest	
Select Main Idea	61.07	61.07	NS	59.70	59.70	NS
Test Strategies	57.86	64.29	NS	49.75	60.15	P = 0.005
Info Processing	50.86	58.29	NS	46.55	61.20	P = 0.003

consists of three scales—Anxiety, Attitude, and Motivation—measuring students' interest and willingness to receive new knowledge and their general attitudes and interest in being in college, which includes putting in the effort and self-discipline required to succeed. As shown in Table 11-2, students in both the control and eportfolio groups showed significant improvement in two of the three scales.

LASSI'S *Self-Regulation Component* includes scales for time management, concentration, self-testing, and study aids. Table 11-3 shows the average scores and significance for students for these four scales. Most of the scales are significantly improved for both groups.

LASSI CONCLUSIONS

The eportfolio students demonstrate significant improvement on eight of the ten LASSI scales, whereas control group students demonstrate improvement on five of the ten scales. Thus, three of the scales show improvement for only the eportfolio students: anxiety, time management, and test strategies. It is interesting to note that each of these scales represents a different component of the LASSI, which suggests that participation in the eportfolio may have a unique impact on the three areas of learner-centered engagement that the LASSI measures. However, as interesting to note are the changes in teaching that followed the efforts to integrate the values-centered eportfolio, independent of the actual use of the eportfolio. Instructors began the Nā Wa`a eportfolio project with the intent to turn students into more independent learners, with a sense of their culture and its relevance in higher education. The faculty in the study, in their interactions with each other and their classroom strategies with the project, concluded that Nā Wa`a was transforming the way they teach. Follow-up data with future semesters are being collected, however, to sort out these findings before any firm conclusions can be made.

Table 11-2. Average Scores for Will Component Scales

Section	Fall 06 Control	Fall 06 Control	N = 9	Fall 06 Eportfolio	Fall 06 Eportfolio	N = 20
Scale	Pretest	Posttest		Pretest	Posttest	
ANX	41.43	47.14	NS	52.30	60.95	P = 0.038
ATT	30.36	42.50	p = 0.007	32.75	40.35	NS
MOT	41.79	55.30	p = 0.03	35.75	45.65	P = 0.016

Table 11-3. Average Scores for Self-Regulation Scales

Section	Fall 06 Control	Fall 06 Control	N = 9	Fall 06 Eportfolio	Fall 06 Eportfolio	N = 20
Scale	Pretest	Posttest		Pretest	Posttest	
Concentration	47.57	61.07	p = 0.02	43.75	51.45	P = 0.046
Self-Test	41.79	57.93	p = 0.02	45.60	57.50	P = 0.005
Study Aids	39.43	53.57	p = 0.03	34.15	48.45	P = 0.005
Time Mgmnt	37.87	42.86	NS	36.55	41.05	P = 0.035

RESULTS: THE NĀ WAʻA EPORTFOLIO SURVEY

Through its participation in the Community College Survey of Student Engagement (CCSSE), Kapiʻolani Community College has benchmark data that relate to student success. The research team chose 12 questions from the CCSSE to ask eportfolio students in order to compare eportfolio results to campus results and national benchmarks. In addition, the eportfolio instructors asked three questions related to the Nā Waʻa eportfolio. In six of the twelve CCSSE survey questions (see Table 11-4), the findings for Nā Waʻa demonstrate a significant positive result in comparison to college and national benchmarks, whereas the other six questions showed no significant difference. Also, because all questions offered an open-ended text box in order to encourage further student input for any of the 15 questions (see Table 11-5), there are comments that may explain differences.

Table 11-4. Eportfolio Na Waʻa Survey Questions Showing Significant Difference

Scoring Options: 4 = Very much; 3 = Quite a bit; 2 = Some; 1 = Very little			
Benchmark Comparison, Nā Waʻa = 38	National	KapCC	Nā Waʻa
Q4 How much has your experience in Nā Waʻa contributed to your knowledge, skills, and personal development in developing a personal code of ethics and values?	2.32	2.41	3.13
Q9 How much has your experience in Nā Waʻa contributed to your knowledge, skills, and personal development in writing clearly and effectively?	2.7	2.86	2.95
Q10 How much has your experience in Nā Waʻa contributed to your knowledge, skills, and personal development in thinking critically and analytically?	2.86	2.83	2.97
Q11 How much work in your experience in Nā Waʻa has emphasized synthesizing and organizing ideas, information, or experiences in new ways?	2.7	2.69	2.99
Q13 How often in your experience in Nā Waʻa have you worked with instructors on activities other than course work?	1.42	1.35	2.22
Q14 How often in your experience in Nā Waʻa have you worked harder than you thought you could to meet an instructor's standards or expectations?	2.54	2.52	2.82

Table 11-5. Eportfolio Na Waʻa Survey Open-Ended Remarks

Sample English 100 students	Sample Hawaiian Language 201/202 students
• It makes me question what is really valuable in life. • I liked the Hawaiian values and having to relate to them. • It is nice to look at life or development as a process that has different steps, all extremely important. • I like the idea of a matrix, like our brains and the associations to our personal experiences. • When I have a moment to reflect, I would like to upload work and relate it to my life. • I really believe this eportfolio concept will help me in many ways. I will continue to use it. I like reflecting on what I've learned or hope to in the future. Makes it so much easier to focus on what it is I'm trying to learn when I know there is a place for me to reflect upon my work at a later time.	• I really appreciated learning about the Hawaiian values and finding things in nature to represent them. • It felt good to evaluate myself with these values. • Hawaiian values can be integrated into every class and every aspect of life. Everyone has their own interpretation of each value. • The values in the Nā Waʻa eportfolio allowed me to look at the way I conduct myself, and reflecting on the Hawaiian values made me more aware of why I do things in a certain way. • Gives me a better understanding of the deeper meaning of Hawaiian words. • Think critically and out of the box. • It raised the bar of my thoughts of Hawaiian language. • Nā Waʻa taught me a lot about myself and made me realize things that I am good in and things that I am not. Things that I have opinions of but lack knowledge of that topic. • Nā Waʻa gave me a firmer foundation to my lifelong learning path.

SURVEY CONCLUSIONS

The six questions that were significantly more positive than national and local benchmarks addressed the use of values, critical thinking, writing, teamwork, and a level of engagement. Students' spontaneous, open-ended comments in the survey support our hypothesis that working on the eportfolio with the values approach is leading students to engage more deeply in their learning, to mention the values in their reflections, and to relate the values to their understanding of their learning. Further research is needed to document various areas that are probably contributing to these findings such as the role faculty are playing as they integrate the Nā Wa`a eportfolio approach into their courses. We believe this new role is based on the ways faculty are transforming their teaching, structuring assignments, and interacting with students.

RESULTS: STUDENTS' REFLECTIVE ANALYSES

Students were required to write reflective analyses to explain how they chose to place a given artifact in the Nā Wa`a eportfolio system. Preliminary analysis of these reflective comments yielded four general categories of personal growth: (a) awareness of one's strengths; (b) recognition of areas where improvement is needed; (c) an increased understanding of the learning process, and (d) recognition of learning beyond course content.

RESULTS: TEACHER FEEDBACK ON REFLECTIVE ANALYSES

In addition to analysis of the students' comments, the research team also analyzed the teacher feedback. In the teacher's effort to help students see the growth demonstrated in their work, she echoed back to them the deeper meaning of their words. Although there were many instances of unique growth, there were also three general themes that

emerged from her responses: (a) increased motivation (e.g., to do well, to improve, to honor one's family, to use research to support one's ideas); (b) increased understanding of oneself through the writing and reflection processes; and (c) awareness of connections between the current learning and future activities such as taking other courses, engaging in professional writing, and participating in one's culture.

SUMMARY OF FINDINGS

The findings from the LASSI and CCSSE surveys, combined with the analysis of both students' reflective analyses and teacher feedback, present a picture of students who feel connected to their learning and who feel empowered to extend what they have learned to other venues. This eportfolio approach, while not conclusively shown to support a specific area of improvement, does generally support learning-centered behaviors and attitudes.

RECOMMENDATIONS

Initially, instructors began the Nā Wa`a eportfolio project with the hopes of transforming their students into more independent learners. At about mid-semester, the instructors realized that Nā Wa`a was transforming the way they teach. The following recommendations are a result of their journey:

1. Integrate eportfolio into the course content. Initially, Nā Wa`a was perceived as an outside entity, an extracurricular activity of sorts that students would work on at home in addition to the course content. The instructors changed their perception of Nā Wa`a in order to influence student participation, including it in both course and classroom. Instructors modified the curriculum to provide students with opportunities to create artifacts for Nā Wa`a.
2. Find interactive ways via a cultural perspective for students to express their knowledge

and/or acquire a deeper knowledge of cultural values. In our case, this perspective was a natural part of Hawaiians' love and craft for *kaona*, hidden meaning and metaphor, hence "The Canoes." Instructors thus generated activities in the natural environment, in cultural practices in Hawaiian literature and oral histories, and in a sharing with community peers and leaders. All of these activities express Hawaiian values through a hands-on approach and create connections between school, community, career, and family.

3. Create an overarching framework fostering student development, especially one connected to local culture. Particularly useful is a cultural framework similar to Nā Waʻa, one possessing metaphors that members of that culture will understand and can adapt to suit their values, practices, and objectives. Such a framework will support the student to be empowered through knowledge of the self.

4. Enhance computer multimedia competence to provide students with opportunities to create more artifacts such as video presentations, audio recordings, and digital storytelling.

5. Create a peer mentor network to provide one-on-one support for students. Developing, initiating, and maintaining Nā Waʻa required a considerable amount of time in and out of the classroom. Peer mentor support not only aided the instructor but also encouraged peer-to-peer, mentor-to-peer, and cross-curricular partnerships.

6. Refrain from prescribing a required number of artifacts that students should present. Instead, students choose how many (or how few) artifacts they choose to upload.

Greg Dening, in his book *Islands and Beaches*, (1980) reflecting on the history of the Marquesas, describes the difference between "metaphor" and "model":

> Both model and metaphor are transpositions, readings of experiences, products of consciousness. Their distinction lies in the fact that metaphors are understood and models imposed. Metaphors enlarge within a closed system; models belong to an observer's perception. . . . It can mean entry into the experience of others in such a way that we share the metaphors that enlarge their experience. . . . Metaphor is an instrument of daily understanding within a closed system. . . . But models are always schizoid: they belong to two systems, the one they describe and the one that constructs them.

Although Dening is writing within the context of recording historical accounts of colonization, his words provide an understanding of how metaphor works in Nā Waʻa. Metaphorically, the student will reach the *Pae Pae* stage where the canoe has landed, and the individual is ready to be supportive of others.

REFERENCE

Dening, G. (1980). *Islands and beaches: Discourse on a silent land, Marquesas, 1774–1880*. Honolulu, Hawaii: University Press of Hawaii.

12

EPORTFOLIOS IN AN UNDERGRADUATE PSYCHOLOGY RESEARCH EXPERIENCES PROGRAM

BENJAMIN R. STEPHENS
Clemson University

The Clemson eportfolio project has taken a disciplinary focus: on how eportfolios in psychology can foster professional identity. More specifically, during the summers of 2003–2007, a total of 37 undergraduate interns completed eportfolios based on their research experiences in Clemson's 10-week summer program in applied psychology. One key support activity was the class in which interns constructed an electronic portfolio documenting their experiences. As explained in this chapter, the intern eportfolios in our program served a central social/professional function: to project one or more facets of self to valued (mainly professional) audiences. In turn, this social function may have increased intern attention to and awareness of the value of three domains: scientific skills, scientific training, and interest in scientific careers.

Students were keenly aware of the various audiences implied from the public nature of their eportfolio presentations. These multiple valued audiences seem to have provided the social contexts required to promote motivation and a professional aspect to the students' projection of their work and career goals. We suspect as well that this social context of the eportfolio enhanced student awareness of growth. As students formulate and project their understandings and accomplishments to a valued audience, they become more aware of those same learnings. In short, increases in intern achievement may be partially mediated via eportfolio construction.

How did the interns structure and project their work and thoughts to their multiple audiences? The first key step is structuring the eportfolio, here defined as the self-presentation style of linking and connecting particular Web pages, documents, and images in the eportfolio. Interns begin in the first few weeks by creating an archive consisting of a chronological listing of work products, biographical information, and artifacts from exercises. A map of this structure is illustrated in the top image of Figure 12.1, which depicts the entry page to the site (the central box), with several links from that entry page to work products, images, and other artifacts.

As the program unfolded over the next several weeks, most interns reorganized their portfolios into hierarchical structures. The lower image in Figure 12.2 illustrates a typical final structure, which begins with an initial page to the portfolio, including an overview or introduction, with links organized according to main themes (research project, class activities, etc.). Each theme often contained links to subthemes and/or artifacts illustrating the

Figure 12.1. A typical initial eportfolio map structure

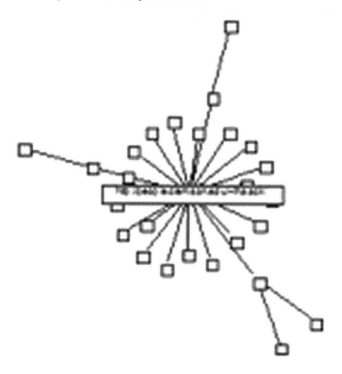

Figure 12.2. A typical final eportfolio map structure

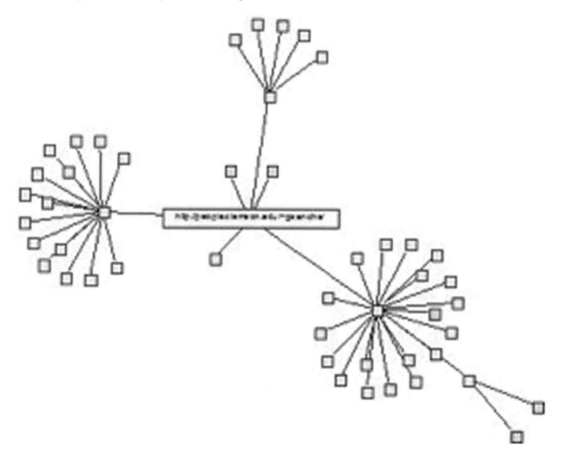

theme: Two examples presented in Figure 12.3 illustrate these final structures. Manger's (2006) eportfolio entry page, for example, presents three columns of links organizing her work in term of "General Information," "Class Activities," and "Research Project." The links in each column lead to external sites (e.g., Clemson University's Web site) or internal sites or artifacts created by Manger (e.g., her "Final Reflection" of the summer program's impact on her learning and career development). Manger's entry page presents both her organizational themes and her supporting links.

Figure 12.3

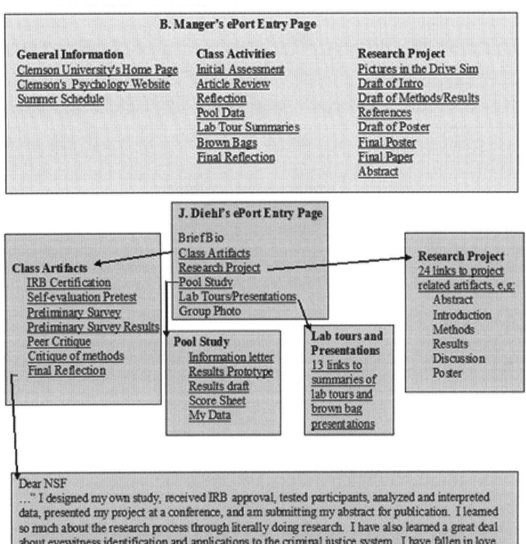

In contrast, Diehl's (2005) eportfolio provides an introductory biographical sketch on her entry page and represents her organizational structure via links to main themes on separate pages. Diehl's structure is conceptually similar to Manger's, but her use of hierarchical linkage enables a stronger sense of organization and inclusion of more artifacts; she includes 24 links to Research Project artifacts, for example. However, Diehl's "Final Reflection" is somewhat distant (located in the third level [L3] of her portfolio under the "Class Artifact" theme), whereas Manger's is more immediately accessible (located in the second level).

Table 12-1 displays the mean and standard deviation for eportfolio structural characteristics for all 37 interns as a group. An overwhelming number of the links were to artifacts within the interns' Web sites (internal links) rather than to external sites. Structurally, the majority of the Web pages and artifacts were located at or above the third (L3) level, although there was noticeable variability in the mean number of L2, L3, and L4 levels. This variability suggests that the structures illustrated by Manger and Diehl represent the 37 interns as a whole. To determine the interrelationship among artifacts, we calculated a "Hierarchy" score, computed as the weighted average of all Web site pages where the entry page was equal to 1.0, pages linked to the entry page were equal to 2.0, and so on. The average hierarchy score for the group was 2.74, indicating that many eportfolios were richly structured within organizing themes.

These structures may reflect the interns' concept mapping of the content of the portfolio designed to appeal to various social audiences for the eport-

folio. Some nodes in the hierarchy seem useful for the mentor and graduate schools (e.g., the research project), whereas others are designed for the instructor (e.g., class activities node). Likewise, many interns constructed nodes that seem directed toward peers; these often contained links to their home institution and/or to photos of summer program peers and social activities. In addition, these concept maps may serve a dual purpose: They may aid both communicator and audience (Wang & Dwyer, 2006). In sum, the development of these maps in our intern eportfolios seems to suggest an awareness of how artifacts connect to self as well as to the needs of valued social audiences.

Within these structures, the content of the eportfolios provided a rich source of qualitative evidence of interns' increased interest, understanding, and commitment to research, science, and scientific careers. As in Diehl's eportfolio, multiple drafts of literature reviews, research proposals, final reports, and poster presentations demonstrate growing maturity in project knowledge and research skills. Reflective comments on weekly colloquia indicate a more mature sense of the scientific domain of applied psychology. And final summative reflections on overall program effectiveness cite multiple positive outcomes. For example, in Diehl's (2005) "Dear NSF" letter, her reflective comments suggest that the program increased her interest in research, provided direction in graduate training, and led to a greater understanding of science. As in the case of the structures of the electronic portfolios, throughout the interns' reflective comments we can trace the identified audience (e.g., NSF), as well as an implied audience (e.g.,

Table 12-1. Means and Standard Deviations for Eportfolio Structural Characteristics

	Mean	SD
Internal Links	34.571	15.687
External Links	4.914	5.967
L1	1.000	0.000
L2	12.800	11.739
L3	19.400	16.141
L4	9.958	13.366
L5	2.389	5.403
L6	0.357	1.082
Hierarchy	2.738	0.592

Table 12-2. Self-Evaluation of Research Skills Survey (after Kardash, 2000).

- Understand contemporary concepts . . .
    - in the field of psychology
    - in applied psychology
    - in the area of research you are working on in this program.
- Make use of the primary scientific research literature (e.g., journal articles) . . .
- Identify a specific question for investigation based on the research . . .
- Formulate a research hypothesis based on a specific question . . .
- Design an experiment or theoretical test of the hypothesis . . .
- Understand the importance of controls in research . . .
- Observe and collect data . . .
- Statistically analyze data . . .
- Interpret data by relating results to the original hypothesis . . .
- Reformulate your original research hypothesis (as appropriate) . . .
- Orally communicate the results of research projects . . .
- Write a research paper for publication . . .
- Think independently . . .

self, mentors, scientists) and a potential audience (e.g., graduate selection committees).

To augment these eportfolio-based qualitative impressions of our interns and the program, we collected survey assessment data. Interns indicated, on a 5-point scale ranging from 1 (*not at all*) to 5 (*a great deal*), the extent to which they believed that *they could demonstrate* each skill in each of three domains, as detailed in Table 12-2. At the beginning of the program, interns rated their abilities for their specific research areas significantly lower in comparison to their abilities for the other two domains (psychology and applied psychology). After the program, the interns reported stronger gains in their abilities in their specific project domains compared to the applied or general domains. This pattern was significantly stronger for some science skills (e.g., understand contemporary concepts) compared to others (e.g., understand the use of controls). These survey data are consistent with the qualitative impressions we formed via reading the eportfolio artifacts and reflections.

One last piece of research on eportfolios focused on how different audiences rate the eportfolios. Immediately prior to faculty ratings, mentors reviewed their interns' eportfolios. Importantly, the faculty evaluations of student achievement were in qualitative agreement with the student interns' ratings. This observation is consistent with the possibility that the interns designed the eportfolio with a pro-

fessional audience as the target and that the content was an effective communication of intern growth and achievement.

In the future, we plan to direct intern attention early and more directly to the interplay of social context, eportfolio content/structure, and intern capability. We suspect this early focus can further enhance the overall effectiveness of the eportfolio for all concerned. For example, in our 2007 summer program, we (1) introduced the concept of integrating artifacts into themes early in the program; (2) asked interns to consider additional themes of a more scholarly nature (e.g., "Scientific and Professional Skills"); (3) encouraged reflection on artifacts early in the program; and (4) suggested a hierarchical organizational structure as an option for eportfolio organization. We suspect that these specific modifications will facilitate and enhance interns' ability to communicate with valued social and professional audiences.

NOTE

This chapter contains work supported by the National Science Foundation and the Department of Defense ASSURE Program under Grant No. SES-0353698. Any opinions, findings, and conclusions or recommendations expressed in this material are those of the author(s) and do not necessarily reflect the views of the National Science Foundation or the Department of Defense.

REFERENCES

Diehl, J. (2005). Psychology internship portfolio. Retrieved March 4, 2007, from http://people.clemson.edu/~jmdiehl/InternshipPortfolio.htm

Kardash, C. M. (2000). Evaluations of an undergraduate research experience: Perceptions of undergraduate interns and their faculty mentors. *Journal of Educational Psychology, 92*(1), 191–201.

Manger, B. (2006). Welcome to Brooke's portfolio: NSF/REU Summer Internship 2006. Retrieved March 4, 2007, from http://people.clemson.edu/~bmanger/

Wang, C. X., & Dwyer, F. M. (2006). Instructional effects of three concept mapping strategies in facilitating student achievement. *International Journal of Instructional Media, 33*(2), 135–151.

13

PERCEPTIONS OF TEACHER CANDIDATES ON EPORTFOLIO USE

NEAL W. TOPP and ROBERT L. GOEMAN
University of Nebraska at Omaha

The University of Nebraska at Omaha (UNO), a metropolitan university with a student population of approximately 15,000 students, is focusing on implementing a campus-wide eportfolio initiative (myMAPP), which will include eportfolios for students, faculty, staff, and units. Currently, all faculty across campus use the myMAPP eportfolio system for annual review, and over 2000 students are engaged with several types of eportfolios in UNO's College of Education (COE).

THE UNIVERSITY OF NEBRASKA AT OMAHA'S COLLEGE OF EDUCATION EPORTFOLIO

In order to achieve more authentic, real-world ways of ensuring the preparedness of education graduates, faculty have begun to include performance assessment, which involves a shift away from traditional curricula and assessment (Britten & Mullen, 2003). Electronic portfolios are a primary mechanism for performance assessment, but they bring with them a new challenge for institutions of teacher education nationwide (Strudler & Wetzel, 2005; Wetzel & Strudler, 2005). UNO's College of Education has taken on that challenge.

The primary purpose of our COE eportfolio is to enhance the learning of teacher candidates. Our model, a database-driven eportfolio, provides a cumulative repository; students can include products from coursework activities throughout their teacher candidate's undergraduate program. In addition, there are two components to the portfolio: the formative portfolio includes many different artifacts; the summative portfolio includes only certain required artifacts, specifically artifacts keyed to the Interstate New Teacher Assessment and Support Consortium (INTASC; 1992) principles (Wetig, Topp, & Clark, 2005). In terms of sequencing, teacher candidates submit their artifacts while they are completing certain courses, which allows faculty to review them. Once the artifact has been deemed acceptable by a course instructor, it is included in the appropriate INTASC (1992) principle matrix box in the student's eportfolio.

THE RESEARCH STUDY

The purpose of this study was twofold. The first purpose was to determine if there were differences in undergraduate teacher candidates' perceptions of the contributions of assessments, both traditional assessments and eportfolio assessments, to the candidates' development of their understanding of education core content areas and contributions of the use of reflections in both types of assessment. The secondary purpose of this study was to determine teacher candidates' knowledge of INTASC (1992) principles given the number of hours spent completing eportfolio classroom assessments.

This study looked at the relationship between certification level (elementary and secondary) and type of assessment based on teacher candidates' scores on the Classroom Assessment Survey (CAPS). In addition, it addressed the relationship between time spent per course working on eportfolio activities and type of assessment on teacher candidates' CAPS content and reflection perception scores.

The participants in this study included undergraduate teacher certification candidates enrolled in their student teaching experience during the 2006 fall semester. A Web-based survey was administered to the participants. Of the 143 eligible respondents, a total of 73 (51%) teacher candidates completed the survey.

INSTRUMENTATION

The CAPS gathered data in four main areas:

- The first set of data included the teacher candidates' demographics. Demographic information included gender, ethnicity, age, certification level, Internet access, technology proficiency, and average hours working within the eportfolio per course.
- The second set of data from CAPS included the teacher candidates' rating of themselves on the knowledge represented by the Interstate New Teachers Assessment and Support Consortium (INTASC, 1992) principles evaluated on a 5-point Likert scale. Each principle was listed, and the teacher candidates chose the appropriate response from the following: very low, low, average, high, or very high knowledge.
- The third set of data included responses to CAPS containing two parts. Part 1 asked

questions based on teacher candidates' understanding of course content; the second part asked questions based on support of reflection. Teacher candidates responded to both parts using a 5-point Likert scale.
- The last set of data included two open-ended questions. The first question asked, "What role has the electronic portfolio played in your preparation as a future teacher?" The second question read, "Please share any comments that could help make the COE electronic portfolio better."

The instrument was created after two pilot studies, and it was tested for validity using experienced education professionals, including a panel of local, regional, and national experts. The reliability of the instrument was estimated using Cronbach's alpha. After making changes based on the factor and reliability analysis, the final draft of the CAPS included 58 items.

VARIABLES

The variables in this study included three independent and three dependent variables. The independent variables were type of assessment (traditional classroom or eportfolio), current certification (elementary or secondary), and number of hours spent on eportfolio assessment activities in each course. The dependent variables were teacher candidates' perception scores on the content area subscale, the reflection subscale, and knowledge of the INTASC (1992) principles.

MAJOR FINDINGS

Two research findings are of particular interest to the eportfolio community.

The first research question asked if there is a significant relationship between certification level (elementary and secondary) and type of assessment (traditional classroom and electronic portfolio) on teacher candidates' CAPS reflection and content perception scores. The results of the study showed that CAPS content perception scores were significantly higher in traditional classroom assessment than in electronic portfolio classroom assessment regardless of level (elementary and secondary). In addition, there was no relationship in overall CAPS reflection scores. Interestingly enough, *within* the reflection scores, secondary level scores were significantly higher in the area of traditional classroom assessment, whereas elementary level reflection scores showed no difference in the same area.

Content and reflection are first referenced in the traditional classroom across all levels; therefore, it is plausible that teacher candidates may not carry over the concept of content to the electronic portfolio. The open-ended response emphasizing *future* use of the eportfolio, from an elementary teacher candidate, supports this finding:

> I believed that the projects that were presented on portfolio were the greatest learning experience for me. I really enjoyed being able to make an I-movie and present it in my portfolio with my lesson and sample work. This process took a significant amount of time, but it helped me reflect upon my own teaching style. This could be a great motivation for some of my future students. I believe this project will be useful in future job interviews. I hope to create movies with my future students.

Another teacher candidate pointed out the disconnection between class activities and eportfolio work: "The only role the Electronic Portfolio has played is documentation of a few assignments for a small portion of classes." Exposure to many different types of assessments could help change the perception of teacher candidates.

As the data in Table 13-1 demonstrate, a statistically significant interaction was found between level (elementary or secondary) and assessment for CAPS reflection. The simple main effects test for type of assessment between levels indicated a statistically significant difference between the elementary and secondary levels for electronic portfolio classroom assessment with elementary-level teacher candidates being more positive. Again, background information helps contextualize this finding. An opportunity to use the electronic portfolio was more available at the elementary level, with eportfolio elements in 26 elementary-majors' courses but in only 18 secondary-majors' courses. Faculty members within the elementary program have continued to be proactive in creating artifacts that represent the curriculum and in turn match INTASC (1992) principles. An open-ended response from an elementary candidate provides an example supporting statement: "I feel it was helpful in making me more genuinely reflective as I was able to actually see myself in practice. Moreover, it provided the opportunity to create technology I can share with others to show my teaching styles. This, I feel, proves as an advantage to all concerned."

Secondary teacher candidates also had some open-ended statements that help explain the findings: "The electronic portfolio needs to be pushed more by profs. Although we are in college and should be internally motivated to use the electronic portfolio, I was busy studying material from the textbook and handouts provided in class." At

Table 13-1. Means and Standard Deviations of the CAPS Content and Reflection Perception Scores by Type of Assessment

	Content		Reflection	
Traditional Classroom	*M*	*SD*	*M*	*SD*
Elementary (n = 41)	3.90	0.51	3.74	0.55
Secondary (*n* = 27)	4.10	0.59	†4.03	0.66
Total	3.98	0.55	3.85	0.61
Electronic Portfolio	*M*	*SD*	*M*	*SD*
Elementary (*n* = 41)	3.26	0.78	*3.84	0.73
Secondary (*n* = 27)	3.19	1.08	*†3.35	0.99
Total	3.23	0.90	3.65	0.87

*$p = .021$
†$p < .0005$

the secondary level particularly, traditional assessment continues to dominate higher education. This study also confirmed that some teacher candidates focus their efforts on what is going on day to day in the classroom. Another teacher candidate stated, "If teachers made it more of a priority, it would have made a better impact on me."

Our second research question asked if there is a relationship between time spent per course working on eportfolio activities and type of assessment (traditional classroom and eportfolio) on teacher candidates' CAPS content and reflection perception scores.

Our results, displayed in Table 13-2, showed no significant findings in the CAPS reflection perception scores in time spent working on the electronic portfolio. However, the results also showed that when we factor in the number of hours spent working on the electronic portfolio, those teacher candidates who spent more time had significantly higher CAPS content perception scores than those who did not. The reported values for time spent working in the eportfolio per course was wide, ranging from 15 minutes per course to 30 hours. The study also showed that when teacher candidates put less than 5 hours of time into working in the electronic portfolio, they had a statistically significant higher perception score in traditional classroom assessment for CAPS content scores.

It only makes sense that if teacher candidates spend more time working in the electronic portfolio, they will have a greater perception score for the

assessment tool in the area of content. Even though the study did not show the same significance in the area of reflection, exposure to the electronic portfolio still varies from course to course and from faculty member to faculty member. Thus, time is not the sole factor: It may be that those who spent less time had a different experience, caused by a lack of activities planned for the electronic portfolio, or a lack of faculty preparation. As one teacher candidate recommended, "Be more consistent and use it when they say they are going to use it." Another teacher candidate also supported this view: "I believed that the projects that were presented on portfolio were the greatest learning experience for me. This process took a significant amount of time, and has aided in my increased use of technology and improved my knowledge base."

RECOMMENDATIONS

One purpose of this study was to provide information for program improvement; therefore, our recommendations are keyed to that purpose. Although the specifics are linked to our teacher education program, the recommendations are useful for programmatic eportfolios in other disciplines as well.

- *The eportfolio should be used in most, if not all, courses in a program.* The respondents that reported consistent use of eportfolios indicated more often that the eportfolio had a

Table 13-2. Means and Standard Deviations of the CAPS Content and Reflection Perception Scores by Time Spent Working on the Electronic Portfolio

	Content		Reflection	
Traditional Classroom	*M*	*SD*	*M*	*SD*
Less than 5 hours (n = 54)	†3.92	0.54	3.79	0.58
5 or more hours (*n* = 19)	4.04	0.60	3.91	0.69
Total	3.95	0.55	3.82	0.61
Electronic Portfolio	*M*	*SD*	*M*	*SD*
Less than 5 hours (n = 54)	*†3.04	0.93	3.49	0.90
5 or more hours (*n* = 19)	*3.67	0.55	3.97	0.74
Total	3.20	0.89	3.62	0.88

$* p = .007$
$† p < .0005$

positive impact on their learning of content. The open-ended comments also confirmed this idea, with several respondents who were generally positive about eportfolio mentioning the consistent use, and generally those who were negative toward eportfolios indicating inconsistent use. Also, elementary education majors were much more positive about eportfolio than secondary education majors, and we know that the elementary program is much more consistent in the use of eportfolios than the secondary program. We believe that consistency in this case would entail introducing the eportfolio in the first course in which teacher candidates are enrolled. (Creating a 1-hour "Introduction to Teaching" course could effectively introduce the electronic portfolio as well as other important topics.)

- Teacher candidates need to spend a substantial amount of time working on eportfolio activities throughout their program. More integrated activities should be included in courses to strengthen the eportfolio experience and help students in their self-assessment of progress toward gaining skills and knowledge required to be a competent teacher.

REFERENCES

Britten, J., & Mullen, L. (2003). Interdisciplinary digital portfolio assessment: Creating tools for teacher education. *Journal of Information Technology Education, 2*(1), 41–48.

Interstate New Teacher Assessment and Support Consortium (INTASC). (1992). *Model standards for beginning teacher licensing and development.* Washington, DC: Council of Chief State School Officers. Retrieved December 5, 2005, from http://www.ccsso.org/projects/ Interstate_New_Teacher_Assessment_and_ Support_Consortium/Projects/Standards_ Development

Strudler, N., & Wetzel, K. (2005). The diffusion of electronic portfolios in teacher education: Issues of initiation and implementation. *Journal of Research on Technology in Education, 37*(4), 411–433.

Wetig, S., Topp, N., & Clark, P. (2005). The digital move. *The Michigan Journal of Teacher Education, 3*(1), 11–16.

Wetzel, K., & Strudler, N. (2005). The diffusion of electronic portfolios in teacher education: Next steps and recommendations from accomplished users. *Journal of Research on Technology in Education, 38*(2), 231–243.

SECTION FOUR

Organizational Learning

In *Electronic Portfolios: Emerging Practices in Student, Faculty, and Institutional Learning,* (Cambridge, 2001), few institutions had expansive visions of offering electronic portfolios as common practice among all campus constituents. Because less was known then about the effects of electronic portfolios on learning in multiple realms, most colleges and universities were taking baby steps with pilots within projects, courses, or programs. As evidence now reveals what can be learned from eportfolio thinking and practice, however, more and more institutions are claiming eportfolios as a central means of learning for their students, faculty, administrators, and communities.

VISION AS FOUNDATION
FOR CHANGE

In this section you will read about expansive plans for supporting learning across and beyond institutions. Such plans benefit from solid theoretical undergirding for building and maintaining the broad set of portfolio practices envisioned by the institutions. For example, Steve Acker from Collective Action, the collaborative group planning comprehensive portfolio access for the state of Ohio, draws on Appreciative Inquiry theory and practice

in calling for the identification of a "desirable destiny," the achievement of a meaningful social good. He contends that "a broadly shared compelling vision contributes to its own attainment." In another example Portland State's reenvisioning of its mission as an urban university thoroughly connected to its community led to the choice of eportfolios to generate, document, and share student, departmental, and institutional learning. These groups and institutions picked eportfolios not from a random list of possible practices but as the best available means to enact the kind of learning that the institutions seek for their students and themselves.

CONTEXTUAL PRESSURES AS
MOTIVATION TO ACTION

Issues prompting the development of portfolios are often, however, pressing matters. Vision provides inspiration for new thinking; pressure provides provocation to action. Although contextual pressures have always influenced an institution's willingness to change, external expectations for assessment and accountability in the last decade have accelerated through intense focus by accrediting bodies and the federal government on student learning outcomes—that is, student success as evidenced by timely graduation and full preparation for the work world and civic responsibilities. Some institutions, including many in the Inter/National Coalition for Electronic Portfolio Research, have rejected simplistic responses to these expectations. They have chosen to honor the complexity of student learning and educational environments by choosing descriptors and assessments that reveal the multitude of elements involved in developmental and integrated learning. They have organized their demonstrations of student and institutional learning in electronic portfolios.

Two universities in this section chose eportfolios for different presenting issues generated by accrediting and federal pressure. Bowling Green State University (Chapter 16), for example, responded to the requirement of program assessment for accreditation by identifying university learning outcomes for students which were used for curriculum redesign and development of new programs. After some trial and error Bowling Green chose an eportfolio system for students that provides a "two-dimensional grid for organizing uploaded artifacts . . . with a common vocabulary for discussing progress, assessing learning, and describing student development." The Ohio consortium (Chapter 14), on the other hand, responded to calls from former Department of Education Secretary Margaret Spellings' 2006 Higher Education Action Agenda for "an educational system that is affordable, accessible, and accountable." The scope of Collective Action's eportfolio infrastructure endeavors to gain economies of scale. The choice of why and where to begin an eportfolio program often emerges from contexts specific to an institution, a state, a region, or a country.

THE IMPORTANCE OF FRACTALS AND PILOTS

According to chaos theory, dynamical systems are sensitive to their initial conditions and to feedback: The system continually changes based on the way in which the parts of the system constantly fold back into themselves. Fractals are the wrinkles in that folding in a dynamical activity. Just as the artist implies worlds within worlds through a single story or painting, fractals imply the continuously recreating elements of a system.

According to *Fractals: The Patterns of Chaos* (Briggs, 1992), the computer made possible the revolution of chaos and fractals because it brought the phenomena into focus. In like fashion the computer has enabled researchers and educators to see the fractals of learning, the elements that fold into themselves again and again as nonlinear learning occurs. Educators react so strongly against testing at a moment in time as evidence of learning because of the importance of development, integration, and social construction in any picture of a learner.

Reporting on a pilot project on transition portfolios from high school to college, Steve Acker (Chapter 14) calls that small and relatively controllable experiment a fractal of the vision of a widely sharable eportfolio system that crossed organizational boundaries. All elements and the benefits of shared portfolio systems were replicated within a small local environment and generated a variety of data useful to argue for a larger project involving more organizations" (p. 120).

At the University of Washington Janice Fournier and Tom Lewis (Chapter 15) lament the lack of an institutional system that would give definition to the many effective pilots at the university. The authors laud innovative uses of eportfolios across campus centers, within disciplines, and in professions but wonder about what additional energy could be released by their identification within a larger dynamic system. Because the campus has not defined *eportfolio*, pilots have fewer commonalities: They are regarded as everything from digital storehouses to vehicles for generating learning.

Pilots are often starting points, as explained in Portland State's account (Chapter 17). Yet, Portland State is a case in point about the relationship of fractals to systems because it is when the university is clearest about its objectives that the symbiosis of the student, departmental, and institutional portfolios is the strongest. When the organization operates as a system, the parts and pilots at those sites are most generative for understanding and sharing learning.

ESSENTIAL COLLABORATIONS

As eportfolios move from pilot status to institutional and cross-institutional adoption, collaboration based on trust becomes more and more essential. Each institution in this section has constituted committees and groups of constituents to work together in developing their eportfolio practices and programs. Especially without mandates, colleagues who care about their students, who are able to deal with ambiguity and change, and who have a track record of working together are key to creating eportfolio cultures. As pilots move from niche programs to institutional scope, the push for higher centralization, lower complexity, and more formal reporting lines needed by a large organization, as Acker points out, may make faculty nervous that their expertise, the intricacies of nonlinear learning, and the need for accounts of individual learning may be discounted.

Fournier and Lewis conclude from their research that strategies to build joint ownership are critical: They commit to "be relentlessly inclusive in the design, development, rollout, or implementation of any eportfolio project, big or small, to create a sense of shared ownership among users"

(p. 132). Ketcheson explains throughout her chapter the essential collaboration of campus leaders, faculty members, and institutional researchers in generating student, departmental, and institutional eportfolios that represent learning for multiple audiences. Hakel and Smith note that an important next step at Bowling Green is helping faculty members to develop, have confidence in, and use common criteria and rubrics to assess student learning as a prelude to a system of eportfolios for the campus.

Chapters in this organizational learning section teach us about vision as foundation for change, contextual pressures as motivation for action, the importance of fractals and pilots, and essential collaborations. Listen for other lessons that fit your context as you learn from experiences of Ohio's Collective Action, Bowling Green State University, the University of Washington, and Portland State University.

REFERENCE

Briggs, J. (1992). *Fractals. The patterns of chaos.* New York: Simon & Schuster.

14

DIFFUSING EPORTFOLIOS IN ORGANIZATIONAL SETTINGS

STEPHEN R. ACKER
The Ohio State University

> How can we better inquire into organizational existence in ways that are economically, humanly, and ecologically significant, that is, in ways that increasingly help people discover, dream, design and transform toward the greatest good?
>
> (Cooperrider & Whitney, 1999)

Cooperrider and Whitney's question about delving into organizational existence is drawn from the research tradition of appreciative inquiry (AI). The core idea of AI is that the energy needed to innovate comes from a relentless drive toward a desirable destiny, the achievement of a meaningful social good. We see powerful destinies imagined and empowered in the visioning and business plans of organizations proposing major, disruptive changes—using alternative energy solutions to supplant fossil fuels and combat global warming or eradicating malaria in Africa with unconventional local methods. NASA's success in putting a man on the moon demonstrates that even the force of inertia (gravity) can be overcome when mass imagination is captured and harnessed toward reaching a goal.

A DESTINY WORTH ACHIEVING

For eportfolio, the core idea, and compelling social good, that pulls us forward is improved and deepened student learning, an outcome to which all educational institutions aspire. The basic argument from AI is that eportfolio systems will be widely adopted when learning organizations have crafted a compelling vision of how eportfolio use is linked to improved student learning, rather than awaiting a carefully defined set of strategies to overcome the wearying list of obstacles to eportfolio diffusion—issues such as a perceived increase in faculty workload, need for user training, and institutional policies for eportfolio archiving.

Once the vision is clear, we must back the claims, with convincing evidence, shared and accepted up, down, and across educational systems, that eportfolio use does support deep learning. Institutions working together can aggregate the needed resources to deliver on the promise of eportfolio and, as an important by-product of reaching toward this vision, address the nagging issues that slow eportfolio diffusion. A broadly shared compelling vision contributes to its own attainment.

The necessary sense of destiny is captured in Darren Cambridge's 2008 description of an electronic portfolio project for which he served as external evaluator. Cambridge applied the phrase *lifewide and lifelong learning* to a project that provides eportfolio access to any Minnesota citizen who requests it. Minnesotans who use this portfolio system gather and reflect on information related at a given point in time (lifewide). Over the years (lifelong), connections among the cross sections of experience show growth and change and support the full potential of the repository of reflection, memory, and experience called eportfolio. To build a modern, living Domesday Book for an entire state is the kind of vision that can empower transformation.

In this chapter, I argue that the Minnesota system developers have the right sense of destiny; eportfolio systems should be designed to meet large, diverse sets of user needs that span lifetimes. Although eportfolio may be productively implemented within a single organization, eportfolio systems with the potential to span organizational boundaries offer much more to students and to participating organizations that make the eportfolio system available to their users. Portfolio installations that accommodate an individual in a variety of daily pursuits (lifewide) and that can pass that rich record across institutional boundaries (lifelong) promise user payback for the time and energy each invests in learning new processes and technologies. Cooperating institutions can invest fewer resources in maintaining a shared technical infrastructure, user support mechanisms, and training events. Partnerships that share a student's starting point, concluding point, and future attainment help both organizations better chronicle the student's growth throughout her or his educational journey.

To deal with scale, like that of the statewide effort in Minnesota, a change agent can begin with a well-controlled pilot that generates data within experimental conditions that can generalize to serve larger, more complex systems. For example, The Transition Portfolio Project in Ohio was a pilot that engaged faculties from two high schools and one university. These communities worked together to prepare high school seniors to understand the different expectations of first-year college composition and senior-year high school writing. Faculty from both high school and college viewed a single piece of student work and offered suggestions for improvement. They also evaluated specific aspects of the draft on a five-point rubric. This parallax feedback, two sets of eyes from both sides of the transition boundary, led to revised student essays judged better overall, as well as on five of six subscales associated with effective college writing (Acker & Halasek, 2008).

This small and relatively controllable experiment was a fractal of the vision of a widely sharable eportfolio system that crossed organizational boundaries. All elements and the benefits of shared portfolio systems were replicated within a small local environment and generated a variety of data useful to argue for a larger project involving more organizations. We learned that institutions involved in this study could share resources needed for training, technology, and support services. We observed that students saw the benefits of carrying their documented learning experiences beyond high school into the college environment. It allowed us to ask if students would be more attracted to ever-larger communities in which to build their portfolios and to investigate whether involving more institutions would leverage and extend benefits found in the smaller collaboration.

COLLECTIVE ACTION—A CASE STUDY IN ESTABLISHING SHARED EPORTFOLIO INFRASTRUCTURE

Data from the Transition Project confirmed that students would benefit from having a storehouse for their high school work made easily accessible in college. And if students are familiar with the software, colleges can spend less time with training and end user support to prepare students for working in the college e-learning environment. Based on this logic validated in the exploratory study and swept along by the Spelling Commission's broad mandate for accountability in higher education, Ohio educators formed The Collective Action Project to build a shared e-learning infrastructure that included the capacity to capture evidence of successful student learning in eportfolios. The Collective Action Web site (http://ohiocollectiveaction.org) presents the project's destiny statement in these words: "Individuals in existing Ohio organizations will act collectively to increase the successes of all Ohio learners. They will do so by coordinating and leveraging various state efforts that contribute to better practices in the usage of technology for learning; and they will determine whether a sharable state infrastructure can be designed to meet the needs of Ohio learners."

The core membership of Collective Action consists of individuals affiliated with the Ohio Board of Regents, the Ohio Learning Network, Ohio-LINK, the Ohio Resource Center, the Ohio Department of Education and its technology support organization eTech Ohio, and faculty members leading specific projects from The Ohio State University and the University of Cincinnati. SIF, the School Interoperability Framework organization, also a member of Collective Action, offers an important context and structure for operating within a K-20 system model. These organizations already are loosely coupled and work together in different combinations on various statewide projects. Each individual representing these various organizations has in common an extended history of collaboration through which trust has been established and a sense that innovation is both possible and necessary, especially given the educational and economic challenges facing the state of Ohio.

These state-level challenges are contextualized by Margaret Spelling's Higher Education Action Agenda (2006), a call for an educational system that is affordable, accessible, and accountable. Collaborative efforts that result in an eportfolio

system within a shared e-learning environment can serve multiple educational communities by capturing economies of scale and scope, contributing to affordability, access, and accountability. A common need to respond to the accountability mandate expands the number of institutions likely to adopt eportfolios. A properly configured eportfolio system provides the toolset to create multiple, individualized contexts in which to display student learning outcomes on top of a common infrastructure. This capacity for "mass customization" (Dolence & Norris, 1995) provides an important economic justification for sharing resources needed to build and operate an eportfolio system.

Recent activities in the commercial sector demonstrate that shared infrastructure can be built and does offer a cost-effective approach for service providers who pool their needs. For example, Amazon offers a shared platform called S3 (Simple Storage Service) and a very cost-effective charging algorithm—$0.15 per month per GB of storage and $0.20 per GB per month for data transferred (http://docs.amazonwebservices.com/AmazonS3/2006-03-01/Pricing.html). Google has built a server farm in a west Washington community that consists of 10,000 servers to meet its own needs and those of external clients. On top of that massive server infrastructure, Google offers collaborative toolkits to support online document, presentation, and spreadsheet creation and sharing capabilities. For users who so choose, virtual private networks can be established for internal work and the output later propagated to wider public networks.

The Amazon and Google models inform Collective Action's approach and rationale for establishing shared services. If the shared services are robust and responsive to the needs of the clients, cost savings strongly encourage their participation. The more interesting question is whether colleges and universities are willing to work together to establish an environment that facilitates the easy migration of students, their work, and learning resources across institutional boundaries. To answer the question, the Collective Action team is pursuing the Russian Doll model, creating a core environment and nesting it as a replicable resource able to serve ever-larger numbers of institutions as awareness and interest grows.

Led by eTech Ohio and the Ohio Learning Network through a related project called the Open Learning Platform, Ohio deployed a hosted Sakai/OSP production-level service starting in autumn of 2007. To build an expandable infrastructure, common (i.e., interoperable) software is highly desirable. Systems built to open standards are necessary, and those with open source software licensing provisions are particularly helpful in encouraging sharing and growth. Open source software licensing permits learning communities to grow in size and across boundaries without violating commercial licensing agreements. For example, the Transition Portfolio project described earlier was conducted on the Ohio Learning Network's Open Source pilot platform that preceded the production-level implementation. Using Sakai/OSP (http://sakaiproject.org), we were able to add faculty, students, and even parents to the user community without concern for whether a commercial license restricted the size of the community or membership eligibility. Such a licensing arrangement, particularly in a shared hosted environment, can smooth the transition from high school to college and also avoid orphaning students who move among higher education institutions, approximately 40 percent of whom transfer at some point during their student career. Early experiences and feedback from 61 schools sharing the open source pilot environment encouraged OLN and eTech Ohio to select Sakai/OSP as the software to take to production. Statewide open standards/open source projects in Arizona (https://www.ideal.azed.gov/node) and California (http://www.calstate.edu/ats/digital_marketplace/) are pursuing similar visions.

ORGANIZING FOR TRANSFORMATIONAL CHANGE

Collective Action began as an affiliation among individuals with previous history together, common tolerance for ambiguity, and shared conviction that higher education must change. But the question remains that if an action-oriented group cultivates a field of dreams, will decision makers beholden to campus-based agendas come?

In addition to setting an aspirational destiny, change agents must understand the motivational structure of the system they wish to impact and what these leaders perceive is in their self-interest. Educational institutions are interested in survival, and they are pretty good at it. In a presentation focused on higher education's response to Spelling's accountability agenda, Milt Hakel cites Clark Kerr's list of 66 entities that have been in existence since 1530. Two of them are churches—the Roman Catholic Church and the Lutheran Church. Two others are governments—the parliaments of Iceland and the Isle of Man. The remaining 62 institutions are universities. One interpretation of these data is that higher education has little motivation to change and will be among the last industries to abandon traditional practices. Another interpretation is that higher education institutions are uncommonly successful at adapting to environmental conditions *when necessary* and thus endure.

We would argue that the environment in which all education operates indeed has changed and that decision makers recognize they must evolve to flourish, if not to survive. For-profit educational institutions have emerged to compete for the student dollar. Open courseware initiatives are growing in number for those seeking quality content outside of traditional class structures and credit-earning contexts. There is general recognition of the goals of the Spelling Commission. For example, Brian Hawkins (2006) described accountability as EDUCAUSE Grand Challenge for 2007. Legislatures and other funders (e.g., parents) are demanding an accounting of both the cost and the benefit sides of investments in higher education. We believe this confluence of environmental forces has convinced the educational leadership that all institutions indeed are faced with a mandate to change. The game plan is to highlight the role eportfolio can play within the accountability agenda.

EPORTFOLIOS, DISRUPTIVE TECHNOLOGIES, AND THE ACCOUNTABILITY AGENDA

Disruptive technologies upset the status quo and can lead to revolutionary change (Christensen, Baumann, Ruggles, & Sadtler, 2006). In early form, disruptive technologies are typically unreliable, messy, rapidly changing, and unsuited for scale. However, their great utility for certain classes of users allows them to develop rapidly through iteration. Eportfolio is immensely useful from the perspective of certain classes of end users, those seeking ways to document student learning.

Eportfolio is a most disruptive technology—it offers to make learning outcomes visible as concrete "authentic" examples of student learning. What if this directly observable data supplanted the proxy data for institutional quality—prestige, reputation, and ranking? To assess colleges and universities based on outcome measures of student learning could well change the perception and public support of premier schools (National Commission on Accountability, 2005; Pascarella & Terenzini, 2005).

Clayton Christensen tells us not to expect innovation leadership from those privileged by the status quo. Dominant organizations rely on their current success and pursue refinement of what has made them successful rather than embark on risky innovation (Christensen, 1997). Examples of disruptive technologies spawned by up-and-coming organizations that "snuck up" on the market leaders abound—the tiny floppy disk that ultimately led to the overthrow of large Winchester drives for data storage is one. Google, and its simple search window that led an assault on the once comfortable world of the library, is another.

Christensen further argues that organizations with few slack resources are also unlikely to innovate; they focus exclusively on surviving day to day. Collective Action, however, may be a model of the kind of hybrid organization ideally suited to instigate change; it aggregates the slivers of free resource that adequately resourced partnering organizations are willing to devote to innovation. Collective Action shares risk capital and limits the exposure of contributing organizations so that it can pursue activities with a definite possibility for failure but the possibility for transformational success as well.

As an entity committed to disruptive innovation, Collective Action has a responsibility to experiment widely, gather and share information broadly and transparently, iterate rapidly, and seek to identify other organizations in need of support to change. By meeting regularly together as a pseudo-organization, Collective Action members take their insights back to their primary organizations and, through the strong organizational links within the institutions, can propagate change.

INSTITUTIONALIZING EPORTFOLIOS— A PHASED APPROACH

In *The Diffusion of Innovations*, Rogers (1983) describes characteristics of innovations that are positively related to diffusion (i.e., trialability, compatibility, relative advantage, and observability) and those negatively related to diffusion (i.e., complexity). His distinction between individual adopters and organizational adopters of innovation has much to do with the programmatic implementation of eportfolio systems.

Innovative individuals pursue the innovation across the initiation and implementation phases and ultimately adapt their behavior to take advantage of the changes offered by the innovation. Individuals adopt eportfolios when the system encourages low-risk, experimental use (trialability), is consistent with current attitudes and behaviors (compatibility), offers advantages to other ways of learning or meeting class requirements (relative advantage), and is easily demonstrated (observability). Intuitive interfaces with good documentation and support (reduced complexity) also encourage individuals to adopt eportfolio. The individual adopts when the relative advantage, scaffolded by trialability, observability, lack of complexity, and compatibility, has been convincingly demonstrated.

However, eportfolios must be adopted by organizations as well as by individuals. Organizational adoption differs from individual adoption because the adoption occurs as handoffs among different departments, often with very different definitions of relative advantage. For example, faculty members typically seek flexible, adaptive technology environments that mold to individual needs. In contrast, those responsible for administering the eportfolio system usually prefer standardized implementations noted for reliability, not flexibility. Low centralization, high complexity, and low formalization encourage organizations to experiment with innovation. Once past the initiation stage, high centralization, low complexity, and more formal reporting lines push the diffusion of innovation, a process much different than the pull that initially attracts those who initiate innovations.

Many promising efforts at change have been thwarted because champions do not properly package an innovation so that it is compatible with the value structures of those who must support the innovation once it has been introduced. If those who champion eportfolios for flexibility in encouraging learning cannot cast the relative advantage of eportfolios so that the technology organizations can address their operational and security needs, the innovation can never fully permeate the organization, and the new innovative practices will be discontinued (Rogers, 1983). Too many eportfolio projects fall victim to this organizational phase change when they try to move from pilot to institutionalization. Organizational innovation requires this awareness from the initiators, as well as the ability to accommodate the needs of the system maintainers as the use community grows.

REVISITING APPRECIATIVE INQUIRY

Initiators and maintainers both benefit from awareness of and immersion in the four stages of Appreciative Inquiry. The Collective Action process and the mechanisms through which shared eportfolio infrastructure can emerge can be mapped into these four key stages: discovery, dream, design, and destiny.

Stage 1: Discovery is mobilizing a whole system inquiry into a positive change core. Collec-

tive Action seeks to diffuse eportfolios not for the sake of eportfolios, but for the belief that learners and users will become better learners and more reflective thinkers. The appropriate starting place is the principal deliverable of the innovation in terms of the people positively affected, rather than in terms of the innovation itself. Literature on learning (Bransford, Brown, & Cocking, 2000; Bruner, 1986) justifies eportfolios. Deep learning juxtaposes features of eportfolios, including work, anchored feedback, iterative knowledge development, and testing and reflection, within a social system (Bruner, 1996).

Stage 2: Dream is creating a clear results-oriented vision in relation to discovered potential and in relation to questions of higher purpose. Having identified the core positive capacity of eportfolios, the dream quest becomes achieving a single overarching eportfolio system. Simply stated, the dream of Collective Action is to scale the eportfolio environment such that all Ohioans seeking its positive contributions to deep learning have access.

Stage 3: Design is creating possibility propositions of the ideal organization, an organizational design that people feel is capable of magnifying or eclipsing the positive core and realizing the articulated new dream.

Cooperrider and Whitney (1999) describe the design stage as critical for encouraging buy-in. In their words,

Once the strategic focus or dream is articulated (usually consisting of three things in our model—a vision of a better world, a powerful purpose, and a compelling statement of strategic intent) attention turns to the creation of the ideal organization, the social architecture or actual design of the system in relation to the world of which it is part. What we have found is that the sequencing is crucial, moving first through in-depth work on Dream before Design, followed with back and forth iterations.

To scale the eportfolio environment so that each Ohioan seeking deep learning has access requires us to answer the following questions: How do we pay for it, how do we establish policies that sustain it, how do we share the benefits accrued, and how do we catalyze the use so that it combusts? The main challenges in answering these questions are three: (a) We must convince local system implementers that the macro system can better serve their needs than dedicated local resources; (b) through appreciative inquiry we need to acknowledge, commend, and reify the contribution of all who collectively make the macro system operate; and (c) we must exchange and build information among the subsystems that is locally meaningful and not contradictory to local circumstance.

Collective Action is addressing these challenges through a set of actions and practices. These actions and practices are all important design elements for this initiative.

- Developing a pilot environment that grew from 40 to 61 institutions in 1 year
- Raising the issue with overlapping constituencies at conferences and meetings, systematically and continuously
- Offering an open source Sakai/OSP infrastructure
- Holding 10 regional workshops on creating a Student Success Plan, each sketched on an eportfolio template and linking individual student portfolios to the institutional success plans
- Offering two state conferences at which to celebrate the success of the schools creating the plans and of the students represented within them
- Establishing partnerships with commercial and noncommercial publishers so that content can be organized around learning objectives, the same pillars that scaffold and display student learning in eportfolios
- Promising to consult multiple times with colleges and schools needing portfolios to meet their objectives
- Creating transition portfolios based on composition, mathematics, and information liter-

acy to help individuals move from high school to college or from the workforce back into additional training and education by knitting school, work, and personal spheres together for lifewide and lifelong learning
- Acknowledging potential obstacles in the design stage, such as the reliability and usability of the infrastructure and software; issues of training users and community creators in mechanics, portfolio thinking, and uses; finding time to reflect; and getting sustainers to think about these issues and move on

Other sites will have different questions, challenges, and actions; but every eportfolio initiative needs to address design issues as central to the progress of that initiative.

Stage 4: Destiny is strengthening the affirmative capability of the whole system, enabling it to build hope and momentum around a deep purpose and creating processes for learning, adjustment, and improvisation over time.

The word *destiny* returns us to a central question: Where is the origin of the energy, purpose, and will needed to attain a risky vision? In 1997 Milt Hakel described a visit to Alverno College, which was engaged in a dynamic vision and set of practices regarding student learning:

The intensity and excitement we observe is mind-expanding, almost intoxicating. It shows possibilities. It opens up a hopeful future. It shows dramatically that there *is* a better way; that things don't have to be the way that they are. The joy of learning is plainly visible for anyone who takes the time to look for it. It isn't easy, and it isn't always pretty, but students are learning not just tons of facts but also how to go beyond knowing to being able to *do* what they know. Their confidence and self-assurance, resulting from genuine achievement, is marvelous.

Hakel (personal correspondence, 2007) reflects on why he still believes in the valued and achievable goal of making changes that affect student learning in positive ways:

> Experience at Alverno College shows clearly that educational institutions can change in ways that help people to change, that is, to discover, dream, design and transform their own capabilities. Student success at Alverno is an existence proof for the rest of us, and ePortfolio technology is an evolving tool that can strengthen the affirmative capabilities of educational systems and *all* their participants.

Learning from organizations inside and outside academia, Collective Action has carefully laid the groundwork for change to an eportfolio system that supports all Ohioans in their lifewide and lifelong learning. Collective Action is designed to, as Cooperrider and Whitney (1999) put it, "increasingly help people discover, design and transform toward the greatest good" (p. 257).

ACKNOWLEDGMENTS

Thanks to Barbara Cambridge, Cable Green, Catherine Gynn, Milt Hakel, Thom McCain, and Peter Murray for review, critique, and enhancement.

REFERENCES

Acker, S., Green, C., Murray, P., & Barber, D. (2006). *Accountability in higher education: Addressing the innovator's dilemma through authentic assessment.* Presented to the 2006 Educause ELI Conference, San Diego, CA.

Acker, S., & Halasek, K. (2008). Preparing high school students for college-level writing: Using ePortfolio to support a successful transition. *Journal of General Education, 57*(1), 1–14.

Amazon Corporation. (2007). *Amazon S3 Pricing.* Retrieved April 23, 2007, from http://docs.amazonwebservices.com/AmazonS3/2006-03-01/Pricing.html

Bransford, J., Brown, A., & Cocking, R. (Eds.). (2000). *How people learn: Brain, mind, experience and school.* Retrieved March 14, 2007, from http://books.nap.edu/html/howpeople1/

Bruner, J. (1986). *Actual minds, possible worlds.* Cambridge, MA: Harvard University Press.

Bruner, J. (1996). *The culture of education.* Cambridge, MA: Harvard University Press.

Cambridge, D. (2008). Audience, integrity, and the living document: eFolio Minnesota and lifelong and lifewide learning with ePortfolios. *Computers & Education, 51*(3), 1227–1246.

Christensen, C. (1997). *The innovator's dilemma: When new technologies cause great firms to fail.* Cambridge, MA: Harvard Business School Press.

Christensen, C., Baumann, H., Ruggles, R., & Sadtler, T. (2006, December 1). Disruptive innovation for social change. *Harvard Business Review, 84*(12), 94–101.

Cooperrider, D. (2000). AI and the conscious evolution of chaordic organizations. In A. Ramsey (Ed.), *AI Practitioner Newsletter.* Retrieved March 23, 2007, from http://www.aipractitioner.com/Pagefiles/10newsletter.htm

Cooperrider, D. (2001). Positive image, positive action: The affirmative basis of organizing. In D. Cooperrider, P. Sorensen, T. Yaeger, & D. Whitney (Eds.), *Appreciative inquiry: An emerging direction for organization development.* Champaign, IL: Stipes Publishing.

Cooperrider, D. (2004). *Advances in appreciative inquiry: Constructive discourse in human organizations.* Amsterdam: Elsevier Publishing.

Cooperrider, D., Sorensen, P., Yaeger, T., & Whitney, D. (Eds.). (2001). *Appreciative inquiry: An emerging direction for organization development.* Champaign, IL: Stipes Publishing.

Cooperrider, D., & Whitney, D. (1999). A positive revolution in change: Appreciative inquiry. In P. Holman & T. Devane (Eds.), *The change handbook: Group methods for shaping the future* (pp. 245–262). San Francisco, CA: Berrett-Koehler Publishers.

Dolence, M. G., and Norris, D. M. (1995). *Transforming higher education: A vision for learning in the 21st century.* Ann Arbor, MI: Society for College and University Planning.

Hakel, M. (1997). What we *must* learn from Alverno. *About Campus, 1*(4), 16–21.

Hawkins, B. (2006). *EDUCAUSE's grand challenge.* Presentation to the EDUCAUSE National Conference, Dallas, TX.

National Commission on Accountability. (2005). *Accountability for better results: A national imperative for higher education.* Retrieved March 28, 2007, from http://www.sheeo.org/account/comm-home.htm

Pascarella, E., & Terenzini, P. (2005). *How college affects students: A third decade of research* (Vol. 2). San Francisco, CA: Jossey-Bass.

Rogers, E. (1983). *Diffusion of innovations* (3rd ed.). New York: The Free Press.

Rosenberg, S. (2007). *Dreaming in code.* New York: Crown Publishers. Retrieved March 15, 2007, from http://www.dreamingincode.com/

Senge, P., Kleiner, A., Roberts, C., Ross, R., Roth, G., & Smith, B. (1999). *The dance of change: The challenges to sustaining momentum in learning organizations.* New York: Doubleday.

Spellings, M. (2006, November). *An action plan for higher education.* Retrieved March 10, 2007, from http://www.ed.gov/news/speeches/2006/09/09262006.html

Waldrop, M. (1996). *The trillion-dollar vision of Dee Hock.* Retrieved March 10, 2007, from http://www.fastcompany.com/online/05/deehock.html

Weatherhead School of Management at Case Western Reserve University. (2007). *Appreciative inquiry commons.* Retrieved March 8, 2007, from http://appreciativeinquiry.case.edu/research/bibPublished.cfm

15

A CATALYST WITHOUT A MANDATE

Building an Eportfolio Culture at the
University of Washington

TOM LEWIS and JANICE FOURNIER
University of Washington

The University of Washington (UW) has been in the eportfolio business for a comparatively long time. As a large, diverse public research university with more than 40,000 undergraduate, graduate, and professional students and almost 30,000 faculty, instructors, and staff spread across three campuses, UW could easily find eportfolios a natural institutional solution for tracking a student's progress through the university. Moreover, UW has been a leader in bringing technology into the service of teaching and learning: Its UWired and Catalyst initiatives received the first ever EDUCAUSE Award for Teaching and Learning.

So it may be surprising that when the Catalyst team began to develop an enterprise eportfolio in 2002 as part of the Catalyst suite of Web-based communication and collaboration tools, it did so without an institutional mandate. Building upon a conceptual framework provided by a group of faculty, advisors, and staff who wanted a tool to guide students through their university experience and with funding from the Student Technology Fee Committee—which was very supportive of eportfolios as a means to showcase work for potential employers—the Catalyst team sought and received

support and ideas from students, faculty, the advising community, and university administrators. These potential users were also deeply involved in the eportfolio design and development process.

The *Catalyst Portfolio* was released in fall of 2002 and by some measures has been a great success. At the end of 2006, more than 26,000 UW students had created almost 63,000 eportfolios. Over 1,600 faculty, advisors, or mentors had created almost 3,400 eportfolio projects for students to complete. Partners in the Center for Career Services, the Freshman Interest Group Program, the School of Nursing, the Honors program, the Department of Geography, the Carlson Center for Experiential Learning, the College of Education, the Information School, the School of Medicine, and the Expository Writing program had all attempted innovative and programmatic uses of eportfolios. Nevertheless, lacking an institutional mandate, this widespread usage and adoption has not yet led to a campus-wide eportfolio culture. Accordingly, the use of the eportfolio has varied: Many use eportfolios, some use them well, some use them not so well, and some have used them and given up entirely.

These disparate outcomes are rooted in the standby eportfolio ontological question: What is an eportfolio? For some, an eportfolio is simply a file management system, a place to put stuff. Very little reflection or self-expression is involved in these uses. Others see an eportfolio as an online scrapbook, a place for students to document their university experiences. Students, however, have lots of options for such documentation and seem to prefer Facebook, MySpace, and blogs. Also common is the view of an eportfolio as an official record of a student's work or as a means to assess learning outcomes, though whether students find any creative spark in assembling these sorts of mandated snapshots is an open question. For those who use eportfolios as part of a developmental or reflective process or in teaching and learning contexts, finding the sweet spot to support both faculty and students doing thoughtful and effective work can be difficult. Finally, a few users see an eportfolio as a giant hammer and go looking for nails—it is a course management system, a digital repository, a content management system. Whatever it is, it seems to no longer be a portfolio, electronic or otherwise.

Having created an enterprise eportfolio system, the Catalyst team has been uniquely positioned to address these challenges. Not strictly a technology group but also not solely positioned to support pedagogy, the Catalyst team helps UW faculty, instructors, students, staff, and researchers meet the daily demands of teaching, learning, research, or work with innovative and effective technologies and services. Catalyst offers Web-based tools, technology-infused learning spaces and facilities, and a host of knowledge services such as technology workshops, face-to-face consulting, Web-based "how-to" content, and original research on effective uses of technology. The tools and services are developed collaboratively, tapping the expertise of faculty, students, and staff, and Catalyst staff routinely work with central administrative units and with individual colleges, schools, and departments. Because almost everyone on campus uses one or another Catalyst service, this familiarity allows Catalyst researchers a certain freedom to do novel studies of Catalyst technologies.

To better understand how the Catalyst team might function on campus to raise awareness about eportfolios as well as to promote best practices, its researchers focused on a simple question: What are the skills students need in order to create successful eportfolios, and how are these skills best learned? The initial approach was to study exemplary portfolios as well as their process of creation by using a campus-wide contest to solicit examples of successful portfolios from undergraduates (created using the *Catalyst Portfolio* tool or other Web authoring software). The hope was to invite a wide range of student work, not just that limited to class projects, and to see what students selected as good work. A panel of faculty judges was assembled to award one grand prize as well as smaller prizes in three portfolio categories: professional, academic, and personal/reflective.

The entries received were instructive in their typology and purpose; out of 123 eportfolios submitted, only 4 (3%) were the type of "learning portfolios" most often promoted in the eportfolio literature. The vast majority (87%) were reflective portfolios created by students in Freshman Interest Groups, a program designed to help students orient to university life. As important, many of the best entries were professional portfolios created by students for prospective employers. As planned, we conducted follow-up interviews with contestants about their portfolio process; their observations sounded several themes:

- Students benefit from instruction on what an eportfolio is and how it differs from other Web-based presentations or written compositions.
- Students desire and appreciate clear criteria and feedback on what makes a successful portfolio for a specific audience and purpose.
- Students with experience in visual design and some level of technical expertise (i.e., knowledge of HTML) are able to maximize the communicative power of their eportfolios.

Clearly students see the value of eportfolios, and what the contest findings showed us is that both students and faculty need conceptual strategies for building eportfolios, actual examples, and a measure of technical training to support a culture of thoughtful and effective work.

Next, Catalyst researchers sought an opportunity to apply these findings to help a program just getting started with eportfolios. The Expository Writing Program (EWP) in the English department had used paper portfolios for years in their required beginning composition course, and there was interest in seeing what value might be added by moving to an electronic format. During the 2005–6 academic year, Catalyst researchers partnered with EWP to pilot the use of eportfolios in nine beginning composition sections.

EWP's prior use of paper portfolios made this program, in many ways, an ideal case for eportfolio adoption—the program already had in place clearly articulated course outcomes and a well-developed portfolio assignment. For the final portfolio, students select five to seven papers and write a cover letter explaining how these works demonstrate achievement of the course outcomes. The greatest challenge was figuring out how to train instructors to use the *Catalyst Portfolio* software. Upwards of 30 sections of beginning composition are offered each quarter, and nearly all are taught by teaching assistants (TAs) in their first year of appointment; many have no prior teaching experience, and even more have no experience teaching with technology.

To ease the work of adoption, the Catalyst team used the *Portfolio Project Builder* to create an eportfolio template that TAs could easily modify. The template, which closely matched the paper portfolio design, was then adapted for the Web—for example, distributing portions of the cover letter over several Web pages and asking students to demonstrate achievement of the course outcomes by linking to their assignments. Drawing upon their previous eportfolio studies, Catalyst researchers also designed scaffolding within the template to guide students in making a successful eportfolio for a specific audience and purpose. In addition, to give both instructors and students a sense of what a finished eportfolio might look like, the researchers created two different sample eportfolios based on student work using the project templates. Finally, the Cata-lyst team offered to conduct all training for students, ensuring that the training was consistent across the pilot sections. In the end this "technological help" included modeling best practices in teaching with eportfolios for the department.

The results of the EWP's pilot suggest that a transition from paper to eportfolios in beginning composition can have significant effects on both students' learning and instructors' teaching practices. In response to the eportfolio template, students wrote more and in greater detail about the connections between their work and the course outcomes than students completing paper portfolios. A portion of students independently included relevant images and links in their portfolios and modified the design of the pages (colors, typeface, etc.) to give their eportfolios a more personalized presentation. Participation in the pilot also caused instructors to reflect on their teaching practices. For instance, several sought ways to integrate the eportfolio earlier and more fully into their curriculum or to capture instructor or peer feedback on papers electronically so that it could be included and referenced in the eportfolio. Although this goal was not fully realized during the pilot, TAs and administrators also saw the potential of eportfolios to help students write for an audience beyond the classroom and to develop skills in visual rhetoric so they could develop eportfolios that resembled a multimedia project more than a simple electronic version of a traditional paper portfolio.

Like other successful program eportfolio projects at UW, what the EWP experience demonstrated is that the trajectory of adoption follows a typical pattern. In the beginning, early expectations were that the *Catalyst Portfolio* software should conform as closely as possible to the traditional paper portfolio model. With greater understanding of the functionality of the software, however, instructors began to see new possibilities for the technology beyond the constraints of the original assignment. Teaching and learning began a transformational process, as the pilot created a fledgling eportfolio culture. Another interesting lesson from the EWP efforts is that such a culture, albeit in a single but significant program, can be created without a mandate. In this case, a simple intervention, providing conceptual strategies, examples, and technical training, yielded significant benefits.

More generally across these two projects, what the Catalyst team has learned from its research is that critical activities can be carried out to support eportfolio adoption and the development of skills critical to creating successful eportfolios on any campus, mandate or no. They include the following:

- Be relentlessly inclusive in the design, development, rollout, or implementation of any eportfolio project, big or small, to create a sense of shared ownership among users.
- Commit to collaboration and iteration in developing curriculum, support strategies, and best practices as you attempt to create an eportfolio culture. Expect some failures.

- Faculty and students need flexible, multifaceted support strategies for the technology and for doing thoughtful work with eportfolios. Real, context-specific examples help. Models of meaningful, context-specific integration help.

As we have learned, eportfolios are no different from other types of portfolios in basic ways: You present yourself to a particular audience for a specific purpose in a way that is visually pleasing, organized, and concise. Successful presentation requires hard work, a range of skills, and guidance. A successful eportfolio culture also requires work and change. Although many times progress will necessarily be incremental, it will be progress, upon which future successes can be built.

16

DOCUMENTING THE OUTCOMES OF LEARNING

MILTON D. HAKEL and ERIN N. SMITH

Bowling Green State University

When Bowling Green State University (BGSU), a state-assisted, residential, doctoral-research intensive university in northwest Ohio with about 22,000 students, announced its aspiration to become the "premier learning community in Ohio and one of the best in the nation," many initiatives were launched. BGSU began implementing academic enrichment programs to improve student learning, including living learning communities and enhanced first-year programs; especially for these programs, documenting student learning outcomes is important.

Describing one major strand of BGSU's evolving and continuing efforts to become a premier learning community, this chapter focuses on the adoption and use of the Epsilen eportfolio system as a means for students to document their learning and performance, telling the story of a research study undertaken to investigate possible benefits of eportfolios to students and the university.

The story begins, as it has for so many higher education institutions, with the introduction of program assessment as a requirement of continued accreditation. As the first step in implementing university-wide program assessment in 1995, faculty members defined student learning outcomes in the majors. From the collected definitions, the assessment committee eventually identified seven university learning outcomes: inquiry, creative problem solving, valuing in decision making, writing, presenting, participation, and leadership (see http://www.BGSU.edu/offices/Assessment). Subsequently, the university used these learning outcomes while developing several learning communities and other student academic enrichment programs, as well as when redesigning its general education program. They also became focal elements in BGSU's eportfolio system.

In the late 1990s, the assessment committee began to consider eportfolios as a means for documenting student learning and outcomes. News from Alverno College and Kalamazoo College generated interest in conducting a pilot test, leading to licensing of the original version of Alverno's Diagnostic Digital Portfolio for use throughout the university. However, that venture was abandoned after 18 months due to incompatible operating systems and the lack of internal technical support.

An article in *The Chronicle of Higher Education* (Young, 2002) led to a revival of interest, and BGSU joined the ePortConsortium (http://eportconsortium.org) and licensed its Epsilen electronic portfolio software in 2003. In the Epsilen system, students can upload a variety of electronically rendered artifacts (e.g., papers, images, spreadsheets, presentations, video and audio recordings) as well as accompanying reflections about the artifacts, keeping them private (the default) or displaying them in a learning matrix or in a "showcase" that might be viewed, for example, by potential employers or graduate/professional schools. The assessment committee found the learning matrix of the Epsilen system to be an especially valuable feature—it is a two-dimensional grid for organizing uploaded artifacts, thereby providing a shared collection of evidence together with a common vocabulary for discussing progress, assessing learning, and describing student development. The Epsilen system also includes resumes, calendars, bookmarks to other Web sites, and secure file storage. Information about and examples of the BGSU electronic portfolios can be found at http://e-demo .with.bgsu.edu/.

The first use of eportfolios by BGSU students occurred in the 2003–4 academic year, with voluntary adoptions in a few first-year student programs and by interested faculty members. Early growth came through word-of-mouth endorsements among students (e.g., "my eportfolio got me an internship!"). Also, local technical support and improved stability of the software made it realistic to undertake a formal evaluation.

RESEARCH DESIGN

As a participant in the ePortConsortium and an early adopter of the Epsilen software, Bowling Green wanted to explore ways to document student learning longitudinally and across all programs. To evaluate whether eportfolio usage delivered the desired benefits, William Knight, director of institutional research and planning; Milton Hakel, chair of the assessment committee; and Mark Gromko, vice provost for academic programs, investigated how eportfolio usage related to several traditional measures of student success. Their preliminary study during the pilot year was expanded in the next year to examine the relationship between eportfolio participation and traditional measures of student success. They identified students having

Epsilen accounts in which at least one artifact had been uploaded (eportfolio group, $n = 821$) and contrasted these students with a stratified random sample (control group, $n = 821$), the strata being defined by college, class rank, and gender in proportion to the students in the eportfolio group. In addition, the eportfolio group was contrasted with a group of students (the "empty accounts" group, $n = 521$) who had opened eportfolio accounts but had not uploaded any artifacts.

Nine features of the eportfolio were examined. These included (a) the number of showcase artifacts (artifacts in the showcase version of students' portfolios), (b) matrix artifacts (artifacts in the learning matrix version of students' portfolios), (c) artifact-specific reflections, (d) general (or overall) reflections, (e) total files uploaded to the eportfolio, (f) events posted to students' eportfolio calendars, (g) bookmarks created in the eportfolio, (h) resumes uploaded to the eportfolio, and (i) the number of resume viewings recorded for each portfolio. Demographic data consisted of sex, race, age, college, class rank, academic status (good standing, dean's list, probation, suspension), living arrangements (on- or off-campus), high school grade point average, and ACT composite score. Educational outcome data included retention from the spring 2004 to the fall 2005 semester, cumulative grade point average, and student credit hours earned by the conclusion of the spring 2005 semester.

RESEARCH FINDINGS AND LESSONS LEARNED

Students in the eportfolio group showed significantly higher grade point averages than those in either the empty accounts group or the control group. Also, students in the eportfolio group had significantly more credit hours earned as compared with the control group. Finally, empty accounts students had earned significantly more credit hours than students in the control group. Retention rates to fall 2005 were significantly different between groups: The eportfolio group was retained at a higher rate than the empty accounts group, which had a higher retention rate than the control group.

The findings show that eportfolios may serve as a key tool for documenting student learning as defined by grades, number of credit hours earned, and persistence. Students who used the eportfolio system showed greater success, measuring success by traditional means. That makes it a "small win" (Weick, 1984), but it is a win nonetheless, one that has led in productive directions for the university.

Two research limitations are notable. The population of students with eportfolios, though considerably larger than the one used in the preliminary study, still represented a relatively small proportion of all students at the university and was skewed in terms of several demographic and educational factors. More importantly, because students' utilization of eportfolios at Bowling Green was and remains a voluntary activity, there is no way to control for differences in motivation between students with eportfolios and others when comparisons are made.

CONSEQUENCES OF THE RESEARCH

Consequences have been internal and external. Within the university the findings led to inclusion in 2005 of the Epsilen system in the suite of Web applications accessible through single sign-on in the university's portal. Streamlining access resulted in substantially increased faculty and student usage. For instance, the number of accounts grew from 250 at the end of the pilot year to 1,400 before inclusion in the portal. Eight thousand five hundred accounts were added the next year, and in 2006–7, our fourth year of implementation, the number of eportfolios accounts grew to over 15,000. There has been comparable growth in the number of uploaded artifacts.

Externally the findings sparked interest in the university. At the Ohio Board of Regents, the findings attracted support for a joint pilot project with Owens Community College to investigate how, through conveying tangible examples of student performance, eportfolios might support student transfer. Together with other program assessment work, implementation of the eportfolio system earned Bowling Green a 2007 Award for Institu-

tional Progress in Student Learning Outcomes from the Council for Higher Education Accreditation. The full submission is online at http://www.bgsu.edu/offices/assessment/CHEA.html.

NEXT STEPS

Bowling Green State University's implementation of eportfolios is still in its beginning stages. Although most students are aware of the eportfolio system and its benefits, its use is voluntary, as decided by individual faculty members. An important next step is for faculty to commit to using common criteria and rubrics to assess student learning. Although the assessment committee has developed prototype rubrics (see http://www.bgsu.edu/offices/assessment/Rubrics.htm), the rubrics have not yet achieved widespread adoption in courses. Another important next step will be to devise a closer integration between the course management system and the eportfolio system, making it easier to save and examine collections of student work for use in advising and also in program assessment (see Portland State's experience with this integration in Chapter 17).

Documentation of student learning outcomes has gained importance in the university's pursuit of its mission. Research findings to date show that using eportfolios can have positive impacts on those outcomes.

REFERENCES

Knight, W. K., Hakel, M. D., & Gromko, M. H. (2008). The relationship between electronic portfolio participation and student success. *AIR Professional File*, No. 107. Retrieved December 1, 2008, from www.airweb.org/page.asp?page=738&apppage=85&id=11

Weick, K. E. (1984). Small wins: Redefining the scale of social problems. *American Psychologist*, *39*, 40–49.

Young, J. R. (2002). E-portfolios could give students a new sense of their accomplishments. *The Chronicle of Higher Education*, *48*(26), 31–32.

17

SUSTAINING CHANGE THROUGH STUDENT, DEPARTMENTAL, AND INSTITUTIONAL PORTFOLIOS

KATHI A. KETCHESON
Portland State University

Organizational change at Portland State University, begun in the early 1990s and centered on general education reform, community engagement, and community-based learning, was realized in both academic and administrative areas of the university. Its initial success was owed, in large part, to a strong and charismatic president and an action-oriented leadership team that based its work in organizational theory and the scholarship of teaching and learning. Change agents emerged in various areas of the university, encouraged by the acknowledgment of the need for change and reconsideration of the university's mission articulated by the campus leadership.

Although not all members of the community supported the change or methods to carry it forward, few would deny that it had a profound impact on all aspects of the university. In 1998 a new president continued the direction of the change effort and expanded it to include international engagement and stronger ties to city and regional governments. Declines in state funding and advances in technology prompted the institution to pursue activities similar to those of an entrepreneurial organization, encouraging experimenta-

tion and risk taking in even the most traditional areas. Years later, the provost's planning initiative focused on engagement, and a faculty senate review recommended strengthening general education curriculum through clearer articulation of learning outcomes to connect general education and the disciplines.

Literature on organizational change emphasizes not only the importance of clear, directed leadership but also the critical role of individual change agents in defining, describing, and communicating the change to constituents. Portland State had change agents in place at a critical time in its history of financial crisis and the spread of the scholarship of teaching and learning and community engagement in the national higher education community. Three key factors prompted organizational change in the university: financial crisis that called for a new and almost revolutionary response; emergence of change agents in the campus leadership and across the campus; and participation in national conversations about community engagement, the scholarship of teaching and learning, and reform of general education.

PORTFOLIOS AS AN EXTENSION OF ORGANIZATIONAL CHANGE

The same three factors prompted the university to view portfolios as a vehicle for communicating its work in fulfillment of the new urban, community-based mission. During the 1990s, portfolios, at the student, department, and institution levels, became a key piece of Portland State's efforts to define and document the distinctiveness of its urban mission through example and reflection. Initially adopted independently by different parts of the university, the portfolios were a logical extension of the university's change effort. As the university moved into the next decade, it recognized that a richer and more complete picture of its activities in teaching and learning, research and scholarship, and community engagement could be communicated through a suite of portfolios accessible to a wide audience through the Internet.

Although the three kinds of eportfolios have different purposes, they are united by a common theme flowing from the institution's mission to promote student learning, conduct relevant research, and foster community and global engagement. Student portfolios were the first to be developed, emerging from the general education program as a method for authentic assessment of student work in the context of the program's four major goals. As Banta notes (2007), electronic student portfolios can "illustrate growth over time in generic as well as discipline-based skills." Although assessment in the departments and disciplines began as a grassroots effort that was not focused on overall learning outcomes for undergraduates, the advance of portfolio assessment in University Studies helped to stimulate a campus-wide conversation about the need to address the whole of the undergraduate learning experience, rather than individual pieces.

Student portfolios were followed closely in the timeline by the institutional portfolio (http://www.portfolio.pdx.edu/) and later by departmental portfolios (http://www.programreview.pdx.edu). These Web sites were developed and maintained by the institutional research office in collaboration with faculty committees and information technology advisors. The institutional portfolio, completed in 2001 as part of a national project, was focused on five themes that encompassed the university's mission: teaching and learning, research and scholarship, community and global connections, student success, and institutional effectiveness. As Barbara Cambridge notes (2001), electronic portfolios "offer ways to make meaning of information" (p. 3) and provide a means for turning information into knowledge. Representing the university's work at the highest level of analysis, the institutional portfolio served as a tool for learning about the university by communicating its assessment, reflection, and accountability efforts as interrelated activities within the larger context of its mission.

The concept of departmental portfolios was slower to take hold than the others, in part because some departments feared an administrative mandate resulting only in increased work for department chairs. The 2005 accreditation review by the Northwest Commission on Colleges and Universities, however, recommended that the university improve the consistency and clarity of assessment across the curriculum. For the accreditation self-study, a subsection of the departmental portfolios Web site had been devoted to assessment, comprising plans, goals and outcomes, tools, findings, and reflective narratives on the use of results to improve learning. Although the Commission applauded the subsection, it found the format difficult in drawing connections across departments and in identifying common learning goals and outcomes for undergraduates. Following the accreditation visit, a new faculty committee on assessment recommended a portfolio approach to begin a reconsideration of the overall structure of the departmental portfolios Web site.

STUDENT PORTFOLIOS

Initiated in 1994, University Studies has a theme-based, interdisciplinary curriculum spanning 4 years of undergraduate study, including the year-long Freshman Inquiry, Sophomore Inquiry, Upper Division Clusters, and the Senior Capstone. Community-based learning is a major component, reflecting Portland State's mission to let knowledge serve the city and its local, regional, national, and international communities.

As electronic student portfolios appeared on the national scene, students volunteered to prepare paper portfolios for faculty to pilot assessment techniques. Because the paper portfolios were not mandatory and not graded, they did not employ a prescribed format. As the process matured, faculty members developed a common template focused on the four program goals of communication, ethics and social responsibility, diversity of the human experience, and inquiry and critical thinking. Students provided examples of their work under each of the goals and included reflective essays on their learning. Additionally, the template allowed for creativity in design and presentation, reflecting each student's personal interests.

These portfolios were introduced first in Freshman Inquiry, with students who entered the university largely without prior college credit. Because Portland State's undergraduate student body consisted mainly of transfer students (60 percent), however, faculty teams worked to develop assessment rubrics to apply to evidence of learning under the four goals in a structured process at the end of each year. With a budget line in University Studies for portfolio development and assessment, faculty over time conceptualized portfolios spanning the 4 years of the program, engaging transfer students along the way through transfer transition courses at the sophomore and junior levels.

A major obstacle to this plan was the lack of a common technology platform for creation, storage, and retrieval of the portfolios. At the beginning of the effort, portfolios resided only on local area servers. Although in 2007 a single course management system was selected instead of an open source option that could provide both course management and assessment support, University Studies faculty did not abandon the goal of creating portfolios across the 4 years. In 2007 the program included eportfolio assessment of a fourth learning goal, international learning, in Freshman Inquiry and in Sophomore Inquiry as part of an international learning assessment project sponsored by the American Council on Education.

This experience with the loss of an open source option underlined the need for a champion outside of University Studies who could garner strong political support across the campus for electronic portfolios and the technology necessary to maintain them. From the outset, many departments regarded University Studies not simply as the university's general education program but as a separate department, competing with others for faculty, students, and resources. Just as the new technology platform was beginning to gain footing, the university experienced a number of administrative changes, resulting in interim positions in key areas. Attention moved away from the technological needs of portfolios (although recognition of their key role in student learning assessment was maintained), leaving them vulnerable to competing needs in other areas of the institution.

INSTITUTIONAL PORTFOLIO

In 1998, around the time that University Studies began to develop electronic student portfolios, Portland State joined five other urban universities in the Urban Universities Portfolio Project, a project conceived originally as a way to communicate the urban university mission to a wider audience and to address the need for changes in the accreditation process toward a greater emphasis on student learning. Portland State, Indiana University Purdue University–Indianapolis, University of Illinois–Chicago, University of Massachusetts–Boston, Georgia State, and California State University–Sacramento quickly decided that electronic portfolios were ideal for those purposes.

When institutional teams began designing the portfolios, they realized the powerful contributions of hyperlinking and Web-based information storage and retrieval. A guiding principle was that the work of an institution could be presented in context, specifically in the context of overall institutional mission, with a focus on self-reflection, analysis, and interpretation. A visitor to the portfolio would be able to make connections among institutional activities, such as teaching and assessment, research, community engagement, or planning and management, through hyperlinks and narratives supplemented by exhibits (including video or audio clips, photographs, samples of student work) that demonstrate rather than describe how the institution is addressing its mission (Kahn, 2001). Key to the information provided in a portfolio was the aspect of reflection, which allowed an institution to focus on continuous improvement and to place failure in context (Cambridge, 2001).

At Portland State, a team of faculty, working closely with institutional researchers, created a set of design principles and content outline for the eportfolio. Rejecting a Noah's Ark approach (i.e., one person from each part of the campus), leaders identified faculty who had demonstrated good practices in teaching and learning through activities sponsored by the teaching and learning center or who were known to be furthering the use of technology in their teaching and scholarship. Faculty participation was seen as key, for as Morse and Santiago (2000, p. 34) state, "Faculty leaders knowledgeable about outcomes assessment can and should take the lead in educating peers about assessment, in setting up institutional structures that facilitate the planning process, and in guiding assessment initiatives toward institutional change."

It quickly became clear that an active and creative team of faculty and institutional researchers was leading the institution toward development of an innovative approach to assessment, reflection, and accountability that would have broad acceptance across the campus. Faculty did what they do best—think and create—in partnership with institutional researchers who both participated creatively but also applied technical expertise in information architecture and communication to bring the group's ideas alive through the Web environment. Faculty told their department programs about their high level of participation in the process and about the powerful new approach to communicating the university's mission represented by the institutional portfolio. The eportfolio project became a model for faculty involvement in campus-wide initiatives, finding application in the creation of various administrative committees on topics such as advising and assessment (Ketcheson, 2002). The project also brought attention to the scholarly components of institutional research as a resource for the entire campus.

DEPARTMENTAL PORTFOLIOS AND ASSESSMENT

Departmental portfolios were intended for use in a newly designed program review process, in annual departmental accountability, and in budget planning. Institutional research provided the resources and personnel to create, support, and manage the Web site, while the vice provosts for undergraduate studies and for graduate studies worked through the dean's council to ensure departmental participation.

Data were organized under five criteria articulated by a subcommittee of the academic dean's council: mission, program, curriculum, faculty, and finances. Many departments took a portfolio approach to the Web site, offering a variety of examples and reflections on program goals and outcomes, whereas other departments included only broad mission statements, with no review or reflection on the provided data for their units.

The Center for Academic Excellence supported assessment at the grassroots level through a faculty committee focused on departmental pilot projects and encouraged discussion, debate, and information sharing. At the completion of these pilot projects, the president launched an Assessment Initiative. A faculty-in-residence for assessment was appointed within the Center for Academic Excellence to expand the grassroots effort.

Preliminary analyses conducted by an oversight group of assistant and associate deans found that this grassroots approach, allowing wide latitude for discipline or department-specific materials, often yielded learning goals similar to those of University Studies. Nonetheless, assessment remained a largely localized activity not connected with the larger context of undergraduate learning so that advancing a portfolio approach that could illustrate connections across the curriculum was not possible. Without a common purpose or central theme, the assessment process proved unsustainable and a different approach became necessary.

Following the accreditation visit, the university committed to articulate institutional learning outcomes for undergraduates by fall 2008. A new assessment committee formulated a process of achieving faculty approval for such a set of outcomes. A new format for the Web site would provide a top-level summary structured around institutional outcomes, with the rich, department-specific materials in the background providing detail about department-specific enactment of the outcomes and their own sets of disciplinary or program goals. With a more structured approach, the university anticipated making connections between general education and the majors and between generic and specific learning outcomes, and communicating publicly through a unified approach of student, department, and institutional portfolios.

PORTFOLIOS FOR ACCREDITATION

To use the institutional eportfolio as the self-study document of Portland State's latest reaccreditation review by the Northwest Commission, a new section in the existing portfolio Web site was organized as a series of narratives, one for each standard, containing links to documents or other Web sites. Student and departmental portfolios were linked to the self-study, giving the evaluation team access to materials from all three levels, while navigational features allowed access into the institutional portfolio as further evidence to support the self-study.

Rather than developing the self-study as a true portfolio, the administration felt that a hybrid model, somewhere between an electronic file cabinet and a portfolio of evidence and reflection, would have a better chance of a favorable review. This decision created, essentially, two documents in one: a thematic institutional portfolio and a more traditional standards-based self-study. Although hyperlinking enabled connections between the portfolio and the self-study, it also raised questions about the relationship of the two. Which should be viewed as the self-study, the portfolio or the narratives?

By using the portfolio as the self-study document, the university had hoped to pilot a new method of documenting assessment and account-

ability efforts that could be used for multiple purposes beyond the accreditation review. In this regard, success was only partially achieved. The standards-based approach did not look much different in the electronic and print forms, except that hyperlinks enabled more efficient access to materials in university Web sites. Given access to the student, department, and institutional portfolios, the visiting team did appreciate the ability to view most materials before the site visit.

Although the self-study used similar navigation, graphics, and layout to the institutional portfolio, it was based on narrative and differed in style and tone. Thus, it appeared to be sitting next to the portfolio, rather than composing a part of it. A thematic or special emphasis self-study may have been more conducive to the portfolio method and might have allowed the institution to use its successful experience in developing the institutional portfolio to advance the development of self-studies that better reflect the goals of student learning and continuous improvement.

EVALUATION OF EPORTFOLIO EFFECTIVENESS

One indication of the effectiveness of the student, departmental, and institutional eportfolios has been their frequent mention over time in the work of various campus committees. Committees addressing planning, assessment, and general education issues used the portfolios to provide background and evidence for their recommendations, sometimes suggesting new ways the information could be presented or used. Although at first, formal evaluation of the eportfolios at the university level was conducted only during the development stage, a systematic process was instituted in 2007 with a new planning initiative focused on accountability and assessment.

University Studies faculty regularly assessed the effectiveness of student portfolios in documenting learning and reflection. Because the portfolios were not initially mandatory, a pilot stage provided input from faculty and students on design, content, and uses. In addition, University Studies faculty participated in national organizations and projects to gather feedback and ideas with other institutions experimenting with portfolios.

For the departmental and institutional eportfolios, critical friends were engaged at various stages to provide feedback on portfolio drafts and final products. During initial stages of the institutional portfolio, a group of individuals representing a Web development firm and possible audiences for the portfolio, including K-12 and community college representatives and a former state senator, brainstormed about content and reviewed initial drafts. Faculty who were the heaviest users of institutional research, who were members of faculty senate, and who had served on institutional-level projects helped shape the portfolio and disseminate the concept across campus.

For the accreditation self-study, a set of critical friends from across the country received an electronic survey for use as they reviewed drafts of the eportfolio pages. Faculty and higher education professionals familiar with Portland State, these reviewers commented on how well the portfolios communicated information and helped users understand key activities supporting the university's mission. Feedback from the process was used to refine departmental and institutional portfolios for presentation to the evaluation team.

The effectiveness of the student, departmental, and institutional portfolios was subject to refinement during a planning initiative, including retooling the survey and developing periodic data collection on eportfolio effectiveness in communicating planning goals and university mission to various audiences. Results would be used in a transparent process of continual review and improvement available to a wide audience through the Web.

CONCLUSIONS

The change effort begun at Portland State in the early 1990s encouraged a variety of innovative approaches to teaching, learning, and assessment, including the adoption of portfolios at the student, departmental, and institutional levels. Resource scarcity and leadership shifts sometimes propelled

and sometimes hindered significant change. Organizational change, however, was sustained after key pioneers were gone, including the innovative adoption of eportfolios.

Embedding a portfolio approach into the culture of an institution takes time. The approach needs leadership, buy-in from faculty, and a clear purpose to be successful. Through the reflective process inherent in the portfolio approach, the university identified missing elements in program and departmental accountability and assessment of student learning outcomes and provided means for faculty members to see how their work fit within the larger framework of the institutional mission. Development of each of the three portfolio types involved collaboration among faculty and administrators and helped to create an improvement process across the campus.

At Portland State, the challenge of sustaining the portfolio approach over time will involve frank discussions about technical and financial resources and methods for ensuring that student learning remains at the forefront of departmental activities. Faculty and administrators must remain committed to the effort. The university has achieved substantial success in the implementation of student, departmental, and institutional eportfolios, and the lessons learned through these processes continue to inform the development of portfolio thinking across the campus.

REFERENCES

Banta, T. (2007). A warning on measuring learning outcomes. *Inside Higher Education*. Retrieved May 2, 2008, from http://www .insidehighered.com/views/2007/01/26/banta

Cambridge, B. L. (2001). Electronic portfolios as knowledge builders. In B. L. Cambridge (Ed.), *Electronic portfolios: Emerging practices in student, faculty, and institutional learning* (pp. 1–14). Sterling, VA: Stylus (originally published by American Association for Higher Education).

Kahn, S. (2001). Linking learning, improvement, and accountability: An introduction to electronic institutional portfolios. In B. L. Cambridge

(Ed.), *Electronic portfolios: Emerging practices in student, faculty, and institutional learning* (pp. 135–158). Sterling, VA: Stylus (originally published by American Association for Higher Education).

Ketcheson, K. (2002). Hands and minds: Collaboration among faculty and institutional researchers in Portland State University's Portfolio Project. *Metropolitan Universities: An International Forum, 13*(3) 22–29.

Morse, J. A., & Santiago, G. (2000). Accreditation and faculty: Working together. *Academe: Bulletin of the American Association of University Professors, 86,* 30–34.

SECTION FIVE

Electronic Portfolio Technology and Design for Learning

Since the publication of *Electronic Portfolios: Emerging Practices in Student, Faculty, and Institutional Learning* in 2001, one of the most dramatic transformations has been the new technologies developed to support electronic portfolio practice. As we suggest in the introduction to this volume, technology is moving from being solely a medium with which to compose portfolios to also serving as a venue in which to support the full process of composing, reading, and responding. This expansion of the role of eportfolio technology has provided portfolio teachers and assessors with new means to guide the portfolio process. As these means have been explored by members of the Coalition, both the potential of the new capabilities and the considerations needed to use them effectively are coming into focus.

Several key themes emerge from the research detailed in this section. First, the new technology provides opportunities to *for drilling down and linking up*, allowing programs and institutions to investigate student learning and institutional performance. Through analysis of work produced at multiple levels (by students, faculty, and organizational units) using multiple methods (quantitative and qualitative), focusing on aggregate patterns across a large group of portfolio authors, and producing thick descriptions of individual experience,

portfolios collected through the new technology environments provide rich resources for research and self-study. What was envisioned in *Electronic Portfolios* is now a reality: These multiple layers and methods can be linked together in the digital space, allowing researchers and readers to navigate between different levels of complexity.

Second, the greater variety of portfolio composition experiences offered by the new tools has reinforced the link between *design* and *deep learning*. While the capabilities of the technology have expanded, portfolio authors who thoughtfully take advantage of the characteristics of the digital medium still often have the highest-impact experiences. Effective visual, hypertextual, and multimodal composition seem to connect to a stronger sense of professional and disciplinary identity. Representing themselves visually and hyperlinking their work together into coherent wholes, students have enriched opportunities for critical reflection that can result in deeper learning.

Finally, the enhanced capabilities provided by the new technologies highlight the importance of clear *alignment between pedagogy and technology*. The kinds of scaffolding offered to students, both online and in the classroom, must match the context of portfolio learning. Some contexts require faculty to provide carefully structured guidance, whereas others necessitate that students have broad creative freedom. Because both the technology used to support portfolio practice and the pedagogy that guides student activity are now means for providing scaffolding, choices of technology and pedagogy must be made in concert.

Cara Lane's overview of eportfolio technology (Chapter 18) demonstrates the importance of context in making technology decisions. Lane shows how the University of Washington's research demonstrates that the best electronic portfolios are skillfully designed in a manner appropriate to their disciplinary and professional situation, leading to significant differences in both content and form. These differences have implications for the functionality eportfolio technology needs in order to support students in multiple programs across the university.

Lane provides a broad overview of the currently available technology options and the kind of pedagogies and assessment methodologies they best support, considering issues of ownership, flexibility, and accessibility. Ultimately, she suggests, no single tool may be able to serve in all contexts; we may need to work toward effective models for supporting the integration of multiple technologies. Although the technical means to achieve it are rapidly maturing, the need for integration may be obscured by the lack of attention to the student experience in much of the academic technology literature on eportfolios, which tends to focus on administrative and implementation issues rather than pedagogy. This focus obscures issues such as the importance of design, which are taken up by later contributors to this section.

Writing about their work in the English Department at the University of Georgia, Christy Desmet, June Griffin, Deborah Church Miller, Ron Balthazor, and Robert Cummings demonstrate the power of new electronic portfolio technology to support large-scale research (Chapter 19). Through analysis of a corpus of writing portfolios in first-year composition courses evaluated both by the faculty of record and by independent raters, they are able to demonstrate that although revision leads to improvement in writing, a result that was expected from earlier research, the dynamics of the relationship between revision and the quality of essays may be more complicated than the literature would suggest. They explore these complications through "drilling down" from numerical results, to qualitative coding of revision strategies, to an in-depth case study of one writer's revisions and reflections on the process. This analysis suggests that sometimes there may be a mismatch between the writer's "meta-rhetorical awareness" of the revision process, as demonstrated through reflection, and how well he or she is able to put this understanding of revision into practice. These results would have been difficult to achieve without the system's support of multiple levels of analysis.

In addition to the ability to drill down through multiple levels of analysis, new eportfolio technologies also enable the linking up of multiple levels of learning, as demonstrated by the work of the Minnesota State Colleges and Universities (MnSCU). Lynette Olson, Lori Schroeder, and Paul Wasko show how the software that supports eFolio Minnesota, a project that provides eportfolio infrastructure to all Minnesotans who choose to use it, was adapted to allow not only individual self-representation but also documentation of institutional learning and performance (Chapter 20). Although research had proven that the existing software is highly effective in supporting lifelong and lifewide learning for students, educators, and workers, new capabilities were needed to support institutional assessment and accreditation. Newly developed linking tools not only enable individuals to align the contents of their portfolios with disciplinary and professional outcomes but also make it possible for institutions to draw from this evidence to present a collective narrative of institutional performance that links to the standards of their regional accreditation agency. The authors develop a multiple stakeholder model to capture the complexity of this new challenge and examine the resulting questions for future research, including important issues of institutional readiness and culture that are investigated in the organizational learning section of this volume.

Although the institutional application of eportfolio technology is an exciting area of growth, many questions remain to be answered by the experiences of individual portfolio authors. Mary Zamon and Debra Sprague of George Mason University consider how the process of composing an electronic portfolio unfolds over time (Chapter 21). Through asking graduate students in education to record their decision making on "thinking sheets" as they composed their portfolios, the authors sketch a developmental process. As students learn to use new technology and strive to understand the portfolio genre, they begin with a focus on technical issues and are driven by the extrinsic demands of the portfolio assignment. As their facility with the technology and their understanding of portfolio practice grows, their focus shifts to issues of visual design and information architecture in service of a more intrinsically motivated representation of themselves as professionals. Zamon and Sprague deem the shift between these two orientations "the moment." As was the case with undergraduates at Washington, design and deep learning seem to go hand in hand.

Carl Young's research at Virginia Tech (Chapter 22) points to a similar central role for design in creating portfolios that help English education students develop their professional identity and critical consciousness. Students had traditionally produced portfolios to show their competence in relationship to professional standards, such as those of the International Society for Technology Education (ISTE). However, asking students to organize their portfolios primarily around these standards produced "evidence dumps" more often than sophisticated representations of "self as English teacher." Young shows how more explicit coaching and careful scaffolding of the process of composition led to electronic portfolios rich in critical reflection that more clearly articulate the students' individual visions of teaching philosophy and practice. As at Washington and George Mason, the strongest portfolios were often those that most powerfully embrace the digital medium. Young discusses compelling examples that use visual motifs and themes that unify the portfolio. Although the portfolios' structures are now determined by the students' visions of their identities, rather than the standards, the portfolios still prove effective in demonstrating competence. As is the case with the work of each of the institutions represented in this section, the redesigned portfolio program's success is the result of careful alignment of pedagogical practice and attention to the capabilities of technology.

18

TECHNOLOGY AND CHANGE

CARA LANE
University of Washington

"A pencil is technology. A chalkboard is technology. A book is technology." If you gather a group of educators together to discuss educational technology, someone will inevitably echo this refrain, observing that digital technologies are not the only ones that influence teaching and learning; everyday instructional items are also technologies that reconfigured education at some point in the past and continue to influence the choreography of teaching and learning to this day. So what distinguishes digital technologies from those that preceded them? The most obvious factor may be the most important: *time*. Although pencils, chalkboards, books, and other such technologies are characteristic components of today's institutions of learning, they no longer embody innovation; digital technologies are the ones changing the steps to the educational dance. Eportfolio technology represents one dancer on this crowded stage. In order to understand how this particular technology influences teaching and learning, it is important to view it as a figure of change, part of a larger transformative movement.

Eportfolio technology actively supports new pedagogical choices. The opportunities these tools provide for self-representation and publication coordinate with the ongoing shift in education toward a constructivist learning model (Brown, 2007). As students go through the process of creating eportfolios—selecting artifacts to include, writing about those artifacts, making design choices, and sharing their finished products with others—they are engaged in an active learning process. As our work at the University of Washington demonstrates, this process also provides an opportunity for students to develop Web and visual design skills, ultimately enhancing their digital literacy (Lane, 2007). Eportfolios are also integral components of educational strategies that promote accountability and authentic assessment, critical reflection and the integration of knowledge, and lifelong/lifewide learning. Taken in sum, the pedagogies supported by eportfolio technology represent a significant shift from traditional attitudes and practices.

Although eportfolio technology can facilitate all of the practices supported above, a particular eportfolio tool is unlikely to support each and every practice. The term *eportfolio tool* applies broadly to a variety of tools with very different characteristics. Some allow a uniform implementation across an entire institution, whereas others are infinitely customizable. Some are indistinguishable from personal Web sites, whereas others appear quite distinct from other types of online publication. At some colleges and universities, students even build eportfolios using Web-publishing software, rather than an eportfolio tool. What binds the various eportfolio tools together is that all provide a means for individuals to assemble materials, comment on them, and share them with others. However, the particular tool employed at an institution has a significant influence on pedagogical options: It can be an aid, enhancing traditional practice; a limitation, presenting obstacles to some activities; or a driver of change, making new options possible.

This section discusses the ways in which eportfolio technology influences, or has the potential to influence, teaching and learning. In the pages that follow, I discuss emerging eportfolio practice and provide more detail on current technology. I conclude with speculation on future eportfolio development. The other essays in this section continue this discussion by sharing case studies of eportfolio use at George Mason University, the University of Georgia, the Minnesota State Colleges and Universities, and Virginia Tech.

EPORTFOLIO PRACTICE

There are several popular definitions of *eportfolio*. In technical terms, "an eportfolio is a digitized collection of artifacts including demonstrations, resources, and accomplishments that represent an individual, group, or institution" (Lorenzo & Ittelson, 2005). More basically, an eportfolio consists of "evidence of curricular or cocurricular achievement and reflection" (Johnson & DiBiase, 2004). These definitions share a common understanding of an eportfolio as a collection of work assembled for the purpose of displaying accomplishments and demonstrating abilities. Some of eportfolios' commonly discussed manifestations include the following: accreditation eportfolios, which demonstrate the achievement of national, regional, or institutional standards; process eportfolios, which offer reflection on and documentation of the learning process; and showcase eportfolios, which summarize educational accomplishments and highlight professional skills. However, these common classifications do not adequately reflect the complex nuances of emerging eportfolio practice. For instance, when used over time, eportfolios may move between the three categories of accreditation, process, and showcase previously outlined. The work of I/NCEPR also reveals eportfolios as fertile sites for research, providing investigators with new options for accessing and analyzing student work in order to better understand the learning process. Similarly, the public aspect of eportfolios raises the possibility that these tools could become vehicles for academic and professional networking. The range of topics covered within the previous sections of this book reflects the expansive scope of eportfolio practice: from Kathi Yancey's essay on the many forms of reflection to Helen Chen's discussion of eportfolios as sites of lifelong and lifewide learning.

The essays in this section provide further examples of emerging eportfolio practice. At George Mason University, Mary Zamon and Debra Sprague have come to understand revision not only as a component within an eportfolio but also as a critical variable in the process of a creating an eportfolio. At the University of Georgia, Christy Desmet and other members of the research team found that the repository of work and reflection captured by their program's eportfolio system allowed them new opportunities for investigating the role that revision plays in student learning. The Minnesota State Colleges and Universities has expanded its software to allow for such investigations in learning processes and outcomes on an institutional scale. Finally, Carl Young, while at Virginia Tech, learned that eportfolios can help beginning teachers identify themselves within a field of practice. In his essay, Young highlights the importance of providing opportunities for self-expression within accreditation eportfolios. Similarly, researchers at George Mason University found that students spent considerable time during the eportfolio creation process thinking about visual design and the organization of materials within its eportfolios. The University of Georgia research team plans to continue their research by analyzing in more depth the role that the *e* in *eport-folio* plays in the revision process.

Our research at the University of Washington also emphasizes the importance of Web and visual design elements within eportfolios. As Tom Lewis and Janice Fournier discuss in their essay on organizational thinking, the University of Washington does not have an eportfolio mandate (see Chapter 15). Instead, various instructors, students, and departments on campus choose to use eportfolios on their own initiative. Our review of entries in the 2005 Catalyst eportfolio contest demonstrated how substantially disciplinary interests shape the look, feel, and contents of eportfolios: Entries submitted by art students were rich in visuals and spare in verbal descriptions, those submitted by new students in the University's Freshman Interest Group Program were informal and personal in nature, and graduating seniors in Technical Communication created technically sophisticated eportfolios to demonstrate their mastery of desirable skills in their field. Our interviews with 12 contestants also emphasized the importance that students placed on the look, feel, and behavior of the eportfolio, in addition to the consideration they gave to content. In sum, our research highlighted the multiplicity of eportfolio practice: On one hand, we saw a variety of uses of eportfolios at one institution; on the other hand, we saw the numerous components within eportfolios that required consideration.

Eportfolio practice is flexible and varied, making it challenging to come to a shared understanding of what is meant by *eportfolio*. It is important to recognize that eportfolio practice undergoes constant changes, with new ideas and issues coming to the forefront and demanding consideration. Although they were central themes for some disciplines that pioneered portfolio practice, such as rhetoric and composition, the emphasis on self-expression and design that threads through this section was not a major talking point in eportfolio discourse in academic technology circles a few years ago. We can anticipate that as eportfolio practice continues to develop, new topics will dominate pedagogical and technological discussions.

EPORTFOLIO TECHNOLOGY

The basic structure of an eportfolio—a collection of digital artifacts and commentary about the collection—can be produced using a wide range of software. What eportfolio tools provide are features that simplify the creation process and enable additional types of interactions, such as file management and feedback loops. Even though eportfolios may look like conventional Web sites, they offer much more: "The ePortfolio author should be able to organize and manage documents stored on the Internet and control access without knowing how to use HTML or build Web pages" (Greenburg, 2004). What make eportfolios unique are these types of added features. However, eportfolio tools differ widely in the features they provide and, thus, the practices they support. Some of the elements that distinguish eportfolio tools from each other are their source of production, the scale of adoption they best support, and the basic pedagogical philosophy that influenced their design.

One fundamental breakdown among eportfolio tools involves their source of production. Commercial vendors, open source project teams, and home-grown development shops all produce eportfolio tools—with commercial vendors developing the majority of widely available tools. Commercial tools come in a variety of types and configurations, but most are sold as an eportfolio package, which pairs a tool that enables students to build eportfolios with a combination of the following services: customization to suit the school or program, report generation, technical support, and/or hosting. This combination makes commercial eportfolios large-scale endeavors, similar to implementing course-management systems. Indeed, some purveyors of courseware, such as Blackboard and ANGEL, have recently entered the eportfolio market, selling the latter product as an add-on to their course systems. On the other hand, open source eportfolio tools are designed within an educational context and are not subject to profit pressures of commercial ventures. The most well-known eportfolio venture of this type is the Open Source Portfolio (OSP), which pools resources from several educational institutions through the larger Sakai Foundation to sustain a larger development effort than any one institution could do alone. Open source projects, such as OSP and Sakai, benefit from a commitment to educational practices and needs and a philosophy of openness and free access but tend to have a slower development timeline than their commercial counterparts. Not all university development efforts occur as part of an open source consortium; some institutions choose to build eportfolio tools on their own. The University of Washington created an eportfolio tool as part of a suite of communication and collaboration tools; the University of Denver built a system featuring a large rubric library; and the University of Nebraska–Omaha developed a database-driven tool meant to help users demonstrate learning over time (Lorenzo & Ittelson, 2005). Another option for creating eportfolios is to use Web-authoring software or similar presentation software. This option may be the only one that exists for users in departments or at institutions without an eportfolio tool in place.

The scale at which eportfolios are adopted varies widely by institution. They can be adopted by an individual, a course, a department, a university or college, or a university system. When an eportfolio is widely adopted, it enables various benefits to be realized: simplified technology training (only one tool to learn), opportunities for analyzing a large quantity of student work for assessment and research purposes, and interactions across a large community. Currently, the wide-scale adoption of an eportfolio tool tends to be driven by assessment and accreditation needs. Indeed, the eportfolio literature in academic technology reflects this trend, with the majority of published articles discussing administrative concerns and relatively few conveying students' perspectives (Ayala, 2006). TaskStream and LiveText are two popular eportfolio tools that were specifically designed to provide wide-scale assessment and accreditation support. Students use these types of eportfolio systems to connect their work to national, regional, and local standards, which then allows administrators to run complex reports documenting student achievement. In addition to measuring student progress, the widespread adoption of an eportfolio system can also be used to help build community and to sustain lifelong learning. The use of eFolio by Avenet in the state of Minnesota is an example of a program motivated by these goals; it makes an eportfolio tool available to all residents of the state of Minnesota (MnSCU 2007; Chapter 20). Darren Cambridge's (2008) research on the use of eFolio Minnesota found that the program was able to reach a wide user base beyond educational institutions. Cambridge found, however, that the community-building aspects of this eportfolio project could be further enhanced with new features and practices that helped connect eportfolios to a larger audience and practices that foster collaboration.

There are also drawbacks of large-scale adoption. The most notable is that one tool may not fit all uses. As our research at the University of Washington demonstrates, students in various disciplines do vastly different things with eportfolios. With the current generation of tools, it is unlikely that the same tool would have the robust visual support that art and technology students need, as well as the easy-to-use interface required by students in nontechnological courses, such as first-year composition. Indeed, at the University of Washington we found that the former group of users appreciated the technical control that Web-authoring software or hand coding allowed them, whereas users in the latter category were well supported by templates within the Catalyst portfolio tool. However, when a variety of tools are in play, much of the eportfolio use at a university may be invisible to the larger university community without a larger effort, such as a contest, to bring it to light. San Francisco State University (SFSU) is working to address this problem by providing centralized information and resources to support numerous eportfolio tools, including eFolio by Avenet, the KEEP toolkit, TaskStream, and individuals building eportfolios on the University's Web space (San Francisco State University, 2007). Because many (if not most) institutions are using multiple tools, this effort provides a useful model of diversity of use coupled with a mechanism for communication and collaboration.

EduTools, a project of the Western Cooperative

for Educational Telecommunications, recently conducted a review of seven popular eportfolio tools, cosponsored by EPAC. The project, for which I was one of the reviewers, focused on identifying and categorizing the different features available with various tools (EduTools, 2007). During the reviewing process, I observed that the locus of control varied between tools: Some gave students nearly complete control over their eportfolios, others allowed instructors to extensively scaffold the eportfolios for their students, and still others gave the majority of control to the program, department, or institution. For example, with eFolio by Avenet, students maintain control over their eportfolios as they proceed through their course of study and enter the professional world. This approach supports a constructivist model of learning where students create content and share it with others. On the other hand, Blackboard and ANGEL, two tools designed to complement course management systems, give considerable control to instructors. In these tools, instructors have the ability to create unique eportfolio templates for the specific courses they teach. This approach supports a pedagogical model where many decisions about course content and assignments are made by individual instructors for individual courses. In contrast, accreditation tools, such as TaskStream and LiveText, set the locus of control at a program, department, or institution level. Choices about how eportfolios will be used and structured are likely to be made for several courses at once. Due to the configuration and customization process that accompanies the implementation of OSP, this tool also tends to be controlled at a higher level, although individual instructors with the training and resources to set up the tool on their own, or who purchase the r-smart group's hosted version, can use it independently.

Although the tools described above tend to best support different types of use, the distinctions between them are beginning to blur. Eportfolio development shops, whether commercial or university-based, recognize the diversity of eportfolio practice and are introducing features that support multiple uses. For example, while eFolio's focus remains on student use and student control, the tool also provides new features that enable departments and institutions to develop templates for students. However, students still maintain ownership of their eportfolio and can reconfigure, update, and repurpose the contents over time. Similarly, during the course of its development OSP has added features for personalization to a tool that began as an institutional matrix-style eportfolio (Coppola, 2006). At the University of Washington, our research has shown the need to enhance the design choices and multimedia capability available in our eportfolio tool in order to further support students' development of design and multimedia skills. Technological flexibility of this sort will become increasingly important as eportfolio practice continues to evolve.

FUTURE DEVELOPMENT

Many current challenges of using eportfolio technology are likely to become easier over time, as two technological developments carry forward: (a) tool developers continue to add new features to meet a variety of users' needs and (b) support continues to grow for IMS standards that would increase compatibility among tools, thus allowing users to easily move work from one tool to another. The first development would enable users with differing needs to find whichever tool is available to them generally useful, whereas the second may eventually make the debate about using one eportfolio tool or many a moot point (Cambridge, 2006). If such industry standards are adopted, some eportfolio tool developers may even choose to create tools that provide rich features to suit a particular type of use (such as a tool aimed at art students or one for individuals presenting professional skills), knowing that users could easily utilize a different tool to meet other eportfolio needs. Conversely, we may find that one tool, or a suite of complementary tools, becomes dominant as flexibility of application (one tool addressing many needs) shapes future development efforts.

Given the current interest in design and digital literacy, as highlighted in the essays in this section, the future eportfolio tools are likely to add features to support a variety of presentation options. At the same time, evolving eportfolio practice is likely to place new demands on this technology. One possibility that I/NCEPR members have contemplated, through discussions of Darren Cambridge's work in this area, is the use of concept maps. These maps—a weblike array of connected nodes—introduce radically different options for structuring content and showing relationships between ideas than those available in current eportfolio tools. If this trend grows in popularity, new technological options will emerge to support this practice. In addition, if and when the goal of using eportfolios to support lifelong and lifewide learning becomes mainstream, these tools will need to find ways to support an array of practices from social spheres beyond educational contexts. These possibilities remind us that eportfolios in the future may look and act quite differently than the eportfolios we use today.

REFERENCES

Ayala, J. (2006). Electronic portfolios for whom? *EDUCAUSE Quarterly, 29*(1), 12–13.

Brown, M. (2007). Mashing up the once and future CMS. *EDUCAUSE Review, 42*(2), 8–9.

Cambridge, D. (2006). Integral ePortfolio interoperability with the IMS ePortfolio specification. In A. Jafari & C. Kaufman (Eds.), *The handbook of electronic portfolio research* (pp. 234–247). Hershey, PA: IDEA Group.

Cambridge, D. (2008). Audience, integrity, and the living document: eFolio and lifelong and lifewide learning with ePortfolios. *Computers & Education, 51*(2), 1227–1246.

Coppola, C. (2006). *Understanding the Open Source Portfolio, version 2.1, 2.2.* Retrieved May 18, 2007, from http://bugs.sakaiproject.org/confluence/download/attachments/22304/understandingOSP-October2006.pdf

EduTools. (2007). *ePortfolio: EduTools ePortfolio review.* Retrieved on May, 18, 2007, from http://eportfolio.edutools.info/static.jsp?pj=16&page=HOME

Greenberg, G. (2004). The digital convergence: Extending the portfolio model. *EDUCAUSE Review 39*(4), 28–37.

Johnson, G., & DiBiase, D. (2004). Keeping the horse before the cart: Penn State's eportfolio initiative. *EDUCAUSE Quarterly, 27*(4), 18–26.

Lane, C. (2007). The power of "e": Using eportfolios to build online presentation skills. *Innovate, 3*(3). Retrieved May 18, 2007, from http://innovateonline.info/index.php?view=article&id=369

Lorenzo, G., & Ittelson, J. (2005). *An overview of eportfolios. The EDUCAUSE Learning Initiative.* Retrieved May 18, 2007, from http://www.educause.edu/LibraryDetailPage/666?ID=ELI3001

San Francisco State University. (2007). *ePortfolio: Academic technology SF State.* Accessed on May 18, 2007, at http://eportfolio.sfsu.edu/faq.php

19

RE-VISIONING REVISION WITH EPORTFOLIOS IN THE UNIVERSITY OF GEORGIA FIRST-YEAR COMPOSITION PROGRAM

CHRISTY DESMET, JUNE GRIFFIN, DEBORAH CHURCH MILLER, RON BALTHAZOR, and ROBERT CUMMINGS
University of Georgia

In search of a more authentic method of final assessment, the University of Georgia First-Year Composition (FYC) Program replaced its traditional 3-hour, high-stakes final examination with an electronic portfolio of selected writings completed during and developed from the course (see Barrett, 2007; Estrem, 2004; Huot, 2002; Yancey, 1999). The eportfolio emphasizes revision, including two revised essays; reflection, including a reflective introduction, exhibits of the writer's composing/revision and peer review processes, and a personalized "wild card" exhibit; and audience awareness and collaboration, including evidence of peer review and double instructor ratings.

Although the pedagogical benefits of the eportfolio were intuitively apparent to many FYC teachers, the electronic writing environment that we use to collect, share, and comment on documents also allows the FYC Program to research and assess our eportfolio-based pedagogy. The "front" end of the EMMA™ application is a familiar-looking word processor; the "back" end is a continually growing database of electronic documents (544,947 as of June 1, 2007). Students do their work in the OpenOffice word processor; they then upload their documents to the EMMA database through a simple Web interface, much like that used to attach files to an e-mail. Students and teachers can then read documents online or print them out. They can also download the documents for comment or revision in OpenOffice. Thus, if teacher and students use EMMA regularly throughout the semester (and an ever-increasing number do), the database offers a rich record of student writing practices. As important, because the database marks each document with a time stamp and never overwrites previous drafts, as a word processor does, we have the potential to follow a student's drafting and revision process without introducing research regimens that might disrupt the normal progress of the student's writing experience (Pullman, 2002).[1]

In the field of rhetoric and composition, process pedagogy has long emphasized the importance of writing as revision. Still, there is a range of views: Some researchers (e.g., Bridwell, 1980) call into

Figure 19.1. Front Page of an EMMA™ ePortfolio for first-year composition.

My classes   My documents   Class documents   Course materials   My profile   Help   My archive   Logout

Claire Paffenhofer

My name is Claire Paffenhofer and I was born in Savannah, Georgia, home to oak trees that stretch out and canopy the road as far as you can see. In Savannah I remember sitting in the back seat of my dad's car and looking out the window to see the trees fly by. Nowadays, having two decades behind me, I live in Athens, GA on Pulaski Street, in a forested neighborhood that reminds me of Savannah. I am only child. My mom is from Alabama and my dad is from Germany, so I grew up on foods ranging from cornbread to rouladen. I am a freshman at the University of Georgia, majoring in English. I love to read and soak-in literature. One Hundred Years of Solitude by Gabriel Garcia-Marquez is my favorite novel. One day I hope to be an editor for a literary magazine or even translate texts from German into English.

Reflective Introduction
Paper 3 - "Atmosphere in Athens Coffee Shops"
Paper 4 - "Logos, Ethos, and Pathos in 'Majoring in Debt' by Adolph L. Reed"
Composing Exhibit
Peer Review Exhibit
Wild Card - Poem

question revision's efficacy; others (e.g., Harris, 1989) think that some writers are single-draft writers whose work is not improved by revision; and still others (cf. Beach, 1976; Perl, 1979) have found that with revision, students' writing might get even worse. Nevertheless, between early studies of composing and the present, a healthy body of work on revision has evolved.[2] Earlier studies that focused primarily on drafts and documents, as our study does, tended to contrast experienced and student writers, or expert and novice writers. Richard Beach (1976) established the idea that weaker writers tend to evaluate their writing on a surface level (defined as proofreading activities), whereas stronger writers employ a more comprehensive approach that takes account of form and content. In her landmark study, Nancy Sommers (1980) found that student writers made local changes, whereas experienced writers made global, holistic revisions of their texts. Building on Sommers's findings, Lester Faigley and Stephen Witte (1981) developed their own taxonomy for defining revision changes, based on "whether new information is brought to the text or whether old information is removed in such a way that it cannot be recovered through drawing inferences." Studying the revision process through writers' successive drafts, they determined that advanced writers made more revisions than inexperienced writers (including more surface corrections) but also made more meaning changes than their inexperienced counterparts. Distinctions among these three kinds of revisions—surface revisions, local meaning-based revisions, and global meaning-based revisions—established by these early studies provide a starting point for our use of EMMA to study student revision in FYC.

THE STUDY AND FINDINGS

The current revision study poses two questions. First, *does* revision improve the written products submitted in FYC eportfolios? Second, *how* do the most successful and least successful writers describe their own revision process, and what insight into that process can their observations give us? To investigate whether revision improves the quality of students' written products in the FYC eportfolio, we focused on a single measure. From a pool of 5,000 essays uploaded to the EMMA server in fall 2005, we chose 450 "before" essays (submitted for a grade during the semester) and 450 "after" essays (submitted as part of the final eportfolio, as in Figure 19.1). It is important to note that the student writers had already taken these documents through several drafts and cycles of revision and had submitted them for grades in their FYC classes. After choosing to include these specific essays in their eportfolios, students then had

Figure 19.2.

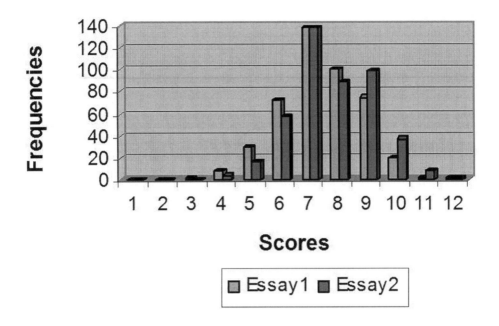

Distribution of Scores

an opportunity (but were not required) to revise the essays further, producing the polished eportfolio documents that we considered as the "after" essays in our study.

Trained, anonymous raters used a 6-point scale (EMMA "Research Initiative Rating Scale") for blind ratings of the documents; the scale reflects the criteria of the program grading rubric but is not identical to it (Figure 19.2). Between the "before" (Essay 1) and "after" (Essay 2) documents, we found a statistically significant improvement in the assigned ratings by holistic raters. For Essay 1, the mean score was 7.36 (in a range of 2–12 possible points), and for Essay 2, the mean score was 7.74. On average across the 450 essay pairings, ratings increased by .38 points.[3] Using this data, we

feel confident that if we were to rate paired essays written by the entire population of FYC students, we could expect the mean improvement to be between .25 points and .50 points on a 12-point scale.

More specifically, 46 percent of the essays revised for the EMMA ePorts ("after" essays or Essay 2) improved by 1 or more points out of 12; 28 percent remained the same; and 26 percent declined by 1 or more points. Table 19-1 shows the distribution of improvement scores (IMP) that were calculated by subtracting the combined scores for "before" essays from the combined scores for "after" essays.

The students who earned lower scores (fewer than 8 on the 2–12 scale) on Essay 1 were more likely to improve their Essay 2 scores, and those with

Table 19-1. Distribution of Improvement Scores

IMP	−5	−4	−3	−2	−1	0	1	2	3	4	5
Freq	1	0	3	27	86	125	121	65	14	7	1
%	0.22	0.00	0.67	6.00	19.11	27.78	26.89	14.44	3.11	1.56	0.22
%				26.00			27.78			46.22	
				Decreased						Increased	

high scores (8 or more points) on Essay 1 were more likely than their less successful peers to receive lower scores on Essay 2, a statistical regression effect (and therefore not significant for our results). Furthermore, those students whose scores decreased generally did so only by 1 point (19.1 percent out of the 26 percent that decreased in their scores), whereas a much larger percentage of students (44.44 percent) made modest gains of 1–3 points out of 12.[4]

While the sheer scope of the EMMA database allowed us to work with large numbers of student essays for the first phase of the study, the collection of class documents in a single electronic "place" also allows us to "drill down" through the collected documents and portfolios of any given student and to examine in some detail both the changes in individual documents and the rhetoric of reflection that provides a context for the students' revised essays. For the second phase of the study, we selected from the 2005 research sample the five students whose essay ratings increased the most and the five whose ratings decreased the most. Successful revisers began with essays ranging between 5.3 and 8.6 on the 2–12-point scale. After revising, their scores increased by between 3.3 and 5 points each. As previously indicated, unsuccessful revisers started with essay ratings a little higher than their more successful peers (their ratings began between 8 and 10); their scores decreased by between 2 and 3 points after the students had revised their essays for inclusion in the portfolio.

To analyze the "before" and "after" essays of our 10 selected students, we decided to use the coding system developed by Faigley and Witte (1981) because their system fits well with the first phase of the study, which focuses on the quality of student writing based on a range of content, rhetorical, stylistic, and presentational criteria derived from the program rubric. This coding system enabled us to quantify the number of changes that were added to or deleted from text as well as changes that rearranged, distributed, or consolidated text; the system also allowed us to note two other changes: whether those changes preserved or introduced a change to the meaning of the original and whether they were changes in microstructure (local meaning) or macrostructure (global meaning).[5]

Both successful and unsuccessful writers made more microstructural changes (meaningful changes on the local level) than any other kind of change. Unsuccessful writers made fewer surface changes; most surprising is that they made fewer than half the number of formal changes as their most successful peers (see Table 19-2). These results—specifically, the centrality of microstructural changes for both successful and unsuccessful writers—go somewhat against the conclusions drawn by both Faigley and Witte (1981) and Sommers (1980). Further analysis revealed more surprising results in our research sample, particularly concerning the impact of formal changes on essay ratings. For instance, one of the most successful revisers, a student whose essay rating increased 4 points on the 2–12-point scale, made only 11 changes to his text, all of them formal. It is worth noting that of the 11 formal changes, 7 were paragraph breaks—the original 1,112-word essay was a single paragraph. What a difference a paragraph break makes!

A SNAPSHOT OF ONE WRITER

The students whose ratings decreased also defied expectations established by composition research and lore. One student, who is the focus of the rest of the chapter, made a high number of meaningful revisions—including the greatest number of macrostructural changes made by anyone in the study (6)—but the essay lost 2 points in the process.

Table 19-2. Frequencies of Combined Revision Changes per 1000 Words in Final Drafts

	Formal Changes	Meaning-Preserving Changes	Microstructure Changes	Macrostructure Changes
Successful Revisers	6.7	8.7	14.4	4.7
Unsuccessful Revisers	3.3	7.9	22.8	6.8

In the "before" essay, a thematic analysis of the film *American Beauty*, the student discusses the ways in which all of the characters contributed to what she argues is the theme of the movie: "*American Beauty* is about the American dream gone wrong and the search for happiness outside of materialistic objects . . . It illustrates the way that the American Dream can cause a person to live a shallow, materialistic, and unfulfilling life." In the "after" or eportfolio essay, she continues to explore this theme, now focusing primarily on a single scene as a means to support her claim about the movie. The student revised the essay radically, cutting two paragraphs from an eight-paragraph essay and writing two new paragraphs to replace them, in addition to making numerous other changes (31 per 1,000 words, compared to an average of 22.8 for unsuccessful revisers and 14.4 for successful revisers).

The student explains her decision to shift the revised essay's focus to a single scene in the Reflective Introduction to her eportfolio (see Figure 19.3 and 19.4). She complains that in the original essay, "The illustrations are very basic and do not illustrate the theme as deeply as possible," whereas the focus on a single scene "is a more accurate representation of the abstract ways the theme is displayed in the movie because it forces me to examine a specific scene very closely, looking for small examples that represent a larger idea." Her critique of the "before" essay is accurate: it contains a number of unsupported assertions about characters' feelings and motivations. The "after" essay gives a great deal of detail but fewer global guideposts about the meaning of these details. For example, the writer deletes four important global ideas (e.g., "The other characters in the film are also seeking happiness. All of them subconsciously realize they are not

Figure 19.3. Revision exhibit.

Revision Introduction:

Below is an example of my revising techinques. For this particular essay, I was asked to perform an in-depth examination of a movie. I chose the movie *American Beauty*. Here, I have traced my development of the theme of American discontent as portrayed in the movie. The selections show my development from writing about this theme in my initial journal to my final draft, which is included in this portfolio. It shows how I was able to go from talking about the theme in very general terms with no specific examples to illustrating the theme within a very specific example. This theme is a very abstract concept that requires a lot of in-depth thinking. Although I always understood the way that *American Beauty* portrayed the idea of American discontent in my head, I was having trouble illustrating it through my writing. As I go further in my drafts, I begin develop this idea on this abstract theme. My evaluations of the theme move from speaking in general terms to illustrating through specific examples.

First Draft: *American Beauty* does not have a particularly memorable plot. What is memorable about it is how every character feels discontent and therefore expresses himself or herself in ways that center around the sub-themes of love, freedom, true happiness, and self liberation. Each character's actions due to their feelings of discontent and emptiness become intertwined and climax in a very memorable and disturbing ending. What I find most interesting about the movie is that it touches on issues that are basic to human emotions. It constantly emphasizes feelings of loneliness, emptiness, discontent, and true beauty. Each character portrays these themes in a different way. For example, Angela tries with all her might to be anything but ordinary by searching for personal fame, love, and beauty in very provocative ways. All of these feelings are explored in the context of society, focusing on how society, particularly American society encourages these feelings.[1]

1 This is the first time I talked about the theme of American discontent being expressed in the movie. Although I explained that it is important to the movie, I did not provide specific examples or illustrations. My audience did not get a good understanding of the way that this theme is incorporated through the characters or the scenes. This paragraph is very general and lacks any form of specific examples.

happy, but most of them continue to seek happiness through materialistic means") but adds only one (i.e., "The scene involving Lester and Carolyn on the couch illustrates all of the points *American Beauty* attempts to display") and makes an important macro-substitution in the subtitle, changing "The Quest for Happiness" to "The Disillusioned American Dream."

Although the author's revision gives the reader more detail and more support for her claim (something one can easily imagine her instructor and perhaps her peers had been asking for), it does not step back and tell the reader what those details mean as clearly as the original had. Thus, the writer chooses one programmatic desideratum (evidence and support) or another (complex thesis).

The discrepancy between this student's ratings and the contextual evidence surrounding her "before" and "after" essays—particularly in the Reflective Introduction to the eportfolio—is suggestive. Studies of revision that move beyond the evidence contained in documents explore the significance of text/context relations to revision. Among the factors they consider are knowledge of writing genres and a combination of what Alice Horning (2002) calls "meta-rhetorical" awareness—that is, writers' knowledge of themselves as writers—and their evaluation of their own intentions and the audience's expectations (Carroll, 1989; Nold, 1982). In her Reflective Introduction, the subject of our case study describes her writing process and offers a detailed explanation of her revision choices:

> My goal in this paper was to examine aspects of this movie [*American Beauty*] that made it merit-worthy. Initially, I began the paper by examining all the deeper themes, character plots, and symbols in the movie. I knew that the abstract themes in the movie were what made it valuable, but *I did not know how to organize this idea for a reader.* My first draft proved very ineffective because, as shown in my revision exhibit, it only examines the topic in very general terms, lacking any form of example or illustration. *A couple of drafts later, I understood the main goal of the paper a little better.* I was able to examine one theme within many

different contexts and circumstances, *providing effective examples that illustrated my point to the reader.* I examined each character in the movie and how their actions portrayed the themes of the movie. However, I still had trouble expressing the depths of these themes completely because my topic was still too broad. I was not able to narrow my ideas down in order to express the theme in one specific example. It wasn't until the draft featured in this portfolio that *I figured out a way to illustrate an abstract theme effectively and in an organized manner.* I did this by examining the theme within one particular scene that illustrated the themes of the movie. (emphasis added)

Clearly, this student made thoughtful and deliberate choices. Her explanation of her composing and revising process offers persuasive evidence that she possesses a clear understanding of her own goals as a writer, of having an audience, and of the significance of attending to their needs. She also shows that she has been attentive to the progressive nature of drafting, narrowing, and focusing her topic through successive drafts, and acknowledges genre expectations of FYC essays in her attempts to find ways to narrow her topic, focus her argument, and illustrate the themes of the movie. Coming through most strongly in the student's writing is a clear sense of her own agency—communicated through not only the use of first-person pronouns but also her narrative of gradual decision making and developing skill—and of the key role played by intentionality in her revision choices. Like Sommers's (1980) experienced writers, the student communicates a sense of discovery in the revision process. The temporal distance she establishes between her past and present provides further evidence of metacognition; as Brodkey and Henry (1992) argue, when students are able to "reposition" themselves in their texts, even their minor surface changes may be more consequential than a purely formal analysis of student texts can provide. Finally, the student's grasp of genre conventions in FYC draws explicitly on the language of the program rubric.

Placing herself not only within the writer-reader dyad but also within a collective of writers bound

Figure 19.4.

Carrie Black

I consider myself an observer. I could sit for hours watching people and never become restless. At times I like to put a hand to the world, step back and study those around me, taking in all that I can from them. Humanity fascinates me. Anything that attempts to portray human life intrigues me, whether it is music, artwork, or an essay on human culture. My name is Carrie Black. I am currently a double major of foreign language education and anthropology at the University of Georgia. I am a member of the UGA Redcoat Marching Band and I would love to minor in music, but with a double major that is simply not possible. I was born in Chicago, Illinois and raised in Watkinsville, Georgia. I currently would like to go into the field of education. I have always known that I would enter a profession that involves working with people. As of now, I would eventually like to end up teaching anthropology on a college level, but I plan to start in high school education.

I believe writing to be an art form. Writing is unthinkably valuable to humankind because it a very important part of what preserves the past and prepares for the future. Writing will inevitably be an important part of my future. If I pursue a career in education, it will be necessary for me to have the abilities to identify grammatical and contextual errors and to be able to critique the writing of others. If I eventually teach at a university level, it will be required of me to have writing abilities to write articles on research. I will need to be able to evaluate and communicate my thoughts on both my own research and the research of others. Fine-tuning my writing skills is very important to my future.

Reflective Introduction: How to Express the Abstract I PDF I PDF single-spaced
Portfolio Essay 1: The Affirmative Action Debate I PDF I PDF single-spaced
Portfolio Essay 2: American Beauty: The Disillusioned American Dream I PDF I PDF single-spaced
Revision Exhibit I PDF I PDF single-spaced
Peer Review Exhibit: Carrie's comments on Keith Barksdale's Boyz n the Hood I PDF I PDF single-spaced
Wild Card: Falsifiable Evidence and Confirmation Bias in Rev. Strobel's The Case for Christ I PDF I PDF single-spaced

together by similar curricular goals, she makes an important first move toward feeling the sense of collaboration that Horning identifies as important for experienced, professional writers.

The evidence of this student's Reflective Introduction places her midway between novice and expert writers. She exhibits the meta-rhetorical awareness associated with even novice writers (Beach, 1976). But she fails to achieve the sense of an overarching structure characterizing expert writers; she describes revision as a set of steps or perhaps epiphanies, drawing systematically on a series of tropes from her rhetorical inventory rather than constructing a new metaphor that could encompass her whole experience. Her sense of the writing process is more segmented than recursive. So while this writer's reflective rhetoric does not place her clearly as either a novice or an experienced writer, as defined by past studies and theories, what seems significant in her case is the strong disparity between the persuasiveness of her Reflective Introduction in the eportfolio and the ratings of her revised essay by anonymous raters. This student communicates a better understanding of revision than she is yet able to put into practice. As a writer, she may still be "in process," but the evidence of her eportfolio gives a more complex and encouraging picture of her achievement in FYC than can the revised, polished essays the portfolio frames and contextualizes.

RECOMMENDATIONS

From the researcher's perspective, perhaps the greatest benefit of EMMA eportfolios is the size and accessibility of the database of electronic documents upon which the eportfolios are built. For a large-scale program like the University of Georgia's FYC (from 3,300 to 4,000 students per semester), the electronic storage mechanism is crucial not only for the exchange of documents during the course of the semester but also for achieving a statistically significant research sample. Any program embarking on such an endeavor, however, needs to secure up front not only adequate server space and a person with the necessary expertise to manage the hardware but also a plan for maintaining and adding to the database. Although server space gets cheaper every year, the database grows exponentially.

Second, to reduce the time and cost of retrieving documents for study, it is crucial to consider carefully how the exhibits can be identified digitally (e.g., as "Reflective Introduction" or "Revised Essay #2") and linked to one another for easy retrieval. Our first collection of essays was seriously hampered by an inability to select appropriate artifacts quickly and easily. To resolve this confusion, our software designer constructed a portfolio template that asked students to identify each piece by kind from a drop-down menu when adding it to the portfolio. This way, students can title essays as they wish and control the order in which documents appear in the portfolio, while researchers can target easily the documents they want to study. A future plan is to ask students to link their revised essays to their original graded essays. Both decisions will save many hours of work by letting the software, as directed by the students, rather than the researchers select appropriate documents for analysis.

Finally, we have found a real tension between the results of our large-scale analysis and the subsequent study of particular writers and documents. To sort out the relationship between the writers' intentions and products, as represented by different pieces in the eportfolio, we will need to supplement the study of writing with the study of writers—in the case of our project, through longitudinal interviews. Moving from the macroscopic level of the database and the microscopic level of the essay offers particular methodological challenges, suggesting the need to scrutinize carefully the relationship between EMMA documents as discourse and as data.

ACKNOWLEDGMENTS

The authors would like to thank Professor Nelson Hilton and the University of Georgia Center for Teaching and Learning for supporting this project with a generous grant and Professor Jaxk Reeves, JianPing Zhu, and Yin Xiong for their statistical analysis of our data.

NOTES

1. Of course, students can delete any documents they wish. But because the eportfolio includes as one of its exhibits a demonstration and discussion of students' composing/revision process, the shape of the curriculum encourages them to preserve their drafts.

2. A good survey of earlier studies can be found in Fitzgerald (1987); a more recent review of the literature is offered by Horning (2002, pp. 15–79).

3. The true mean improvement was between .2567 and .5077. Improvement was, of course, not equally distributed across essay pairings, and no student increased his or her score by exactly .38 points.

4. Another question worth examining is the effect that other features of the eportfolio (e.g., Reflective Introduction, Composing/Revision and Peer Review exhibits, and the Wild Card) have on the final grades assigned to the portfolios by two different readers.

5. The language that Faigley and Witte use comes from Walter Kintsch and Teun van Dijk's well-known theoretical model of text processing.

REFERENCES

Assessment rubric for UGA FYC ePortfolios. (2005). Retrieved July 18, 2008 from http://www.english.uga.edu/freshcomp/portfolio_grading/port_rubric.htm

Barrett, H. (2007). *The electronic portfolio development process.* Retrieved February 9, 2007, from http://electronicportfolios.org/portfolios/aahe2000.html

Beach, R. (1976). Self-evaluation strategies of extensive revisers and non-revisers. *College Composition and Communication, 37,* 160–164.

Bridwell, L. (1980). Revising strategies in twelfth-grade students' transactional writing. *Research in the Teaching of English, 14*(2), 197–222.

Brodkey, L., & Henry, J. (1992). Voice lessons in a poststructural key: Notes on response and revision. In S. P. Witte, N. Nakadate, & R. D. Cherry (Eds.), *A rhetoric of doing: Essays on written discourse in honor of James L. Kinneavy* (pp. 144–160). Carbondale, IL: Southern Illinois University Press.

Carroll, J. (1989). Disabling fictions: Institutional delimitations of revision. *Rhetoric Review, 8*(1), 62–72.

Description of UGA FYC courses and ePortfolio evaluation. (2005). Retrieved July 24, 2008, from http://virtual.park.uga.edu/freshcomp/fresh-hand0506.htm#04

<emma>™. (2007). Retrieved July 21, 2008, from http://www.emma.uga.edu/

<emma>™. (2007). *Research Initiative Rating Scale.* Retrieved July 24, 2008, from http://www.english.uga.edu/cdesmet/revision/revision_rating_scale.pdf

Essay grading rubric for UGA FYC. (2007). Retrieved July 24, 2008, from http://www.english.uga.edu/freshcomp/rubrics_page/Rubric04-05.rtf

Estrem, H. (2004). The portfolio's shifting self: Possibilities for assessing student learning. *Pedagogy: Critical Approaches to Teaching Literature, Composition, and Culture, 4*(1), 125–127.

Faigley, L., & Witte, S. (1981). Analyzing revision. *College Composition and Communication, 32*(4), 400–414.

Fitzgerald, J. (1987). Research on revision in writing. *Review of Educational Research, 57*(4), 481–506.

Harris, M. (1989). Composing behaviors of one- and multi-draft writers. *College English, 51*(2), 174–191.

Horning, A. (2002). *Revision revisited.* Cresskill, NJ: Hampton Press.

Huot, B. (2002). Toward a new discourse of assessment for the college writing classroom. *College English, 65*(2), 163–180.

Nold, E. (1982). Revising: Intentions and conventions. In R. Sudol (Ed.), *Revising: New essays for teachers of writing.* Urbana, IL: NCTE.

OpenOffice. (2008). Retrieved July 24, 2008, from http://www.openoffice.org/

Perl, S. (1979). The composing processes of unskilled writers. *Research in the Teaching of English, 13*, 317–336.

Pullman, G. (2002). Electronic portfolios revisited: The Efolios Project. *Computers and Composition, 19*, 151–169.

Sommers, N. (1980). Revision strategies of student writers and experienced adult writers. *College Composition and Communication, 31*(4), 378–388.

Yancey, K. (1999). Looking back as we look forward: Historicizing writing assessment. *College Composition and Communication, 50*, 483–503.

20

MOVING EFOLIO MINNESOTA TO THE NEXT GENERATION

From Individual Portfolios to an Integrated Institutional Model

LYNETTE OLSON, LORI SCHROEDER, and PAUL WASKO
Minnesota State Colleges and Universities

Minnesota State Colleges and Universities (MnSCU) sponsors and manages eFolio Minnesota and eFolioWorld. eFolio Minnesota is a nationally recognized and award-winning electronic portfolio infrastructure system. Minnesota students, faculty, and workers are able to create, maintain, and publish a unique Web-based portfolio to electronically showcase profiles, knowledge, artifacts, reflections, and achievements. Research demonstrates that many individuals are intrinsically motivated to do so and report significant impact on their learning and professional relationships (Cambridge, 2008). Recently, the eFolio Minnesota software tool has been expanded to offer comprehensive support for accreditation purposes and for continuous institutional performance improvement.

The eFolio system is managed by Academic Innovations, a unit within the Office of the Chancellor. The Minnesota State Colleges and Universities System consists of 32 state universities, community colleges, technical colleges, and consolidated community and technical colleges located on 53 campuses across the state. In 2007 the MnSCU launched eFolioWorld, an initiative that broadened the eFolio Minnesota user population to education institutions throughout the United States.

A challenge for higher education is devising ways to respond efficiently and effectively to the needs of federal and state education departments, accrediting agencies, and higher education systems to obtain data and information. The MnSCU system is engaged in a Chancellor initiative that uses electronic portfolios to address institutional accountability and assessment needs while showing the interconnection of student competencies and program outcomes. This new initiative builds on eFolio Minnesota's success in supporting individually focused lifelong and lifewide learning.

Since The Higher Learning Commission/ Academic Quality Improvement Program has endorsed the use of eFolio Minnesota for accreditation purposes, MnSCU institutions have been able to use this tool to facilitate these interconnections, to foster excellence in teaching and student learning, to facilitate institutional effectiveness, and to provide an efficient method for communication, accountability, and accreditation.

This chapter addresses how the eFolio Minnesota software has been adapted to allow users to demonstrate, support, and foster interconnections between purpose and practice among students, faculty, and institutions, empowering both individuals and institutions. These changes require new research on the use of eportfolios in accountability and assessment.

BACKGROUND OF EFOLIO MINNESOTA

On August 1, 2002, after over a year of discussion, design, and development, MnSCU launched eFolio Minnesota (http://www.efoliominnesota.com), the nation's first statewide electronic portfolio management system. The eFolio system offers a multimedia electronic portfolio designed for users to create a living showcase of their education, career, and personal achievements. All Minnesota residents, including students enrolled in Minnesota schools, educators, and others, can use eFolio Minnesota software to reach their career and education goals.

Initial funding for eFolio Minnesota was obtained through congressional awards administered by the federal Department of Education through its Fund for the Improvement of Postsecondary Education (FIPSE) offices. MnSCU funds also were targeted to lay the foundation to serve and support 21st-century e-learners.

In 2007 eFolio Minnesota began its 5th year of operation with over 60,000 registered users and with well over a million hits per month. It is being widely used by diverse populations that include Minnesotans from K-12, higher education, and the workforce.

The eFolio Minnesota engine allows both individuals and institutions to build on a content management engine (http://www.avenet.net) created by Avenet, Inc. enabling individuals to control the display of the selection and reflection of learning and the achievement of learning outcomes. Special tools in eFolio Minnesota have been designed for individuals to create, store, and share a portfolio of accomplishments with anyone, anywhere, and anytime. The eFolio system is based on a software design that allows even the most inexperienced computer user to build an electronic portfolio site. Site owners can manipulate icons and use navigation strategies with which most computer users have familiarity, as illustrated in

Figure 20.1. eFolio software functionality.

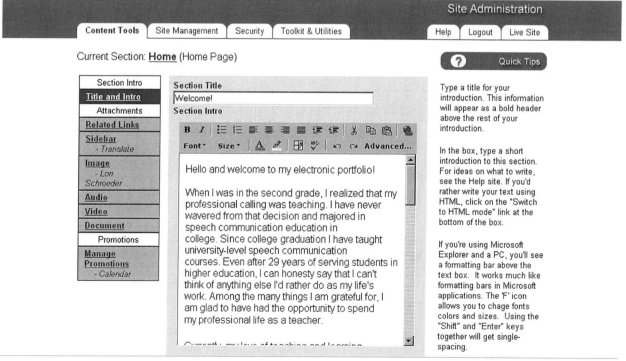

Figure 20.1. Site owners who have a computer and Internet access can build, change, and instantly publish their work on the World Wide Web. Key software features include the ability to upload documents, images, and multimedia files. In addition, users can create hyperlinks to external Web sites.

This anytime and anywhere accessibility and ease of software use are key factors in the success and popularity of the individual eportfolios.

INDIVIDUAL AND INSTITUTIONAL APPLICATIONS OF EPORTFOLIOS

Research on the use of electronic portfolios in higher education reveals that institutions have found eportfolios to be an effective vehicle to (a) document learning and map to lifewide and lifelong learning; (b) support institutional core and program competencies; and (c) promote academic quality and institutional operational efficiencies.

In a study of approximately 500 eFolio Minnesota portfolio owners conducted in 2004, Cambridge (2005, 2008) concludes that eFolio Minnesota offers electronic portfolios for lifewide and lifelong learning (Table 20-1). Cambridge reports that in addition to supporting learning in the classroom, eFolio Minnesota encourages users to document their lifewide learning and performance as it is manifested in the workplace, family, and community. In addition to supporting students and educators during their formal engagement with MnSCU institutions, eFolio Minnesota invites all residents of and students within the state of Minnesota to capitalize on their learning before,

during, and after formal education, regardless of provider. The ease of use and flexibility of the eFolio software was a significant factor in this success.

Cambridge suggests that in its embrace of electronic portfolios for lifewide and lifelong learning for all, eFolio Minnesota is unique in the United States. However, at the time of his study, eFolio Minnesota did not yet include robust support for more institutionally focused application of electronic portfolios. Use of institutional portfolios to support accreditation at Portland State and Indiana University Purdue University–Indianapolis (IUPUI) suggest new opportunities.

Portland State University used an electronic portfolio in its 2003 self-study to initiate efforts to advance the university's mission (http://portfolio.pdx.edu/Portfolio). The self-study, embedded within the portfolio, could be reviewed as a separate document that specifically focused on the Northwest Commission on Colleges and Universities (NWCCU) Standards (Chapter 17). Each standard's narrative was written by members of individual subcommittees and edited and reviewed by the self-study leadership team. Portland State University reports that an effort was made to make the process of self-reflection as inclusive as possible and to allow faculty, staff, and administrators multiple opportunities to participate and provide their perspectives on the university's work. Each of the portfolio's themes (Community & Global Connections, Institutional Effectiveness, Research & Scholarship, Student Success, and Teaching & Learning) reflects an overarching set of institutional goals and illustrates how they are manifesting themselves in practice throughout the institution. During

Table 20-1. Percentage of eFolio Users Using eFolio for Function by Role (Cambridge, 2005)

Function	Used (%)	Satisfied (%)	Found Helpful (%)	One or More Times per Semester (%)	One Semester or More (%)
Educational Planning	56	65	40	37	44
Documenting Knowledge, Skills, and Abilities	75	45	42	38	42
Tracking Development	42	53	48	47	46
Finding a Job	47	33	37*	27**	40
Evaluation Within a Course	40	47	45	54	53
Performance Monitoring	36	49	47	36	34

* Found somewhat helpful
** Less than once per year

the self-study each theme served as a focus for discussion, analysis, and reflection among faculty, staff, students, and community members. In addition to the five major themes, the portfolio includes a section on vision and planning, and a template for the university's reaccreditation self-study report that was completed in 2005. Portland State University also plans to use the electronic portfolio as a tool for reflection, to assess where it is excelling, and to identify areas that need improvement. Portland State University's use of the electronic portfolio illustrates how it can successfully promote institutional effectiveness, facilitate assessment, and foster communication.

Similarly, IUPUI uses an electronic portfolio for self-evaluation, reflection, and planning (http://iport.iupui.edu/selfstudy/criteria). Originally developed as part of a national initiative that experimented with the use of electronic media to inform university stakeholders about campus work and effectiveness, it also is intended to reach a number of key IUPUI audiences (Hamilton, 2001). In addition, the electronic portfolio was used for accreditation purposes with the Higher Learning Commission of the North Central Association (NCA) (http://www.ncahigherlearningcommission.org). The institution reports that in developing the portfolio, it focused on using the features of the Web—menus, navigational tools, and drill-downs—to allow users of the site to make efficient connections between arguments and supporting evidence and between general statements and more detailed information. The multimedia capabilities of the electronic environment enabled IUPUI to capture authentic samples of student and faculty work, accomplishments, and performances in audio, video, graphical, and written forms.

FUNCTIONALITY TO SUPPORT OUTCOMES ASSESSMENT AND INSTITUTIONAL PORTFOLIOS

To support the use of eFolio Minnesota for similar institutional assessment, new functionalities have been developed. The Academic Innovation unit of the Office of the Chancellor developed software to help institutions publish their *Systems Portfolios* and to thereby facilitate continuous quality improvement processes. Higher education institutions are now able to use eFolio software to address institutional accountability and assessment needs while showing the interconnection of student competencies and program outcomes.

eFolio Minnesota offers an electronic portfolio that logs an institution's activities with regard to the nine key processes of the Academic Quality Improvement Project (AQIP), which is an accreditation program of the Higher Learning Commission of the North Central Association of Colleges and Schools. The Systems Portfolio demonstrates the context in which the institution implements each of the nine components, the processes that the college uses in its fulfillment of the components, the results that were achieved from the efforts, and the improvements the institution has made and is making based on what it has learned from its assessments and measurements.

Supporting institutional assessment requires software to support two new processes. First, individuals must be able to align the evidence in their portfolios with institutionally defined standards. Second, connections between evidence and outcomes must be able to be made for the institution as a whole. The first function is supported by Toolkit, while the second is supported by LinkBuilder.

The Toolkit utility is a new feature of the individual portfolio system, added in late 2005, that allows individual site owners to access a library of discipline-based standards, goals, and competencies. Students may use this utility to map their portfolios to preinstalled standards through linking to appropriate sections and items. Individuals such as paraprofessionals, Peace Corps volunteers, superintendents, and principals, have been able to successfully demonstrate that they have met discipline outcomes and program standards, as illustrated in Figure 20.2. Toolkit functionality also supports students' efforts to pursue credit for prior learning. Similarly, faculty are able to use the Toolkit functionality to map their professional development plans and activities to appropriate sections and items.

Figure 20.2. Student demonstrates learning related to pre-installed Toolkit-embedded competencies.

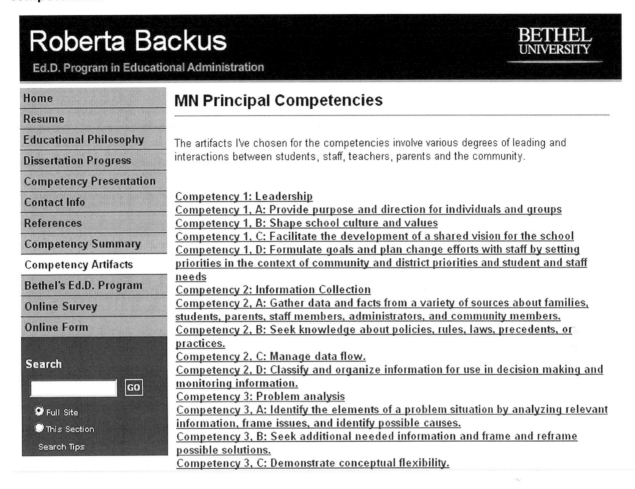

Institutions are able to develop sites to suit their purposes employing the same user interface and experiencing the same instant Web publishing capability of the anytime and anywhere technology as individual eFolio site owners do. In addition, the current system has developed software mapping functions that enable institutions to do the following:

- Exhibit data and documents collectively that articulate the institution's mission, vision, and goals, demonstrating aligned compliance to approved criteria and standards and helping an institution create a fact-based culture supporting its operations, decision making, and planning
- Enhance interaction among institutional work teams, promoting collaboration and bridging gaps between outcomes and strategic decision making
- Foster a vehicle to showcase educational effectiveness and the fulfillment of licensure competencies by students in specific programs in a user-friendly, user-generated environment
- Build upon internal and external accountability procedures by creating a valuable tool designed to be shared and updated on a continuous basis

Similar to the individual eFolio Toolkit software, institutions may use LinkBuilder functionality to map eFolio content to sets of preinstalled standards or competencies. Institutions are able to control the content they wish to display in terms of how they have met discipline and program outcomes, standards, competencies, and accreditation criteria.

Figure 20.3. Super Forms as "feedback form."

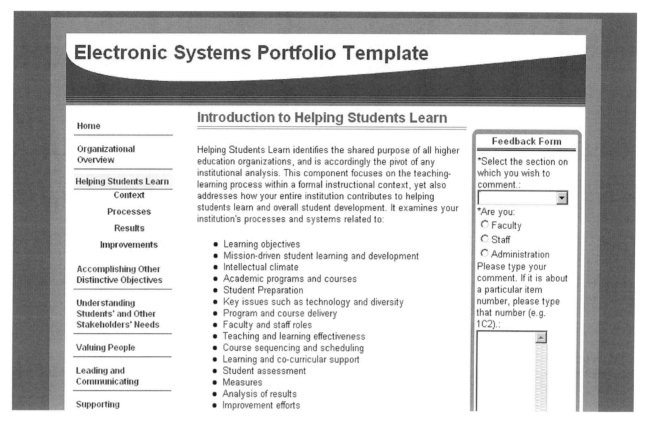

In addition to the Link-Builder tool, institutional users are able to invite colleague feedback with a number of feedback devices, such as Guest Book and Super Forms. The software tools enable site developers to build and maintain a dynamic institutional portfolio, inviting relevant stakeholders to share ideas and input in order to facilitate accreditation efforts and to foster continuous quality improvement (Figure 20.3). The software also allows the entire site or particular sections of the site to be private and password protected. Site builders can configure feedback to be public or private; with some software tools, such as Online Surveys, feedback is anonymous.

Currently 25 higher education institutions in the United States have deployed accounts to support institutional and program accreditation efforts. In addition, these institutions have submitted their eSystems Portfolios for AQIP review: Metropolitan State University, Ridgewater College, Minneapolis Community & Technical College, MSC–Southeast Technical, and Northwest Tech-

nical College, Bemidji. In addition, the institutional Electronic Portfolio Project is interested in developing eFolio system software to support program accreditation efforts with other external organizations such as ABET, NCATE, PEAQ, and the Minnesota Department of Education and the Minnesota Board of Teaching, integrating skills and licensure competencies for Paraprofessional, Assistive Technology, Dental Assisting, and Superintendents and Principals Licensures.

Leaders of these institutions testify to the increased efficiency and expanded opportunities for collaboration that eFolio's new capabilities bring to institutional assessment processes. John Huth, Academic Quality Improvement Program (AQIP) coordinator, Minnesota State College–Southeast Technical, says this about his experience using eFolio Minnesota:

We have used our eFolio site to facilitate our institutional effectiveness efforts, including conducting anonymous surveys and the review of critical documents requiring comments from our personnel. It is a tool with many possibilities for communication, management of information, and group facilitation. (J. Huth, personal communication, January 22, 2007)

William Lowe, provost and vice president for academic affairs, Metropolitan State University, concurs: "Metropolitan State University made very successful use of eFolio in the first iteration of our Systems Portfolio (as part of our participation in the AQIP). It is difficult to imagine going back to hard copy approach" (personal communication, 2007).

A STAKEHOLDER MODEL

Both within and beyond MnSCU, an increasing number of educational institutions are turning to electronic portfolios as tools not only for individual learning and self-representation but also for or-

ganizational collaboration and communication. A new conceptual model is needed for this expanded role that connects purpose and practice. The re-designed eFolio Minnesota software enables institutions to use a Web-based medium to illustrate interconnections between and among stakeholders, as illustrated in Figure 20.4. This model visualizes how eFolio Minnesota is designed to support and document interconnections among these three key stakeholders:

- Student focus demonstrating learning outcomes
- Faculty focus modeling program competencies
- Institutional focus mastering evidence of learning

The **student focus** suggests the potential impact of integrated learning across co-curricular and curricular activities using eFolio Minnesota. A

Figure 20.4. eFolios to demonstrate interconnections between and among stakeholders.

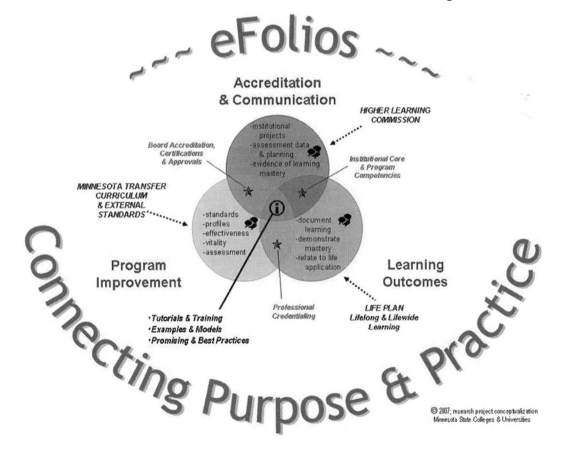

successful electronic portfolio tool supplies links to document that student learning expectations and common student learning outcomes have been met. Student electronic portfolios that showcase and document student learning provide program faculty a means of student assessment based specifically on program outcomes.

The **faculty focus** points to how eFolio Minnesota software can allow and support the intersection of institutional, program, and individual portfolios and how faculty can guide students in using eFolio Minnesota to document achievement of learning outcomes, an important component of effective teaching and learning.

The **institutional focus** illustrates how new mapping functions can support institutions in terms of these benefits: (a) exhibiting data and documents to collectively articulate the institution's mission, vision, and goals, demonstrating aligned compliance to approved criteria and standards, and to support an institution's efforts to create a fact-based culture supporting its operations, decision making, and planning processes; (b) enhancing interaction among institutional work teams, promoting collaboration and bridging gaps between outcomes and strategic decision making; (c) showcasing educational effectiveness and the fulfillment of licensure competencies by students in specific programs in a user-friendly, user-generated environment; and (d) building upon internal and external accountability procedures by creating a tool designed to enable information to be shared and efficiently updated on a continuous basis.

KEY QUESTIONS FOR RESEARCH

Although eFolio Minnesota's effectiveness in supporting lifelong and lifewide learning for individual portfolio authors is now well documented, new research is needed to determine the strengths and weaknesses of eFolio Minnesota for supporting the stakeholder model. Such research, joined with that conducted by other members of the Inter/National Coalition for Electronic Portfolio Research investigating the development and implementation

of electronic portfolio software for institutional use (see Chapter 14), will serve to develop best practices and to discover problem areas that need to be rectified within the tool or with its implementation. Problem areas may include the following:

- Challenges with organizational readiness
- Lack of reviewer ease with navigating technologies
- A possible paradigm shift required when moving from static, hard-copy documents to dynamic media such as video, audio, linkages, and graphics
- Lack of portfolio developer facility with the technology
- Limitations in the software functionality

Such research should also address factors that contribute to the legitimacy of using an electronic portfolio tool to demonstrate how institutions are able to connect purpose with practice. If successful, this inquiry will provide information to strengthen electronic portfolios' use, applicability, and validity and to improve institutional process efficiencies.

The impact of institutional electronic portfolio research will depend on how effectively it is disseminated. Results of research conducted by MnSCU, especially findings linked to assessment, effectiveness, and outcomes at the program, institution, and system level, will be made available throughout the MnSCU system and to higher education institutions nationwide. Authentic projects using eFolio Minnesota, which include collections of work, provide internal and external stakeholders with visible examples that demonstrate how an electronic portfolio can be used to document outcomes, competencies, and criteria related to effectiveness and continuous improvement processes. A gallery of MnSCU institutions that have developed eFolios for accreditation purposes is available at the Institutional Electronic Portfolio Resource Center Web site (http://www.portfolio.project.mnscu.edu).

An increasing number of educational institutions are turning to electronic portfolios as tools for collaboration and communication, to document how they have met accreditation criteria, and to serve as living, dynamic showcases of their activities, mission, and vision. The issues that Minnesota faces are not unique to this state. Educational institutions seek ways to foster excellence in teaching and learning, to develop students' abilities to document and reflect on their learning, and to display how students have met competencies, standards, and licensing and credentialing requirements. Powerful electronic portfolio software, developed and implemented according to the results of careful research, is a crucial tool in meeting these challenges.

REFERENCES

Cambridge, D. (2005). *eFolio Minnesota for lifewide and lifelong learning: Research results.* Retrieved June 21, 2007, from http://portfolio.project.mnscu.edu/Cambridge

Cambridge, D. (2008). Audience, integrity, and the living document: eFolio and lifelong and lifewide learning with ePortfolios. *Computers & Education, 51*(3), 1227–1246.

Campus Technology. (2006). *2006 campus technology innovators: Technology area: ePortfolios: Innovator: Minnesota State Colleges and Universities.* Retrieved September 6, 2006, from http://www.campus-technology.com/article.asp?id=18937

Hamilton, S. (2001). Snake pit in cyberspace. In B. L. Cambridge (Ed.), *Electronic portfolios: Emerging practices in student, faculty, and institutional learning* (pp. 159–177). Sterling, VA: Stylus (originally published by American Association for Higher Education).

Higher Learning Commission, a Commission of the North Central Colleges and Schools. (2006). *Academic quality improvement process (AQIP).* Retrieved September 6, 2006, from http://hlcommission.org

Minnesota State Colleges and Universities. (2006). *eFolio Minnesota.* Retrieved September 8, 2006, from http://www.efoliominnesota.org

21

ASSESSING THE LEARNING POTENTIAL OF EPORTFOLIO THROUGH THINKING SHEETS

MARY E. ZAMON and DEBRA SPRAGUE
George Mason University

Our eportfolio project was conducted at George Mason University (GMU), a state-supported, three-campus institution located in Fairfax, Virginia. Founded in 1971, GMU has a current enrollment of nearly 30,000 students and has grown into a major educational force. In particular, it has earned a reputation as an innovative, entrepreneurial institution.

PROGRAM CONTEXT

This report represents findings from a case study with six participants: four Ph.D. and two MS students recruited from the College of Education and Human Development (CEHD) at GMU. As part of their programs, these students were required to complete either a paper-based or electronic portfolio: The participants in this study all elected to create eportfolios. All students were volunteers, and although choosing to do an eportfolio, they exhibited a range of technical skills. Because the programs required portfolios, all the students in this pilot were given program guidelines about materials to include—specifically, reflective artifacts. These guidelines, as evidenced by student discus-

sion, provided an important context for eportfolio work. (See http://gse.gmu.edu/programs/phd/guidelines.htm for portfolio guidelines for Ph.D. students.) Another contextual factor was a specific eportfolio course offered as an optional elective to Ph.D. students. The four Ph.D. students had taken or were taking this course, which walks students through the processes of creating and uploading a Web-based electronic portfolio. Thus, this group had access to assistance and advice.

RESEARCH QUESTION

How do we know? This most important question in any research is perhaps the most difficult one to tackle. It becomes no less difficult in this specific study of what thinking and learning take place when students create electronic portfolios as part of their academic program requirements.

The power of eportfolios is not in the creation of the product, we believe, but in the thinking process students go through as they create the portfolio. The issue for eportfolio researchers is to find a way to capture the thinking process while it is occurring. To address this problem, we created "thinking sheets," a technique for capturing students' thinking at the precise moment that thinking occurs.

Two central questions framed this project:

1. What is the thinking process that students go through as they develop eportfolios?
2. How can we assess the learning that occurs during this thinking process?

THEORETICAL CONTEXT

Paulson, Paulson, and Meyer (1991) describe portfolios as a collection of student work, guided by performance standards and demonstrating evidence of a student's self-reflection. Portfolios are used to demonstrate competencies, show progress and experiences, and reflect on learning as well as function as a tool for assessment (Russell & Butcher, 1999). Although researchers agree that the power of portfolios lies in the quality of the reflection in which students engage, little research has focused on capturing that reflection as it is evidenced during the creation of the portfolios. What are students thinking as they engage in the design process? Why are they making specific choices such as the artifacts they select and the links they create?

The use of thinking sheets to elicit the data for this study was inspired by an account of teachers trying to discover the thought processes of students solving math problems (Zawojewski, Chamberlin, Hjalmaarson, & Lewis, in press).

Their study used thinking sheets containing potential solution methods, allowing students to choose one or more and explain their work. Our research adapted this idea to see if it is possible to capture students' reflections as they create their eportfolios.

Students were asked to complete a sheet each work session, regardless of how long the session ran or where it occurred. No set number of sheets was required, but two reminders were sent in an effort to obtain the sheets. A reduced-size version of the sheet is reproduced in Table 21-1.

Although students were given print copies and an electronic version of the sheet at the start of their participation, no students elected to complete elec-

Table 21-1. Thinking Sheet Questionnaire

Name: _____   Date _____

Length of time for this session _____

_____

_____

_____

_____

_____

Feel free to use the back of this sheet as necessary.

1. What do you intend to accomplish this session?

_____

_____

_____

2. As you work on the portfolio this session, please note what artifacts (text, links, documents, pictures, audio/video, etc.) or design elements you create or change and briefly explain your reasons for doing them.

_____

_____

_____

tronic versions. In addition, the sheets do not represent the entirety of the students' eportfolio thinking process. Our project included students commencing with thinking sheets at the same time, but some of the Ph.D. students had already begun the portfolio (the master's students were both beginners).

Participants also participated in two interviews, 15 minutes for the first and 45 minutes for the second. During the second interview, participants demonstrated their eportfolios and discussed the reasons for the decisions they had made.

MAJOR FINDINGS

Qualitative data collected from the thinking sheets and interviews were imported into NVivo and common themes were identified:

1. Technology issues
2. Design elements
3. The role of guidelines
4. Personalization
5. The portfolio audience

The total replies exceed the total number of statements because statements were often coded into more than one category. There were between 12 and 15 responses to each of the questions and approximately 75 thinking sheet responses. Work session times averaged 2.5 hours.

The thinking sheets clearly captured the struggle with technology issues. Although four of the students participated in an eportfolio design course offered through CEHD, all students indicated that they were initially more concerned about the technical learning curve than the integrative and reflective connections among the artifacts they chose. As students started the eportfolio process, their major concern was with the technology skills needed to accomplish the task at hand, even though all participants reported using NVu software, a fairly simplified composer. For example, one master's-level student spent 3 hours fixing links because "images are not appearing" and "all links need to be re-done for CD as source designations changed" (Subject #5). These technology

concerns can serve as a distraction from the creation of the eportfolio as a demonstration of competencies that go beyond technical skills.

The thinking sheets also demonstrated that students spent a lot of time on the design elements of the portfolio: colors, design, format, and structure. Although design elements were mentioned in initial interviews, most of the comments about design were made in the final interview/presentations (16 references). By the time of the second interview, though, students were moving away from the technical aspects of the design and reflecting more on the meaning behind the structure they were creating. Students began their interviews by talking about the look of the portfolio. "I wanted clean lines and for it to look professional, not personal," Subject #1 explained, whereas Subject #2 said, "I wanted the background to be soft, the design related to my undergraduate degree in agriculture studies." Participants then progressed to reasons for choosing certain artifacts over others. "I included course artifacts that were required [by the program], ones that represent my best effort. I chose what I was most proud of for each class," said Subject #3. Completion was important to Subject #2: "I included final papers from each course as these were more complete. I did not include other papers as I felt the work was incomplete. I did not want to put in the working/thinking parts of the courses."

Students mentioned the portfolio class as a source for influencing their decisions (six references). These decisions were about design components but also the artifacts chosen, as Subject #2 suggests: "My portfolio is very linear at this time; I followed the Ph.D. directions for elements to include." Subject #3 concurs: "I followed Ph.D. [directions], it is not creative, but based on directions." The class also influenced themes and document format: "Included major themes, followed Ph.D. directions" (Subject #4), and "The files are in PDF because it is more secure than Word files. This was discussed in the portfolio class" (Subject #2). It will be interesting to follow the Ph.D. students. Their portfolios have a program-long life of several years, culminating in the last step to official proposal status. It is possible that as they continue to develop their eportfolios, reflective and integrative concepts will be more frequently cited.

As students progressed through the semester, they began to move beyond the program guidelines. At this point the portfolio changed from a program requirement to a personalization of their selves and their experiences. We began to think of this change in outlook as "the moment," plotted visually in Figure 21.1, because it is a fairly distinct point at which reflection on choice of artifacts began to emerge. The students began to connect course studies to other aspects of their lives, as Subject #1 explains: "Artifacts have yet to be uploaded. I want to include artifacts from my profession, not just focused on my Ph.D. coursework. I feel the Ph.D. will enhance what I am already doing in my professional career." Subject #3 makes the same point, but with a specific example: "I included my testimony to Congress with video. This related to personal and professional aspects, what I care about, my story." The Ph.D. students reached "the moment" more frequently than the master's students, possibly because the time limit on the master's students is a single semester, whereas the Ph.D. project extends over the life of their graduate program. We intend to explore the possibility that longer time influences the coming of "the moment" as more master's-level students are added to the participants. It seems logical that the progression to higher-order thinking/reflection will happen the longer students spend with the development of the portfolio.

The last theme to emerge was audience related: Who would have access to the portfolio and how would they use it? All students mentioned their committee members or professors having access, which is not surprising given that they were creating the portfolio as part of program requirements. At the same time, however, three students discussed using the portfolio to help potential employers know them, while two discussed allowing family members, friends, and fellow students access to their portfolio. Subject #1 saw the portfolio in the context of an interview ("I could see sharing the portfolio for a prospective job—employer could browse before the interview. It can also supplement a face-to-face or over the phone interview"); Subject #2 as a preface to an interview ("It

Figure 21.1

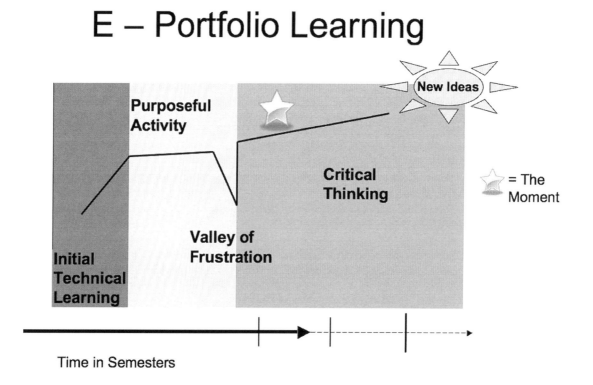

could be sent to potential employers, a cover letter will invite them to the URL"); Subject #3 as material to share with friends ("Perhaps fellow Doc students and friends"); and Subject #4 as material for colleagues ("I could take to conferences to show what I am doing").

Clear evidence of moving toward higher-order thinking came from Subjects #2 and #6, who commented on thinking and perspective: "I liked this session because it gave us a chance to think about our reflections as we design our portfolio" and "I can understand or view my portfolio from the 'Helicopter' perspective." Another type of thinking emerged as students began to evaluate software capabilities. Subject #5, for example, reported using FrontPage near the end of the series of thinking sheets, commenting that "IE is better than Firefox for FrontPage clipart compatibility." Although still somewhat concerned with technology issues, this comment indicates a different level and kind of engagement with technology and its possibilities. In their concluding sheets and interviews, students also reported a desire to add audio or other elements to their portfolios, thus demonstrating a wider view of eportfolio affordances.

IMPLICATIONS

As this project continues, three points will be part of our efforts at George Mason:

1. We need to have more participants and to obtain more sheets over time. The pilot participants turned in an average of four sheets in a semester. Master's students were essentially finished with the portfolio at that point; however, Ph.D. students will continue for several more semesters, with additional reviews of portfolios.

2. More information on initial technical skills should be collected. It was not clear in all cases if students had any prior experience with hyperlinks or Web pages.

3. As we collect additional data, we hope to take them to the program directors so that

Figure 21.2

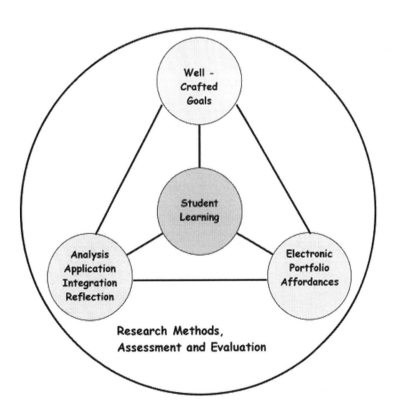

changes tied to eportfolio creation and development, especially the support and instructions, can be made.

CONCLUSIONS/RECOMMENDATIONS

Because this was a small case study, our conclusions are tentative:

1. The learning curve for technical skills appears to increase focus on developing skills and deflect the focus on larger learning purposes of the programs. Accordingly, programs considering portfolios should take into account the time span that students may need to complete their portfolio, depending on two factors: (a) the technical expertise of the students and (b) the demands of the eportfolio technology. Achieving more than an electronic file box may take more than one semester.
2. Most of these students initially viewed eportfolios as linear compositions, although some branched into more complex structures later in the project. The structures students had in their heads as evidenced by the initial drawings were very simple. The information from the last presentation interview was more complex. Eportfolio coaching could attempt to help students develop more complex internal modeling sooner.
3. Directions currently supplied to students developing eportfolios do not differentiate between electronic and paper versions and thus may limit efforts of students to address the potentialities of integration through, for example, internal and external links. Consideration of ways to communicate the affordances of eportfolios to students through specific directions may be important to improving student higher-order thinking.
4. Reflection on nontechnology issues was not as evident as expected. This may be linked to other factors mentioned here as well as to the fact that reflection was directed to be in the artifacts themselves. In other words, the reflective nature of a portfolio separate from reflection in the artifacts themselves is not apparent to students. Encouraging reflection could be done in the coaching or coursework.
5. If these eportfolios are part of the program's summative or formative evaluation, then it is valuable to have published standards and directions related to differences eportfolio use can enable in comparison to paper portfolios.

REFERENCES

George Mason University. (2006). *About George Mason University.* Retrieved February 8, 2007, from http://www.gmu.edu/about/

Paulson, F. L., Paulson, P. R., & Meyer, C. (1991). What makes a portfolio a portfolio? *Educational Leadership, 48*(5), 60–63.

Russell, J. D., & Butcher, C. (1999). Using portfolios in educational technology courses. *Journal of Technology and Teacher Education, 7*(4), 279–289.

Zawojewski, J. S., Chamberlin, M., Hjalmaarson, M. A., & Lewis, C. (in press). Designing design studies for professional development in mathematics education: Studying teachers' interpretive systems. In A. E. Kelly, R. Lesh, & J. Baek (Eds.), *Design research in mathematics, science & technology education.* Mahweh, NJ: Erlbaum.

22

THE MAED ENGLISH EDUCATION ELECTRONIC PORTFOLIO EXPERIENCE

What Preservice English Teachers Have to Teach Us About EPs and Reflection

CARL YOUNG

North Carolina State University

My research focuses on English education students' perceptions of and experiences with the MAED English Education Electronic Portfolio requirement at Virginia Tech, where I served as assistant professor from 2001 to 2006 and as program advisor from 2004 to 2006. Candidates in the Teacher Education in the Sciences and Humanities (TESH) MAED Program create an electronic portfolio as their culminating project prior to graduation. The purpose of the portfolio is for students to reflect critically upon their experiences in the program and in the field, as well as to demonstrate their pedagogical ability, their knowledge of their content area, and their completion of all program requirements and related standards. Requirements include standards from the International Society for Technology Education (ISTE) and the Interstate New Teacher Assessment and Support Consortium (INTASC), as well as standards from content area professional organizations (i.e., National Council of Teachers of English).

Students begin work on the portfolio in the fall semester and complete it in the spring semester of a 15- to 18-month graduate program. At the end of the spring semester, following student teaching, students present their portfolios to their cohort and to a panel of at least three evaluators, which typically includes the program advisor, an additional program faculty, and the university supervisor. Ultimately, students are evaluated on their ability not only to choose multiple strong artifacts that meet each standard but also to reflect critically about how these evidentiary texts meet the standards.

Throughout their program, students are encouraged and required to reflect critically upon their coursework and upon their experiences in the field. For example, my English education students completed an extensive course- and self-evaluation reflection for their initial methods class. In addition, most major assignments for the course included reflective self-evaluation components. Students also maintained an online reflective field journal for their early field and student teaching internships. Here, they posted entries regularly and replied to peers' postings; it is an interactive and collaborative reflective endeavor. They also kept individual print reflection field logs. Although the electronic portfolio itself became a public artifact, at least for their peers and the evaluation committee, there were many opportunities for individual reflection as well. In addition, English education students always received detailed responses to their work and self-evaluations. The electronic portfolio was evaluated using a rubric encompassing all of the required standards. Over time, the portfolio came to represent reflection that was both verbal and visual.

RESEARCH MOTIVATIONS AND QUESTIONS

When I began as a faculty member in the TESH program, I observed that the electronic portfolio requirement was an artificial experience for most students. Rather than an authentic representation and reflection of who students were as beginning teachers and what they knew, the portfolio process was a race to fulfill an external requirement for finishing the program, earning the degree, and receiving licensure—not the kind of technology preparation or practice called for by leaders in the field (Pope & Golub, 2000; Young & Bush, 2004). The 10 INTASC principles became the typical framework for students' portfolio design—10 standards links with a few artifacts and reflections—with little consideration for visual or thematic design representing student identity. Even the reflections were minimal in depth, typically just describing the artifact rather than delving into the teaching context and learning experience associated with it. As a result, most of the portfolios were very similar in design, lacking a sense of personal and professional identity, authenticity, and depth. Drawing on my knowledge of portfolio practice and theory (Calfee & Freedman, 1996; Elbow, 1991; Elbow & Belanoff, 1991, 1997; Yancey, 1992, 1996a, 1996b, 1996c, 1997), as well as my own experience as a writer and teacher of writing, I believed that my students should and could be getting much more from this experience. Although I understood the need to meet NCATE standards and maintain NCATE accreditation, I also saw the potential for the electronic portfolio experience to be more than a rote INTASC "evidence dump."

As a result of this motivating discontent, I conducted evaluation research on the MAED English Education Electronic Portfolio experience—which served in lieu of a thesis or an exam—over a 5-year period. I was interested in determining how effective the current electronic portfolio requirement was as a culminating reflective component for the program, as well as how the electronic portfolio experience affected student development as a beginning teacher—in terms of both preparation and practice. My questions included the following:

- What are English education students' perceptions of the MAED Licensure Program Electronic Portfolio experience? What effect does their experience have on their preparation as teachers and their practice in the field?
- How are their technology skills, abilities, confidence levels, and so forth affected by the electronic portfolio experience?
- To what extent does their portfolio experience affect their interest, desire, and ability to integrate technology into their teaching, and the probability of their integrating technology into their own teaching in the classroom as a preservice teacher and as a beginning teacher?
- To what extent does the electronic portfolio experience affect their identity as a teacher? To what extent does the electronic portfolio experience facilitate reflection? For example, does it foster identity as a reflective practitioner?

Methodology for the project featured a mixed-methods approach, including the following strategies: case studies, informal interviews and observations, surveys and survey data analysis, and artifact analysis. The next section highlights preliminary results from my research.

PRELIMINARY RESEARCH FINDINGS

Data were coded and analyzed using Erickson's analytic induction method (1986), resulting in the following general assertions:

1. The MAED English Education Electronic Portfolio experience does affect student identity by helping students define themselves more explicitly as beginning English teachers.
2. More explicit coaching toward incorporating an identity-based focus in terms of design has improved the quality of students' electronic portfolios, specifically in improving students' ability to situate themselves within the profession with regard to beliefs, philosophy of teaching and learning, knowledge of the field, and teaching practice.
3. More explicit coaching toward developing critical consciousness and critical reflection has improved the quality of students' electronic portfolios, in this case in assisting them to develop the ability to look and look again, to move beyond surface descriptions of artifacts and experiences to critical reflections representing their abilities as reflective practitioners who are able to use higher-level thinking skills, to critique experiences, and to pose informed ideas for change, revision, and improvement.
4. Providing students with multiple opportunities to revisit a particular item for reflection, to revise an initial reflection at various points over the course of the program, facilitates much more explicit and critical reflection.

EVIDENCE FOR FINDINGS

The key piece of evidence for my research findings has been the design evolution of students' electronic portfolios, especially in making the transition from standards-driven design (i.e., 10 INTASC principles as outer links) to design supported by standards. In the second version, students developed their own categories that served as links for the outer layer of their portfolio as well as a visual design and theme reflecting who they are personally and professionally. For example, Kelly's portfolio, one of the early models, illustrates well the typical layout from students: little consideration is given to theme or visual design; it is impersonal in tenor other than the brief greeting and links to her philosophy and resume; and it is organized through links dominated by INTASC standards. Although clean and efficient in design, it is also generic (see Figure 22.1).

However, because Kelly's artifacts and related reflections were rated as stellar, her portfolio was considered a model at the time. To her credit, Kelly achieved this level with very little support or scaffolding from program faculty.

Atypical of this time period is Sara Beth's portfolio, which features an opening page with a striking black-and-white photograph of adult hands cradling a tiny baby's feet accompanied by the following quotation from Thomas Henry Huxley:

Figure 22.1

Welcome to my Teaching Portfolio!

I have designed this electronic portfolio to demonstrate my dedication to inspired, student-centered teaching and learning. The content of these pages represents two years of coursework and practice in English teaching.

The contents of the portfolio are organized under ten guiding principles established by the Interstate New Teacher Assessment and Support Consortium (INTASC) to identify the "knowledge, dispositions and performances deemed essential for all teachers." I have been happy to work with these standards, as they are very much aligned with my own philosophy of teaching and learning.

My goal for each principle was to provide ample evidence that I have met the expectations for a new teacher. It is a difficult task, as the best way to really know a teacher is to watch them teach or, better yet, to be their student!

The blue navigation bar on your left allows you to move through the ten principles. Each principle has its own page, which will appear in this frame. Each page links to a variety of lesson plans, student work, theoretical papers, and other artifacts. When you follow these links, you will always be able to return to the page you left by using the blue navigation bar.

Happy browsing!

Figure 22.2

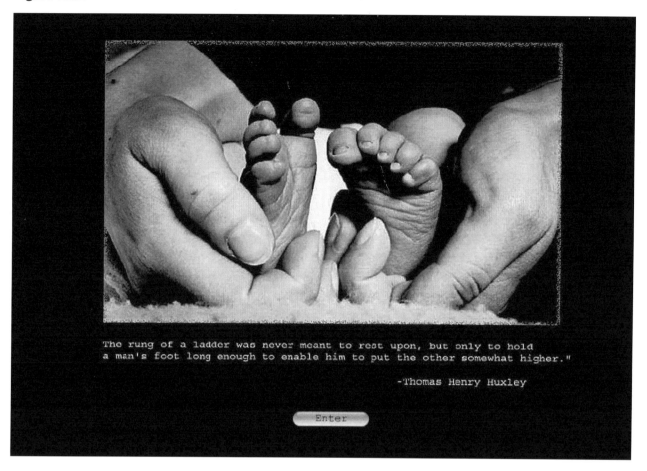

The rung of a ladder was never meant to rest upon, but only to hold a man's foot long enough to enable him to put the other somewhat higher."

-Thomas Henry Huxley

Enter

"The rung of a ladder was never meant to rest upon, but only to hold a man's foot long enough to enable him to put the other somewhat higher" (see Figure 22.2).

The home page then continues the theme established on the opening page with images of footprints and geometric blocks, indicating a journey and challenges to overcome (see Figure 22.3). Another quotation builds on the first and asserts the teacher's role of helping each student to find his or her individual strengths and gifts rather than creating a path where they all become similar or equal in their similarity. Likewise, Sara Beth has a variety of links—only one of which focuses on INTASC standards.

Her opening page and home page both demonstrate an implicit reflective element through the visual images and quotations she has chosen and the thematic design they represent. Put differently, she creates a visual thread that weaves throughout the portfolio and holds it together. These two portfo-

lios became models for me to use in discussing how to work toward in-depth reflection as well as how to create a meaningful design.

This evolution from a more generic design to a more thoughtful one has continued to become more prevalent and is evident in the portfolios of later students such as Sara (http://www.soe.vt .edu/englished/portfolios/liles/Electronic%20 Portfolio/Electronic%20Portfolio/home.html), Jonathan (http://www.soe.vt.edu/englished/ portfolios/duty/Home%20Page.htm), and Katie (http://www.soe.vt.edu/englished/portfolios/ walters/homeintro/index.html) and the rest of her 2005–6 cohort (http://www.soe.vt.edu/ englished/portfolios.html). Both Sara's and Jonathan's portfolios represent the transition to a visual and thematic design highlighting professional identity. Sara includes images of trees, tree branches, and leaves throughout her portfolio, indicating her growth as a beginning English teacher,

Figure 22.3

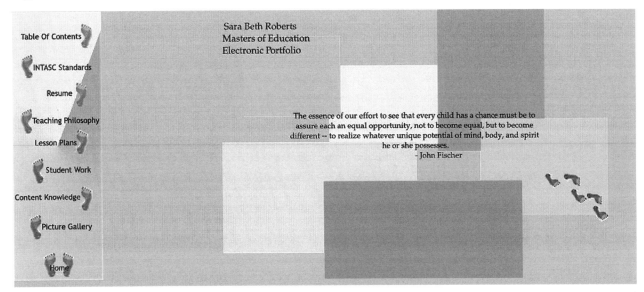

as well as her philosophy that learning is an ongoing process, one that continues as a teacher (see Figures 22.4 and 22.5).

Jonathan's design includes a blueprint as the background for his menu of links (see Figure 22.6).

He even provides an explicit explanation of his thematic design—"under construction"—which is the way he characterizes his quest to become an English teacher. Katie and the rest of her cohort's portfolios represent this transition, but they also take it one step further.

Figure 22.4

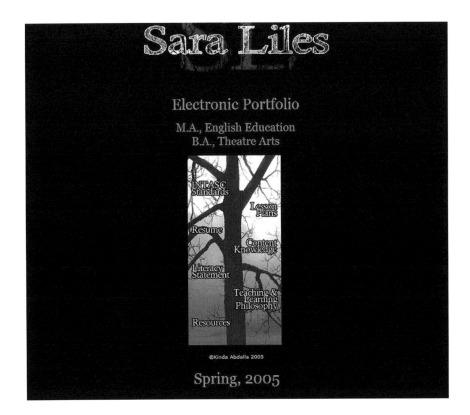

Figure 22.5

Katie includes an opening page with an image of a flower opening at the end of a tree branch with a related quotation from Mark Twain superimposed: "Why not go out on a limb? That's where the fruit is" (see Figure 22.7).

She maintains this theme throughout her portfolio with similar images of seeds, plants, and nurturing and with her insightful reflections about the necessity of taking risks as a teacher and the benefits of being insightful and learning from one's teaching experiences. Unlike past students' portfolios, her organization is neither standardized nor keyed to the INTASC standards. Katie's eportfolio, like those of the rest of the 2005–6 cohort (eight students), includes individualized categories demonstrating how students use artifacts, reflections, and standards to highlight character traits they feel best represent who they are as beginning teachers of the English language arts. For Katie, these characteristics include literacy, knowledge, community, leader-

ship, and technology, and each link includes detailed explanations addressing context, application, artifacts, and reflection (see Figure 22.8).

Appendix A includes a list indicating students' initial ideas for categories; overall, their choices for categories reflected well the characteristics they felt were most important in establishing their identity and competence as beginning teachers of English language arts. Moreover, their choices for categories easily allowed them to embed all the necessary standards requirements *within* the portfolio in a much more integrated and natural way. Through this design evolution over the 5 years, student portfolios have progressed to include a much stronger sense of personal and professional identity, authenticity, and ownership, as well as depth in terms of critical reflection.

Another key piece of evidence warranting these assertions includes the students' narrative reflections describing their MAED English Education Portfo-

Figure 22.6

lio experience composed *after* the completion of the portfolio presentations. One major finding from these documents is the extent to which students have come to understand how much the electronic portfolio serves as a tool for critical reflection. The following two excerpts from selected reflections address this realization specifically:

- I believe my EP as a whole serves as a tool for reflection. I believe this for a number of reasons. First, I believe the theme of my EP speaks towards reflection. I know that I am not an outstanding and or veteran English teacher (yet☺); therefore, it was important for me to understand where I was coming from as a future English Educator. I have been built from the ground-up when it comes to teaching English; therefore, I found it necessary to choose the theme "under construction" for my EP. I also believe

my EP serves as a tool for reflection because it shows all of the decisions I have made as a pre-service English Educator. When I look at my EP, I see decisions that I have made that I agree with and decisions that I have made that I would change if faced with the same situations again. With this in mind, I believe my EP serves as an ever-lasting tool of reflection for now and for years to come. (Jonathan, December 2005; note: he graduated fall 2005 and was actually in the 2004–5 cohort, but he presented to the 2005–6 cohort.)

- The portfolio served as a way for me to channel my reflective efforts throughout the program. By zeroing in on specific artifacts, I was able to paint a picture of the entire year and reflect on specific moments through the artifacts. It was as if I was making an organized collage, or a time line. As I went along the

Figure 22.7

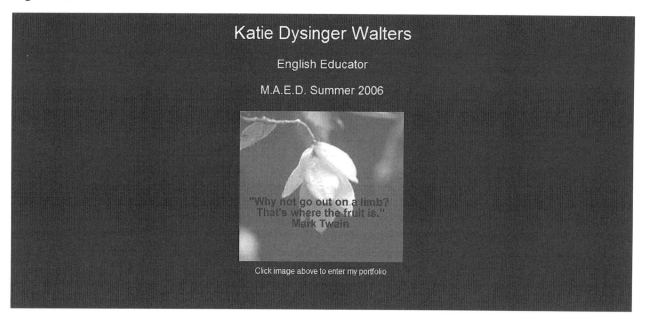

timeline, I was able to further examine my own examinations of artifacts, and see why I made the decisions I did. (Todd, May 2006)

In terms of a more implicit and, perhaps, more compelling result of the electronic portfolio experience, Katie (May 2006) responded as such:

- Being a reflective practitioner means thinking critically and deeply on the many processes of teaching. It means considering a day's lesson plan and asking myself what went well, what didn't go well and how can I fix it. It means thinking about how you relate to students as a group and individually and what is in individual histories that inform and direct those relationships. It means identifying a problem, its possible sources and potential solutions. It means actively seeking and experimenting with solutions to problems you face as a teacher and continually examining the effect it has on my practice. As such, reflection will be the most important factor in my growth as a teacher. Without it, I will not change my practices or my underlying beliefs.

Collectively, these students' responses demon-

strate the potential the MAED English Education Electronic Portfolio experience has for fostering, facilitating, and enhancing the potential for deep, critical thinking and reflection about teaching and learning. Time was a critical factor as well, with students commenting both on the immediate effect of the electronic portfolio experience in assisting these students in processing their graduate program and accompanying field experiences and on its influence in their ability to define themselves as future teachers and leaders modeling similar practices for their students. Not least, the 2005–6 cohort has shown evidence of extraordinary professional commitment. Despite our being spread across the state of Virginia and now into North Carolina, in the fall of 2005, cohort members presented with me at the Virginia Association of Teachers of English Fall Conference on multigenre reading and writing; in the fall of 2006, at the National Council of Teachers of English (NCTE) Annual Conference in Nashville on media literacy; and in the fall of 2007, at NCTE in New York City on the MAED English Education Electronic Portfolio experience.

Ultimately, my experience over the last 5 years has reinforced the importance of critical reflection for my own practice. I trusted my instincts about problems I saw with a portfolio requirement that

Figure 22.8

Katie Dysinger Walters

English Educator

M.A. Summer 2006

home

introduction

literacy

knowledge

community

leadership

technology

Welcome!

As a teacher of English I am committed to helping my students learn to navigate the world. By navigation, I mean to assess and react to the experiences and events they face with understanding and knowledge so that they can become advocates for themselves and for others. In order to realize this objective, I must be and do what I ask my students to be and do. My journey to become a teacher is as much becoming an informed citizen of the world as it is developing the knowledge and skills necessary to implement effective, engaging lessons in the classroom.

I invite you to explore my electronic portfolio to learn more about me as a teacher and the reflective process that has fostered my growth. For my organizing categories, I chose literacy, community, leadership, and technology because they represent the branches of being a well-balanced teacher.

click here to contact me by e-mail

was decontextualized, unauthentic, and too focused on external factors. I also learned not to take reflection for granted, that it is indeed a skill that can and must be developed over time with careful consideration for providing models and scaffolds. Appendix A represents part of my evolution in working with students on electronic portfolio design and the scaffolding that can inform that process. As Beers (2003) poignantly revealed about reading—that we cannot expect kids to "just do it"—I know the same is true for reflection. For me, the 2005–6 cohort represents the tipping point not only in terms of a much higher-quality MAED English Education Portfolio experience but also in terms of the greater potential electronic portfolios have for enhancing teacher education and producing much more confident and competent reflective practition-

ers who have a coherent vision for teaching now and on into the future.

Although my experience is context specific, there are implications and lessons that I believe would benefit others who are facilitating similar electronic portfolio programs at other institutions and in other programs:

- Like any good educational reform or instructional method, electronic portfolios take time and preparation. Faculty and students must be provided with the proper support, training, and resources, including hardware, software, and access.
- Electronic portfolios have the potential to provide preservice English teachers with the valuable and necessary experience of manipulating and integrating technology for an

authentic purpose—namely to demonstrate content and pedagogical knowledge and ability, but also to shape one's identity as a beginning teacher and reflective practitioner (see also Young & Figgins, 2002).

- Although various professional standards can be the source for requiring an electronic portfolio system or program, they do not have to limit the design, purpose, or content of the portfolio. Instead, they can be used to support portfolio content, design, and reflection. When students have the opportunity and resources to create a more authentic electronic portfolio, one involving choice, empowerment, and flexibility, they will be more motivated to create and complete a compelling product.

- Providing models and examples and discussions about these models, and including the explicit expectations for the eportfolios, is also necessary. Models should include both content and design features.

- Multimodal and visual literacies can be key components of electronic portfolio design and, as such, can provide compelling insights that go beyond print to demonstrate in dynamic ways how beginning teachers view themselves and convey their professional identities to others.

- Well-chosen artifacts and critical reflection should be the cornerstones of an effective electronic portfolio. Reflection can and should be taught and modeled explicitly as a scaffolded process.

- The directions for reflecting on artifacts are part of the scaffolding process. I required reflective annotations in which students completed three tasks: (a) name and describe the artifact; (b) provide a description of the explicit context associated with the artifact; and (c) provide a critical and insightful *reflection* that demonstrates clearly how this particular artifact (and, if applicable, all of its parts) meets the particular standard for which you have assigned it. I explained that the crucial third step should demonstrate their thoughtful consideration and abilities as reflective practitioners.

- Another strategy for helping students develop the skill of reflection is for them to reflect on the same item multiple times over the course of a semester, year, or program. Two assignments directly connected to disciplinary and professional practice were required artifacts for all: a literacy statement/definition and a technology statement/definition. Students completed versions of their statements/definitions at the beginning, midpoint, and conclusion of their program experience; in other words, reiteration was built into the model of reflective practice. Each time, students reflected upon the previous version as well as drew upon new material introduced into their methods courses as a means of crafting a more detailed and informed statement/definition. In a final reflection they compared the various versions and described the experience. For examples, see versions of Sara's literacy statement and her final reflection at http://www.soe.vt.edu/englished/portfolios/liles/Electronic%20Portfolio/Electronic%20Portfolio/litstatement.html and versions of Katie's literacy statement and final reflection at http://www.soe.vt.edu/englished/portfolios/walters/cat/lit/lit_mpq.html

- Electronic portfolios are multimedia experiences and, as such, should be shared, demonstrated, and discussed with audiences appropriate for their purpose and focus.

REFERENCES

Beers, K. (2003). *When kids can't read: What teachers can do: A guide for teachers 6-12.* Portsmouth, NH: Heinemann.

Calfee, R. C., & Freedman, S. W. (1996). A national survey of writing portfolio practice: What we learned and what it means. In R. Calfee & P. Perfumo (Eds.), *Writing portfolios in the classroom: Policy and practice, promise and peril* (pp. 63–82). Mahwah, NJ: Lawrence Erlbaum Associates.

Elbow, P. (1991). Forward. In P. Belanoff & M. Dickson (Eds.), *Portfolios: Process and product* (pp. ix–xvi). Portsmouth, NH: Boynton/Cook.

Elbow, P., & Belanoff, P. (1991). State University of New York at Stony Brook portfolio-based evaluation program. In P. Belanoff & M. Dickson (Eds.), *Portfolios: Process and product* (pp. 3–16). Portsmouth, NH: Boynton/Cook.

Elbow, P., & Belanoff, P. (1997). Reflections on an explosion: Portfolios in the '90s and beyond. In K. Blake Yancey & I. Weiser (Eds.), *Situating portfolios: Four perspectives* (pp. 21–33). Logan, UT: Utah State University Press.

Erickson, F. (1986). Qualitative methods in research on teaching. In M. C. Wittrock (Ed.), *Handbook of research on teaching* (3rd ed., pp. 119–161). Washington DC: American Educational Research Association

Pope, C., & Golub, J. (2000). Preparing tomorrow's English language arts teachers today: Principles and practices for infusing technology. *Contemporary Issues in Technology and Teacher Education* [Online serial], *1*(1). Retrieved from http://www.citejournal.org/vol1/iss1/currentissues/english/article1.htm

Yancey, K. B. (1992). Portfolios in the writing classroom: A final reflection. In K. B. Yancey (Ed.), *Portfolios in the writing classroom* (pp. 102–116). Urbana, IL: National Council of Teachers of English.

Yancey, K. B. (1996a). Dialogue, interplay, and discovery: Mapping the role and the rhetoric of reflection in portfolio assessment. In R. Calfee & P. Perfumo (Eds.), *Writing portfolios in the classroom: Policy and practice, promise and peril* (pp. 83–102). Mahwah, NJ: Lawrence Erlbaum Associates.

Yancey, K. B. (1996b). The electronic portfolio: Shifting paradigms. *Computers and Composition: An International Journal for Teachers of Writing, 13*(2), 259–262.

Yancey, K. B. (1996c). Portfolio, electronic, and the links between. *Computers and Composition: An International Journal for Teachers of Writing, 13*(2), 129–133.

Yancey, K. B. (1997). Teacher portfolios: Lessons in resistance, readiness, and reflection. In K. B. Yancey & I. Weiser (Eds.), *Situating portfolios: Four perspectives* (pp. 244–262). Logan, UT: Utah State University Press.

Young, C. A., & Bush, J. (2004). Teaching the English language arts with technology: A critical approach and pedagogical framework. *Contemporary Issues in Technology and Teacher Education* [Online serial], *4*(1). Retrieved from http://www.citejournal.org/vol4/iss1/languagearts/article1.cfm

Young, C. A., & Figgins, M. A. (2002). The Q-folio in action: Using a Web-based electronic portfolio to reinvent traditional notions of inquiry, research, and portfolios. *Contemporary Issues in Technology and Teacher Education* [Online serial], *2*(2). Retrieved from

APPENDIX A

Your Ideas for Initial Outer Layer Portfolio Categories / Links (from 8-27-05)

Professional Conduct
Control of Classroom
Organized
Comfort with Students in Front
 of Class
Well-thought-out Lesson Plans
Flow of Class
Supportive of Students' Needs

Knowledge
Communication
Involvement
Leadership
Technology

Lesson Planning
Classroom Management
Community Involvement
Curriculum Development
Technology

Professional Growth
Knowledge of Objectives
Flexibility
Organized

Student Motivation
Interaction
Compassion / Involvement
Effective Evaluation
Drive and Dedication

Comprehensive Units
Organized Planning
Related Lessons (to each
 other & to class as whole)
Effective Planning
Effective Implementation
Fair & Logical Assessments
Distinguished Subject Knowledge
Originality

Flexibility
Commitment to Students & Community
Creative & Efficient Lesson Plans
Subject Knowledge
Organization
Classroom Management

Possibilities for General Layout of Portfolio

Outer Layer: "You"
A theme page that links to your main page with *your* categories / links or a combination of both; establish your theme through text, images, layout, design, etc. (then maintain thematic element throughout)

Inner Layers Option 1:
The artifacts you collect that fall under the categories you establish for outer layer plus your demonstrating how these artifacts show you have met INTASC and/or IRA/NCTE Standards

Inner Layers Option 2:
The standards that you see fitting under these outer layer categories and then the artifacts you see as demonstrating how you have met these INTASC and IRA/NCTE Standards

Inner Layers Option 3:
You create your own path that you share, explain, and negotiate with Dr. Young. Your pathway must still address standards, include related artifacts, and provide focused reflections.

Artifacts (includes the artifact and a reflective annotation)

Your artifacts should be accompanied by annotations that do 3 things:

1. *Name* and *describe* the artifact

> Note: *Keep in mind that one artifact might have multiple parts; e.g., multiple drafts and revisions of your definition of literacy, multiple drafts and revisions of your definition of technology, an assignment that you created that is accompanied by examples of student work, etc.*

2. Provide a description of the explicit *context* in which it was used, created, taught, collected, evaluated, etc.
3. Provide a critical and insightful *reflection* which demonstrates clearly how this particular artifact (and, if applicable, all of its parts) meets the particular standard for which you have assigned it. This is crucial and should demonstrate your thoughtful consideration and abilities as a reflective practitioner.

> Note: *Again, your reflection might cover your growth over time on an artifact that is multiple parts (e.g., literacy definitions, technology definitions, students doing a pre-test v. post-test which doesn't have to be test in traditional sense, i.e., defining poetry at the beginning of a poetry unit v. definition at end!)*

Conclusion

MOVING INTO THE FUTURE

BARBARA CAMBRIDGE, DARREN CAMBRIDGE, and KATHLEEN BLAKE YANCEY

Electronic Portfolios 2.0 concludes by highlighting three transitions central to the future of eportfolio practice: moving research from a national focus to an international articulation; transforming accountability driven by testing into richer conversations around inquiry into learning; and opening a detached, hierarchical academy to engagement across the multiple knowledge spaces of the digital world. The work of the Inter/National Coalition for Electronic Portfolio Research documented in this book points toward the coming of these transitions; the continuing work of the Coalition will move them forward.

FROM NATIONAL TO INTERNATIONAL

During the last five years, the use of eportfolios has moved beyond its American origins to take root in numerous countries around the world, most prominently in the United Kingdom and Europe. The Coalition has evolved to embrace this trend. Published in 2001, *Electronic Portfolios: Emerging Practices in Student, Faculty, and Institutional Learning* focused on the use of electronic portfolios in the United States. Created in 2003, The National Coalition for Electronic Portfolio Research sponsored much of the collaborative research detailed in *Electronic Portfolios 2.0*. In 2006 the organization changed to the Inter/National Coalition for

Electronic Portfolio Research in order to reflect Cohort 3 members from England and Canada, including the University of Wolverhampton (England) and the University of Waterloo (Canada). The following year, the Coalition launched Cohort 4, the first composed of campuses primarily from beyond the United States and in collaboration with educational leaders in the United Kingdom. Future cohorts and collaborations will continue to globalize our collaborative inquiries, and the results will enrich our understanding of the rapidly disseminating set of practices associated with eportfolios.

The punctuation of the first word in the Coalition's title, Inter/National, reflects the balance such national and global work entails. On the one hand, the use of eportfolios in higher education occurs in national contexts that differ in significant ways. National policy environments vary, as do institutional histories and cultures. For example, in the United Kingdom and Europe, national governments actively support lifelong learning initiatives to which many eportfolio projects are connected, while in the United States, support is left largely to the states and the private sector, leaving lifelong learning eportfolio projects to depend on the initiative of individual higher education institutions and nonprofit organizations. Although sometimes subtle, differences in the use of terminology can also be challenging to negotiate. We see these differences even in the very punctuation in the Coalition's name: although we call it a "slash," our U.K. colleagues would say "stroke." In addition, in each national context, different organizations are best positioned to connect the research to broader efforts toward educational transformation. The Coalition's work was successfully launched through sponsorship of the American Association for Higher Education; the impact of its work in the United Kingdom is multiplied through shared leadership of Cohort 4 with colleagues at the Higher Education Academy and The Center for Recording Achievement.

On the other hand, across national boundaries eportfolio educators face similar issues that benefit from international dialogue, and they are developing practices that can be fruitfully shared across borders. Members of the Coalition from each of the five countries represented so far have confronted challenges that cross national contexts: motivating learners and teachers, integrating eportfolio practice into programs, balancing learning and assessment, working across disciplinary and professional boundaries, and supporting and evaluating reflection. Presentations by European scholars and practitioners at the conferences on eportfolios organized by the European Institute for E-Learning each of the last five years reflect all of these themes, and preliminary results from a comprehensive survey of eportfolio practice in Australia show that these issues top the agenda there as well (Lambert, McAllister, & Brooks, 2008).

The fruit of cross-border collaboration is already evident within the Coalition. For example, Sheffield Hallam University in the United Kingdom is using the developmental scales for assessing reflection developed by Alverno College in the United States, and Coalition members from Stanford University and the University of Waterloo (along with colleagues from Scotland) have published a shared conceptual framework for ways that eportfolios can be used to support learning throughout a lifetime (Tosh, Werdmuller, Chen, Penny Light, & Haywood, 2006).

The technology used to support eportfolio practice also is increasingly being used across borders. For example, iWebfolio, produced by the American company Nuventive, is being used in regional lifelong learning eportfolio work led by the University of Nottingham in England, a member of Cohort 4.

Conversely, PebblePad, originally developed at a Cohort 3 member, the University of Wolverhampton, has been used in pilot studies at American Coalition members George Mason University and Pennsylvania State University. Open Source projects, such as the Open Source Portfolio, Elgg, and Mahara, also involve developers from multiple countries. A similar international group of technologists is creating technical standards for eportfolios through organizations such as the IMS Global Learning Consortium and HR-XML.

However, such efforts also reflect national contexts from which they originated. The Open Source Portfolio's most easily identifiable strength is supporting assessment, a key concern in the United States, while Elgg's appeal comes from social networking capabilities well-suited to the emphasis on widening participation in higher education of the United Kingdom and Europe. As with issues of teaching, learning, and assessment, understanding eportfolio technology in the future will require balancing national and global elements, going inter/national with the slash/stroke.

Although Coalition work and most published work on eportfolios have so far focused on Europe and the Anglophone world, the use of eportfolios is becoming a more thoroughly global phenomenon, with important work underway in dozens of countries, including Japan, Korea, China, the United Arab Emirates, Brazil, and South Africa. Because eportfolio scholarship and practice as we now know it reflects distinctively Western beliefs about individual identities and institutional dynamics, more research is needed to learn how eportfolio purposes and forms change in these new cultural contexts. How will the idea of the portfolio be transformed by educators and learners worldwide? Because an ever increasing percentage of students in higher education in most Western countries come from non-Western cultures, the answers also have the potential to help the educators in the West better embrace the diversity of their learners.

Increased inter/national dialogue is essential for exploring changes as eportfolios go global and globalization comes into the eportfolio classroom. We hope to support such inquiry through future cohorts of the Coalition, both nationally-focused and broadly international.

FROM TESTING TO INQUIRY: HOW CAN EPORTFOLIOS HELP RECONCEPTUALIZE ACCOUNTABILITY?

As the international growth in eportfolio practice demonstrates, in a knowledge economy many countries around the world realize the centrality of learning for their citizens. Regularly generated statistics show the relative success of students at all academic levels in important subject matters. As nations become more and more concerned with identifying, documenting, and assessing student learning outcomes, they often develop large-scale accountability systems. Distortions, however, can rear their ugly heads if accountability usurps the place of learning as the central activity of schooling.

Assessment, of course, is an integral part of the learning process. As learners develop, it is important that they receive feedback on their learning, identify how their learning occurs and progresses, and develop their own abilities as self-assessors. Formative assessments that literally help *form* students' process and progress in learning are essential. Eportfolios as evidenced in this book provide opportunities for formative assessment in deep and extended ways. Through their own reflections, students practice self-assessment. As students post learning objects and reflect on them, they invite response from peers, teachers, and other readers of their portfolios, both formally and informally. Then, through analyzing their own reflections and the feedback of others, students become more knowledgeable about the progress of their own learning. Eportfolios are, therefore, ideal vehicles for formative assessment.

Accountability, however, requires summative assessment, most often scaled to levels beyond the classroom or institution. Because scaling involves costs of administration, evaluation, and dissemination, governments, through a variety of accountability and accreditation systems, rely most often on one-time tests. Although literature about assess-ment and evaluation establishes that, to be valid, assessments must be varied and multiple, one-time tests dominate both nationally and internationally. Moreover, policy decisions about funding and structuring of education are often made based on data from these tests that fail to reveal the extent or depth of student learning.

Eportfolios are an antidote to the inadequacies of testing. Even if testing is so entrenched that it is unlikely to be replaced soon, institutions and governments can build into accountability systems additional information for more and better-informed decision making. As described in this book, at such institutions as the University of Georgia, Indiana University Purdue University Indianapolis, and Portland State University in the United States, colleges and universities have demon-strated that eportfolios can provide institutions with rich evidence of student learning on which to base curricular, pedagogical, and budgetary decisions. Work in the state of Ohio to build an infrastructure that coordinates eportfolio use and availability of eportfolio evidence for decision making statewide is paralleled by the California State University system in a newer cohort of the Inter/National Coalition for Eportfolio Research. In the United Kingdom, eportfolios are a natural outgrowth of nationwide-mandated personal development plans. If foundation and governmental funding were channeled to support eportfolio system develop-ment in the same way that such funding has sup-ported test development and implementation, eportfolios would emerge as essential complements to tests. More importantly, in the future, they can replace testing as a more responsible method of documenting student learning, especially as institu-tional and governmental control of education con-tinues to dissipate with ubiquitous sources and sites of learning.

In fact, as the sources and sites for learning change, the definitions of teacher and student shift significantly. In eportfolios, faculty members, work supervisors, and peers learn from students, em-ployees, and colleagues whom they may know through face-to-face or online connections. As students move among many sites for learning—in formal schooling, in the workplace, and on their social networking sites—they must take with them the evidence of their continuous learning to demonstrate what they know and can do.

This new world of distributed learning sites and of multiple identities as teachers and learners mandates investigation into how learning occurs in these new circumstances. The scholarship of teaching and learning includes designed inquiry into important questions about learning, with findings shared for critique and use. One reason that the movement called the scholarship of teaching and learning has gained momentum internationally is that every discipline and educational environment must study the implications of new learning sites and modes in order to prosper. The growth of the International Society for the Scholarship of Teaching and Learning evinces the widespread commitment of educators to study and apply new knowledge concerning students' lifelong and lifewide learning.

Educators are, however, not the only inquirers into student learning. Because students are at the center of such inquiry, they can become co-inquirers, and increasingly, as they gain experience with reflection and integration, independent inquirers into learning processes and products. In their book *The Advancement of Learning: Building a Teaching Commons,* Mary Huber and Pat Hutchings (2005, pp. 119–120) recommend that students have a greater role in discussions about learning. Eportfolios provide a place for that greater role as students document, reflect on, and analyze what occurs during their own learning processes. As described in this book, students can participate in the intellectual work of discovering how they learn through keeping a continuous record, making links among occasions and products of learning, and building on past experience as they move into deeper and deeper learning. When Huber and Hutchings call for "new genres and forms to document the work of teaching and learning," they echo Peter Smith's call for a new kind of learning passport that enables students to move among educational sites (see Introduction). The new genres and forms need to be transportable to many sites, understandable by multiple audiences, and guided by learners themselves, all features of electronic portfolios.

FROM IVORY TOWERS TO KNOWLEDGE SPACES

The capacity of eportfolios to support inquiry into learning may also help the academy negotiate the challenge of the digital age. In *The Digital Revolution and the Coming of the Postmodern University* (2002), philosopher Carl Raschke identifies three moments of historical transformation in the making of knowledge. First, he says, was the invention of language; second, the invention of writing; and third, during our own time, the digital revolution. Located in this current moment, he sees the Internet as the new "incubator" of knowledge, its proliferation of "knowledge spaces" both democratizing in effect and potentially threatening to those in the academy. More specifically, he argues that these new, flexible, and dynamic spaces, with their capacity to welcome all people and all projects and to support organization, communication, and circulation of information, may mark the demise of U.S. higher education as we have known it. He identifies other factors accounting for the potential demise of higher education, to be sure—the hierarchical nature of the academy, for example, and the reluctance of faculty to engage in new pedagogies and technologies. But his argument is clear and radical: in clinging to an authority that is increasingly anachronistic, universities risk losing that authority altogether.

As a thought experiment, we might consider how the concept of knowledge spaces fits in with or informs the academy. Thinking in terms of knowledge spaces and the academy as one, we can see the knowledge spaces of the academy in dialogue with other knowledge spaces outside the academy. We might thus see how both kinds function similarly and how, increasingly, they overlap. Students in a myriad of credit-based learning experiences—including course-based service learning projects, design projects for capstone requirements, internships, student teaching and other clinical experiences, and co-ops—all engage in learning that crosses the academy "divide," such students drawing from and synthesizing the learning that occurs in diverse knowledge spaces. We might identify these experiences as Web 2.0 in type or sensibility, given their connections among theory, research, and practice; their locations in communities; and their opportunity for making knowledge. The sensibility that Web 2.0 offers is more about community than technology, more about the opportunities to work together to gather and share information than about who is organizing it or who owns it, more about the multiple-contexts-situating texts than about the texts in isolation, and more about positioning all participants as learners, creators, and contributors.

Given this context, how might eportfolios be useful? As the chapters in this book demonstrate, eportfolios may be the most likely vehicle to help us make the transition to an academy that maintains both its relevance and its authority as it welcomes students' experience in increasingly significant and transformative ways. This shift is evident in chapters where a key assumption underlying the research reports is that student accounts of their learning can help us understand learning differently. In other words, we invite student accounts of learning, especially through reflection, because those accounts, from a Vygotskian perspective, promote and enhance *student* learning. Inside eportfolios, as students use multiple systems of representation to map learning in new ways, they help *faculty learn* about how learning actually works; faculty understand learning in new ways. In such accounts, for example, students like the accounting major at the University of Waterloo (Chapter 7) articulate and show the distinction between two outcomes: mastering concepts, which is not difficult, and determining the relationships linking them, which is. This student explains this doubly, through verbal explanation and visual map, both inside of an eportfolio. Through the student articulation, we literally *see* distinctions between novice and expert in new ways from the vantage point of the student. Likewise, the student teachers at Virginia Tech (Chapter 22) show

us another aspect of learning: how they have adopted and adapted the theory of the classroom to the everyday realities of classroom practice, and what that adaptation means for their professional futures. Such knowledge can only be made by these former students, who help us see the value of our curriculum as they enact it in real-world contexts. And as members of a community, these new teachers continue—two years beyond graduation—to engage in reflective practices together, committing to a profession that in the United States loses 50 percent of its early professionals within five years. And, in the blogs of the Wolverhampton eportfolios (Chapter 5), we see Web 2.0 tools enriching eportfolio learning through documentation, dialogue, and community. These practices—documentation, dialogue, and community—are characteristics of the Coalition as well, a real and virtual community of learners working on institutional projects and on projects across a larger international network.

The introduction to this book, looking backward to an earlier account of eportfolios, traced movement from the past to the present: from implementation to designed inquiry, from formal schooling to lifelong and lifewide learning, and from local contexts to larger contexts. This conclusion, pointing from the present to the future, suggests that all learners will operate more and more in an international context, that designed inquiry will become even more the purview of learners themselves, and that the digital revolution will challenge formal schooling in even more ways. Eportfolios provide a unique way to feature student inquiry and knowledge, to benefit from what technology offers as a mode of and vehicle for learning, and to place each individual's learning in the broadest of contexts.

As the Inter/National Coalition for Eportfolio Research continues to coordinate teams of researchers in future cohorts, it will report on findings from their research. The prospect of ubiquitous eportfolio use is not a pipedream, but a distinct possibility if educators and learners continue to develop, study, and implement eportfolio practices. The eportfolio revolution marks a digital revolution that demands and enables new theories, practices, and knowledge for all learners.

REFERENCES

Huber, M., & Hutchings, P. (2005). *The advancement of learning: Building a teaching commons.* San Francisco, CA: Jossey-Bass.

Lambert, S., McAllister, L., & Brooks, C. (2008, February). Audit of ePortfolio practice in higher education in Australia: Methodology, data and trends. Paper presented at Australian ePortfolio Symposium. February 7. Brisbane, Queensland, Australia.

Raschke, C. (2002). *The digital revolution and the coming of the postmodern university.* London: RoutledgeFalmer.

Tosh, D., Werdmuller, B., Chen, H., Penny Light, T., & Haywood, J. (2006). The learning landscape: A conceptual framework for ePortfolios. In A. Jafari & C. Kauffman (Eds.), *Handbook of research on ePortfolios* (pp. 24–32). Hershey, PA: Idea Group.

INDEX

Rodriguez, Michael, 63
Rogers, R. R., 17
roles, 81–82
RSS, 47

safe space, electronic portfolio as, 56
Sakai Foundation, 152
Salvas, Krista, 89
Santiago, G., 140
scaffolding, for reflection, 190
Schön, Donald, 7, 26
Schroeder, Lori, 165–173
science, technology, and math (STM), at Alverno, 27–28
self-assessment, 9, 19; framework, 21, 22*t*
Self-Regulation Component, LASSI, 98–99, 99*t*
selves, types of, 41–48, 43*t*, 51–52, 70
Serrano, Angelica, 62
shell, 8, 9*f*
showcase eportfolios, definition of, 150
Shulman, Lee, 32
Simple Storage Service (S3), 121
Skill Component, LASSI, 98, 99*t*
Smith, Erin N., 133–135
Smith, Peter, xiii
Sommers, Nancy, 156
Spelling, Margaret, 121
Sprague, Debra, 175–180
Sproule, Bob, 69–79
stakeholder model, 171–172, 171*f*
Stanford University, 29–35
Stephens, Benjamin R., 12, 103–108

STM. *See* science, technology, and math
story, and lifelong learning, 32
students: and assessment, 88–89; categorization by, 186, 192; and integration, 63; reflections by, evaluation of, 181–192, 183*f*–189*f*; and stakeholder model, 171–172
Super Forms, 170, 170*f*
symphonic self, 41–42, 51–52, 52*f*; and activities, 44–46; and electronic portfolio, 57, 57*f*; and genres, 46–47; versus networked self, 43*t*; and technology, 47–48; and values, 42–44

TaskStream, 152–153
teacher education, electronic portfolios and: at UNO, 109–113, 111*t*–112*t*; at Virginia Tech, 181–192
technology, 145–146; disruptive, 123; future of, 153–154, 194; Lane on, 149–154; and thinking sheets, 177; types of selves and, 47–48
thinking sheets, 14, 15*f*, 175–180, 176*t*; moment of engagement with, 178, 178*f*; theoretical context for, 176–177
Thomas College, 87–90
time: for portfolio preparation, 189; and technology, 149
Toolkit, 168–169, 169*f*
Topp, Neal W., 109–113
Transition Portfolio Project, 119–127
Twain, Mark, 186

university, reinvention of, 15–16
University of Denver, 152
University of Georgia, 155–163
University of Illinois-Chicago, 139
University of Massachusetts-Boston, 139
University of Nebraska-Omaha, 13, 109–113, 152
University of Washington, 8, 9*f*, 129–132, 149–154
University of Waterloo, 69–79
University of Wolverhampton, 51–58
Urban Universities Portfolio Project, 139–140
UWired, 129

values, 81–82; Kapi`olani Community College and, 97–102; types of selves and, 42–44
vision, 115; Ohio State University and, 119–120

Wasko, Paul, 165–173
Western Cooperative for Educational Telecommunications, 152–153
Whitney, D., 119, 124
Will Component, LASSI, 98–99, 99*t*
Witte, Stephen, 156

Yancey, Kathleen Blake, 5–16, 41, 45, 193–198
Young, Carl, 181–192

Zamon, Mary E., 175–180